YASCHA MOUNK is a writer, academic, and public speaker known for his work on the rise of populism and the crisis of liberal democracy. A contributing editor at the *Atlantic*, where he has a regular column, his journalism has also appeared in the *New Yorker and Harper's*, among other outlets. He is currently an Associate Professor of International Affairs at Johns Hopkins University and a term member of the Council on Foreign Relations. His most recent book, *The People vs. Democracy*, was published by Harvard University Press in 2018.

Also by Yascha Mounk

The People vs. Democracy

The Age of Responsibility

Stranger in My Own Country

THE GREAT EXPERIMENT

How to Make Diverse
Democracies Work

Yascha Mounk

BLOOMSBURY PUBLISHING

LONDON · OXFORD · NEW YORK · NEW DELHI · SYDNEY

BLOOMSBURY PUBLISHING
Bloomsbury Publishing Plc
50 Bedford Square, London, WC1B 3DP, UK
29 Earlsfort Terrace, Dublin 2, Ireland

BLOOMSBURY, BLOOMSBURY PUBLISHING and the Diana logo
are trademarks of Bloomsbury Publishing Plc

First published in 2022 in USA by Penguin Press, an imprint of Penguin Random House
First published in Great Britain 2022
This edition published 2023

A catalogue record for this book is available from the British Library

ISBN: HB: 978-1-5266-3013-1; TPB: 978-1-5266-3014-8; PB: 978-1-5266-3015-5;
eBook: 978-1-5266-3006-3

2 4 6 8 10 9 7 5 3 1

Text design by Alexis Farabaugh
Printed and bound in Great Britain by CPI Group (UK) Ltd, Croydon CR0 4YY

MIX
Paper | Supporting
responsible forestry
FSC® C171272

To find out more about our authors and books visit
www.bloomsbury.com and sign up for our newsletters

To Friendship
(personal and civic)

Contents

INTRODUCTION

A moment before the show went live, I realized how nervous I was. German is my mother tongue. But after going to college in Britain and grad school in America, I am now more comfortable talking about politics in English. So when I sat down for a live interview with *Tagesthemen*, one of the most popular news programs in Germany, I was afraid that I might make a fool of myself by sounding incoherent or saying something I didn't really mean.

When the host set me up to talk about some of the main arguments in my latest book—What, she asked, are the causes for the recent rise of authoritarian populism?—I started to find my groove. Little by little, my nerves steadied.

There is widespread anger at economic stagnation, I said. There is the rise of social media, which makes it easier for demagogues to reach a big audience by spreading lies and inciting hatred. And then there is a third reason, one that is particularly pertinent in a country still grappling with the recent arrival of a million refugees from Africa and the Middle East.

"We are," I told the host, "embarking on a historically unique experiment—that of turning a monoethnic and monocultural democracy into a multiethnic one. That can work. I think it will work. But of course it also causes all kinds of disruptions."

After the interview, a wave of relief washed over me. My German had mostly sounded natural. I had managed to get across some of the core arguments from my book. Most important, I had not done anything crazy or embarrassing. The worst outcome of any live interview—that you inadvertently go viral—had not, I thought, materialized.

I headed to the railway station with a big smile. With not a minute to spare, I caught a train to Frankfurt, checked into an airport hotel, and fell into a deep sleep.

Only when I switched on my phone the next evening, after a ten-hour flight back to the United States, did I realize that the interview had gone viral after all. My inbox was overflowing with angry messages: "Stop telling us how to live!!" one said. "How dare you experiment on us?!" another asked. "Thanks for admitting to your vile conspiracy," a third read.

I was taken aback by how vitriolic these messages were. But I was even more baffled by their content. To what conspiracy had I admitted? Who was I supposedly experimenting on?

A search of the internet quickly supplied the answer. A few minutes after my interview, *Tichys Einblick*, a far-right website, had posted an article implying that Angela Merkel and I were deliberately experimenting on the German people. "Who agreed to this experiment?" its author demanded to know.

From this short post, the rage at my supposed admission had spread with astonishing speed. Far-right radio hosts, YouTubers, even elected politicians were citing the interview as proof that nefarious forces were undertaking a "great replacement" designed to annihilate Europe's native population.

Finally, the word reached *The Daily Stormer*, an American neo-Nazi website. Putting my name in triple brackets to indicate that I am Jewish, the headline warned readers about ((((Yascha Mounk)))'s Unique Historical Experiment. Invoking ARBEIT MACHT FREI, the perfidious inscription on the gate to the Auschwitz extermination camp, the article was tagged: Diversity Macht Frei—The Hebrew People Are at It Again.

In one sense, my fifteen minutes of fame among the far right and the five minutes of hate they elicited are based on a straightforward misunderstanding. To state the obvious, Angela Merkel and I are not in cahoots to run some grand experiment on the German people. Nobody is. The rapid change in the ethnic and religious composition of countries from Germany to Sweden, and from Australia to the United States, does not stem from the deliberate preferences of some secret cabal; it is the oft-unintended consequence of a series of choices that politicians have made for a variety of economic, political, and humanitarian reasons.

And yet I do not regret using the word "experiment." For I still believe that, understood in the right way, this word best describes the situation in which most developed democracies around the world now find themselves.

In one sense, an experiment is carried out by scientists who consciously set parameters before they begin. According to *The Oxford English Dictionary*, it is "a scientific procedure undertaken to make a discovery, test a hypothesis, or demonstrate a known fact." This is how my critics interpreted the claim that many countries have now embarked on a unique historical experiment. In their mind, where there is an experiment, there must be an experimenter—preferably a Jew with an unplaceable accent and an affiliation with elite institutions like Harvard University.

But in another sense, an experiment can simply consist of trying to make some important endeavor succeed in unaccustomed or unforeseen circumstances. It is, in the words of the same dictionary entry, "a course of action tentatively adopted without being sure of the outcome."

This, of course, is what I had in mind.

In the eighteenth century, the Founding Fathers of the United States embarked on a great experiment in modern democracy when they set up a self-governing republic at a time when similar undertakings had miserably failed in every country where they had been tried. Though they could not be sure of the outcome, they recognized that a "long train of abuses" left them with no other choice if they were to be true to their ideals.

Today, we are embarking on a similarly novel endeavor. At a time when there is little precedent for them, we have stumbled into a great experiment in building highly diverse democracies that manage to endure and, hopefully, treat their members fairly.

This great experiment is the most important endeavor of our time. It was set in motion in the absence of a conscious experimenter. We lack widespread agreement about the kinds of rules and institutions that can help it succeed. And increasingly, we are losing sight of the goal: a vision of the future that members of both majority and minority groups can wholeheartedly embrace.

The purpose of this book is to trace the nature of this experiment, to chronicle the prohibitive costs we would pay if it failed, and to offer an optimistic vision for how it can succeed.

DIVERSE DEMOCRACY AND ITS DISCONTENTS

It's tempting to think that it should be easy to make the great experiment work.

From Sweden to the United States, politicians like to claim that "diversity is our strength." And those who value democratic institutions naturally believe that these are better able than dictatorships to keep the peace between different ethnic or religious groups. So shouldn't building diverse democracies be pretty straightforward?

Unfortunately, there are two oft-neglected reasons why both diversity and democracy can actually make it harder for societies to succeed. First, clashes between different identity groups have historically been one of the major drivers of human conflict. For many societies, diversity has turned out to be a stumbling block rather than a strength. And second, democratic institutions can do as much to exacerbate as to alleviate the challenge of diversity. In many cases, rule by the majority has served to enflame violence between ethnic or religious rivals and to deepen the exclusion of minority groups.

If the great experiment is to succeed, we need to take an unflinching look at the obstacles that stand in its way.

In some of history's most bloody conflicts, victim and perpetrator shared what, to modern eyes, would appear to be the same identity. Humans are perfectly capable of waging war on their own compatriots and coreligionists, of inflicting untold misery on people who share the color of their skin or are members of their own family.

But the history of countries from India to Indonesia also shows that diversity significantly increases the danger of violent conflict. In many of humanity's most heinous crimes, "ascriptive identities" like race or religion played a decisive role. From the mass deportations carried out by the Assyrian Empire in the ninth century BC to the expulsion of Muslims from medieval Spain, from the Holocaust to the Rwandan genocide, one group's supposed iniquity or inferiority has, time and again, served as a pretext for violence and murder on a massive scale.

A clash between groups who are descended from different ancestors or who worship a different god has, historically, been one of the main causes for violent conflict, state failure, and even civil war. That is the first difficulty facing diverse societies.

Can key features of democracy, like regular elections, help to avoid the pitfalls to which diverse societies have so often fallen prey?

The historical record is far from sanguine. The citizens of the world's most celebrated democracies have prided themselves on their ethnic purity. From Athens to Rome, and from Venice to Geneva, premodern attempts at self-government were restricted to an ethnic in-group.

Meanwhile, the most celebrated examples of diverse societies were, with few exceptions, empires or monarchies. From Baghdad in the ninth century to Vienna in the nineteenth century, episodes in which a great variety of different groups lived together peacefully, and influenced one another's cultures, came at times when the people had little say over their collective fate.

That is no mere coincidence. If you are the subject of a king or emperor, the relative number of people in your own group does not directly impact the laws you have to follow. So long as you trust the monarch to tolerate your community, you can look upon an influx of people from a different ethnic or religious group with relative equanimity.

If you are a citizen of a democracy, by contrast, the relative number of people in your own group directly impacts your ability to shape political outcomes. So long as you are in the majority, you get to call the shots. If you suddenly find yourself in the minority because of immigration or other forms of demographic change, the laws to which you are subject could change drastically. The very logic of self-government, with its constant imperative to cobble together a majority of like-minded voters, makes it tempting for citizens to exclude those they regard as different from full participation in their polity.

This is the second difficulty facing diverse democracies. Democratic institutions often make it harder, not easier, to keep the peace between competing identity groups.

Diversity often leads to conflict. Democratic institutions frequently aggravate ethnic and religious tensions. So if diverse democracies are to endure, or even thrive, it would be helpful if they could look back at a long history of trying to forge fair and inclusive societies.

Sadly, that is not the case. Most democracies have a long tradition of ethnic and religious exclusion, and so they have worryingly little experience with how to handle the diversity of identity groups that is now their reality.

Only in the past five or six decades have most democracies embraced erstwhile outsiders as compatriots on a significant scale. At the end of World War II, fewer than one in twenty-five people living in the United Kingdom had been born abroad. Today, it is one in seven. Until a few decades ago, Sweden was one of the most homogeneous countries in the world. Now one in five Swedish residents have foreign roots. Countries from Austria to Australia have undergone similarly rapid changes.

The reasons for this demographic transformation differ from place to place. In Germany and Switzerland, it was mostly driven by the need for unskilled labor that would fuel these countries' "economic miracle" in the 1950s and 1960s. In France and the United Kingdom, much of it was a consequence of the imposition, and later dissolution, of brutal empires. In Denmark and Sweden, generous asylum laws played a significant role.

But despite important differences, all these countries share a key commonality: their transformation is owed to the unforeseen and unintended consequences of policies that had objectives unrelated to the ultimate outcome. None of these countries intentionally chose to turn themselves into diverse democracies, and so none of them ever developed a coherent plan for how to deal with the key challenges they would face.

A version of this story also holds true for North America.

Because the great majority of their citizens have roots in distant lands, Canada and the United States could never pretend that a long history of common heritage or shared experience bound one compatriot to another. Unlike most European countries, they thought of themselves as nations composed of immigrants from their inception. And yet the major democracies of the New World have, for much of their existence, been deeply ethnically exclusionary in their own ways, and have blundered into the great experiment with just as little foresight.

The link between race and citizenship is particularly close in the United States. For the first ninety years of the republic's existence, African Americans were denied the most basic protections of citizenship: the right to keep the fruits of their own labor, to choose where to live or whom to marry.

When the peculiarly cruel institution of chattel slavery was finally abolished, in 1865, and the country embarked on a hopeful period of reinvention, African Americans briefly seemed to gain full civic rights. But as the backlash to Reconstruction built, they were, once again, disbarred from full participation in the nation's public life. Under the oppressive laws that held sway in the country's South for the better part of the next hundred years, they were segregated from their nominal compatriots, denied access to many basic social services, and prevented from participating in electoral politics.

For much of its history, America has also been less open to immigration from outside of Europe than the story it traditionally tells about its origins might suggest. When Chinese laborers started to arrive on the West Coast in significant numbers in the latter half of the nineteenth century, politicians began to worry about the impact that the influx of this "alien race" would have on the ethnic makeup of the American population. Starting in 1875, a series of laws barred "undesirable" East Asian immigrants from entering the country.

When the share of foreign-born residents climbed to a record high in the first decades of the twentieth century, Democrats and Republicans agreed to tighten the screw further. Laws passed in the 1920s capped the total number of newcomers at 165,000 per year and imposed additional restrictions on non-Western immigrants.

Only in 1965 did the Immigration and Nationality Act begin to remove the strict limits on immigration from outside the Western Hemisphere. Even then, leading politicians sought to ensure that the new regime would not alter the country's demographic composition. In his signing statement, President Lyndon B. Johnson insisted that this "is not a revolutionary bill. It does not affect the lives of millions. It will not reshape the structure of our daily lives."

At first, the number of immigrants from Asia, Africa, and Latin America grew slowly. But as the proportion of immigrants from continents other than Europe gradually rose, and the new arrivals made liberal use of their right to sponsor family members to follow them to the promised land, they came to make up the lion's share of newcomers. During the 2010s, about four out of every five immigrants legally admitted to the United States came from Asia or Latin America.

Even in the United States, the great experiment is more a result of mistaken assumptions about the long-term impact of public policy reforms than a testament to a principled commitment to the benefits of diversity. Neither Woodrow Wilson and Franklin Delano Roosevelt nor Lyndon Baynes Johnson and Ronald Reagan took a conscious decision to set up the great experiment. They all stumbled into it.

That helps to explain many of the problems from which diverse democracies around the world now suffer.

Many democracies have, since their inception, pledged to treat all their citizens equally, irrespective of their religion or ethnicity. They are doing their best to make the great experiment work. And yet the stories they tell about themselves still hinge on the fiction of their homogeneity.

If you had asked residents of Stockholm, Vienna, or Tokyo five decades ago who truly belonged in their country, they would likely have given you a version of the same answer: someone whose ancestors spoke the same language, lived in the same territory, belonged to the same ethnic group, and perhaps even worshipped the same god. Even today, many of these countries make it harder for minority groups to practice their religion or find cultural recognition. They pass lightly over the darkest chapters of their countries' past. And in some cases, they continue to insist that a "true" member of their country must share the same culture and ethnicity.

Especially in countries that have long prided themselves on their cultural cohesion, and have not experienced a significant influx of immigrants for very long, this raises the risk of a permanent division between insiders and outsiders. In parts of Europe and East Asia, many immigrants and members of other minority groups fear that they will never quite belong in the only country they have ever known.

As a result, the risk of cultural fragmentation is now real. Some immigrant groups have formed a socioeconomic underclass. In the poorest banlieues or inner-city neighborhoods, a few are vowing to reject the most basic rules of their societies, to voice sympathy for violent extremists, or even to engage in acts of homegrown terrorism.

Other democracies, which have been highly diverse since their founding, have for centuries endorsed a much more explicit scheme of domination. Much of their history consists of a slow struggle to overcome an overt racial hierarchy that placed white Anglo-Saxon Protestants at the top, a diverse array of religions and ethnicities in the middle, and black or indigenous people at the very bottom.

Their success in doing so should not be belittled. The astonishing difference between the rights and opportunities African Americans enjoy today and those to which they had access fifty or a hundred years ago testifies to the ability of even the most deeply flawed democracies to refashion themselves.

And yet the brutal history of domination continues to cast its long shadow over these societies. Those whose ancestors have been subjugated in the past still suffer from serious socioeconomic disadvantages. Mistrust between different demographic groups continues to run deep.

And even though these countries have long ago embraced legal equality for all their citizens, the echoes of past subjugation continue to reverberate in shocking injustices, like the abhorrent police killings of unarmed black men.

The history of diverse societies is grim. And though many things have improved over the last few decades, the past continues to haunt the present. All of that makes it unsurprising that many people are now growing pessimistic about whether diverse democracies will be able to endure.

THE RISE OF THE PESSIMISTS

To while away the time before the start of the match, the fans got a few chants going: "Here it is, the mosquito," a man with closely cropped brown hair intoned, his body turned to the crowd. "It bites you in the front and the back," he added as the crowd stomped its feet. "Quick, go get some bug spray," he concluded, to raucous applause, "and the mosquito is kaput."

Then the man took a long swig of beer and raised his right arm in a fascist salute. The crowd eagerly followed suit, a hundred men, and about a dozen women, reciprocating the gesture.

One of the few people who did not raise his hands was standing right next to me. "I have to be careful how I cheer these days," Paolo Polidori, a middle-aged Italian man wearing a navy T-shirt, beige khakis, and blue trainers, told me. "Wouldn't want people to make a thing of it. . . ."

Born in Trieste, Polidori has been coming to the Curva Furlan, the home of the most devoted fans of the local soccer club, since he was a little boy. Though he was not attending that day's game in an official capacity, he has, over the past years, become a powerful man in this midsized city in Italy's northeast.

The longtime leader of the largest faction on Trieste's city council, Polidori recently became the town's deputy mayor. If his party, the far-right Lega, wins Italy's next parliamentary elections, he may move on to more august responsibilities. "Polidori," one local journalist told me, "is a man on the make."

During a conversation that morning, at the picturesque Caffé degli Specchi in the town's central square, Polidori cycled through a litany of far-right talking points that I had also heard from activists during reporting trips in countries from Poland to Brazil. Mainstream politicians, he insisted, are secretly doing the bidding of George Soros. The governments they prop up hide the harmful effects of vaccines to boost the profits of big pharmaceutical companies. And immigration, especially from Muslim countries, is a terrible danger to Italy. That is why his party, with its proud opposition to a multiethnic society, is the only political force that can save the country.

Back at the stadium, the game had finally started. When the opposing keeper took a goal kick, the crowd broke into loud monkey noises. "It's OK because he's white," Polidori said to me, a mischievous smile on his lips. "A bit of a paradox . . ."

In many developed democracies, pessimism about the great experiment is now the defining hallmark of parts of the right. Like Polidori, the racists and demagogues of this world agree on a key credo: the historical success of democracies from Italy to the United States is rooted in their cultural inheritance and ethnic makeup. Immigration and demographic change present an existential threat to both. They are bound to impoverish countries and cultures, and to incite chaos or civil war.

Over the past decades, these voices have migrated from the fringes of public and political life to its very center. There are a lot of important differences between far-right leaders like Donald Trump and Marine Le Pen, Viktor Orbán and Jair Bolsonaro, Narendra Modi and Recep Tayyip Erdoğan. They hail from different religious traditions, have an allegiance to different ideological tribes, and direct their ire at different enemies. But one thing they share is a strong strain of ethnic majoritarianism: all of them cast the most visible minority group in their country as a central threat to its well-being—and promise to stand up for the majority.

Between them, these leaders now rule some of the largest democracies in the world. In dozens of countries that had once seemed stable, they are quashing dissent, undermining independent institutions, and attacking the rule of law. In some places, they have even succeeded in reshaping the nature of democratic citizenship in fundamental ways.

Across the world, from Italy to India, big parts of the right are now dominated by devoted detractors of diverse democracy. But what is most surprising about this historical moment is not that parts of the right oppose diversity; it is that parts of the left have, in their own way, also been growing remarkably pessimistic about the prospects of the great experiment.

As a child, Heidi Schreck worshipped the American Constitution. Growing up in Wenatchee, Washington, she made a name for herself by giving patriotic speeches about America's founding document in American Legion halls around the country.

But as Schreck came of age and learned about America's past and present injustices, she grew more skeptical, both about her country and about its founding document. How, she began to ask herself, could things have gone so badly wrong? Is the Constitution failing to deliver on its original purpose?

In a one-woman play that took Broadway by storm, winning nominations for both the Tony and the Pulitzer, Schreck answers this question in the negative: "I actually don't think our Constitution is failing. I think it is doing exactly what it was designed to do from the beginning, which is to protect the interest of a small number of rich white men."

At the end of her smash hit, Schreck asks a member of the audience to judge whether Americans should abolish the Constitution. She leaves viewers in little doubt as to her own predilections; even so, one review in *The Atlantic* took the show to task for not making a stronger case against "the decrepit national albatross."

For much of America's history, even the most ardent critics of the country's injustices argued that its founding ideals could help to shine a light toward a brighter future. In his speech about the meaning of the Declaration of Independence, Frederick Douglass pointed to the bitter irony of celebrating freedom while slavery remained the law of the land: "This Fourth of July is yours, not mine," he insisted. "You may rejoice, I must mourn." And yet Douglass did not reject the principles put forward by the Founding Fathers: "Notwithstanding the dark picture I have this day presented of the state of the nation," he concluded, "I do not despair of this country. . . . I therefore leave off where I began, with hope. While drawing encouragement from the Declaration of

Independence, the great principles it contains, and the genius of American Institutions."

Surveying the cruelties of Jim Crow a hundred years later, Martin Luther King Jr. echoed Douglass, complaining that "America has defaulted on [its] promissory note" to guarantee all people "the unalienable rights of life, liberty, and the pursuit of happiness." And yet he too remained determined to "cash this check," refusing "to believe that the bank of justice is bankrupt."

Today, a new generation dismisses these sentiments as naive. For writers like Schreck, racial injustice is not a betrayal of America; it is its defining quality. Racism is not a terrible sin committed by particular people; it is an omnipresent social force of which all whites are inescapably guilty. And the past fifty years are not a story of fitful and uneven progress toward greater justice and equality; they have offered, at best, a few momentary reprieves from the white supremacy that makes up the country's DNA.

Refusing to see significant progress in the past half century, these writers naturally have little hope for the next half century. In their minds, "whites" and "people of color" will always face each other as implacable enemies. If countries like the United States should make significant progress toward greater racial justice, it is only because the historically oppressed will triumph over their historical oppressors in an all-out struggle for power.

Many of the injustices against which these writers inveigh are real. Even so, this fatalism no more amounts to a realistic vision for how to build thriving diverse democracies than does the xenophobia of the ethnonationalist right. If the great experiment is to succeed, we need to develop a more optimistic vision.

THE NEED FOR AN OPTIMISTIC VISION

Pessimists about the great experiment don't paint a realistic vision of the current state, or likely future, of diverse democracies.

Some of these pessimists claim that immigrants and other members of minority groups are failing to join the societal mainstream because they are stupid, lazy, or evil. Others rightly reject this analysis, blaming the lower socioeconomic standing of minority groups on the oppression they have suffered in the past and the obstacles they still face today. What both perspectives miss, though, is that these groups have actually been making significant strides toward equality.

In most diverse democracies, both the descendants of immigrants and members of minority groups are quickly climbing the social ranks. They are gaining university degrees at much higher rates. Their income is rapidly rising. In fields from business to culture and politics, they are reaching positions of power and prestige that would barely have seemed imaginable to their parents or grandparents.

Mainstream views about race and religion are also rapidly shifting. From Sweden to Australia, citizens are far less likely to have hostile views toward racial or religious minorities, and far more likely to recognize that somebody who does not have the same religion or skin color can be a true Swede or a real Australian.

Within living memory, America was a country of official segregation and open hatreds, in which the force of the law made it hard for black and white Americans to be friends, and illegal for them to marry. Today, strict laws punish businesses that engage in illegal forms of discrimination and jail individuals who commit hate crimes. The number of interracial friendships, relationships, and families is growing by the hour. And though the racial gap in income and education, in life expectancy and incarceration, remains significant, it is steadily shrinking.

Despite the shadow of the past, most democracies are making real strides toward incorporating their diversity into their self-conception.

An overly pessimistic assessment of the current state of diverse democracies is not only wrong on the merits. By painting a deeply unappealing vision of the future, it also harms the prospects of the great experiment.

Those who are most interested in politics tend to have highly polarized views about hotly debated topics. Many of them either favor diverse democracies and believe that any difficulties in creating them are largely the fault of a majority population that is racist and intolerant or oppose diverse democracies and blame all their current problems on the actions of immigrants or minority groups. Most citizens, however, are far less interested in partisan politics, and have much more ambivalent feelings about key questions of public policy. They want the great experiment to succeed. But they are also concerned about the ways in which rising diversity might create real problems or change their country in unaccustomed ways. Similarly, they genuinely abhor the injustices suffered by many of their compatriots. But they also worry that more immigration could lead to a rise in crime or terrorism.

Anybody who wants diverse democracies to thrive will need to get decent people who have such ambivalent feelings about the nature of the great experiment on board. But those who are ambivalent are unlikely to be swayed if they are told that they need to adopt an unremittingly negative assessment of their own country. Nor are they likely to work toward the realization of more just democracies if they come to believe that these will, even in the best-case scenario, be consumed by an existential struggle between different identity groups.

There are real reasons to fear that the great experiment could go wrong. It is entirely possible that diverse democracies will, even twenty-five or fifty years from now, suffer from many of the injustices that now characterize them. But it is far too early to resign ourselves to a vision of the future in which most people will still eye anyone who has a different religion or skin color suspiciously; in which members of different identity groups have little contact with one another in their daily lives; in which we all choose to emphasize the differences that divide us rather than the commonalities that could unite us; and in which the basic lines of political and cultural battle still fall between Christian and Muslim, native and immigrant, or black and white.

Deriding more ambitious visions for what the future might bring as naive or utopian can seem smart or sophisticated. But in reality, the great experiment is more likely to succeed if its most devoted advocates attempt to create societies that most people would actually want to live in.

To build that kind of society, we should insist that the limitations of today need not become the realities of tomorrow. It is possible for members of diverse democracies to build ever closer links of cooperation and even friendship. National cultures can come to accommodate newcomers as full and equal members. People drawn from different ethnic and cultural groups can, without needing to give up their own identities, embark on a meaningfully shared life. And ascriptive identities like race can come to play a lesser role than they do now—not because a lot of people blind themselves to their present importance, but because we will have dismantled many of the injustices that now make them so salient.

Anybody who is serious about creating diverse democracies that endure, and thrive, needs to put forward a positive and realistic vision for how the great experiment can succeed. That is what I set out to do in this book.

In part 1, I explain why it is so hard for the great experiment to succeed. Humans are very prone to forming in-groups and discriminating against outsiders. This helps to explain why diverse societies have often suffered from anarchy, domination, or fragmentation. To avoid these common pitfalls, they need to find ways to keep humanity's instinct toward groupishness in check.

In part 2, I put forward an ambitious vision for what diverse democracies might one day look like. Their citizens can be true to their deepest convictions, charting their course through life in the confident knowledge that they are free from both the oppressive powers of the state and the restrictive norms imposed on them by their own elders. They feel a shared commitment to their country rooted in its civic traditions and its everyday culture. Their public spaces resemble a vibrant park where each group can do its own thing, but people from different backgrounds often choose to interact. And finally, the informal rules that govern how people treat one another encourage them to seek out greater mutual understanding and solidarity, holding on to the idea that the citizens of diverse democracies can come to create a meaningfully shared life.

Finally, in part 3, I explain why it is realistic to pursue this ambitious vision for the future of diverse democracies, and speak to what both citizens and policy makers can do to help turn it into reality. Over the past decades, diverse democracies have made genuine progress toward raising the living standards of minority groups and accepting them into the societal mainstream. They can build a more integrated culture and political system, avoiding a dystopian future in which the main political cleavage runs between natives and immigrants, or whites and "people of color." And while there is no panacea for the serious challenges and injustices that remain, realistic changes in public policy, electoral politics, and the choices we make in our everyday lives can hasten the arrival of such thriving diverse democracies.

Before we start, it is also worth noting what this book won't do. Diversity comes in a great number of varieties. Human societies have, for example, always been split along the lines of class and gender. Countries, like France, whose "original" residents look relatively homogeneous to a contemporary observer, are composed of regions that once prided themselves in their own rules, laws, traditions, and dialects. And a number of democracies, like Belgium or Canada, have had to figure out how to sustain a joint government even though they are made up of culturally and linguistically distinct territories. While I will at times draw on historical examples that speak to these different dimensions of conflict, my primary focus will be on the challenge to the success and survival of the world's leading democracies that now appears most urgent in many parts of the world: states whose residents are divided over some of the most salient ascriptive identities, like race and religion.

Optimism does not come easily at this difficult historical juncture. And as someone who warned about the serious threat that authoritarian populists would pose to diverse democracies long before Trump won the 2016 election, I may not be the most obvious person to muster it. Even so, I must admit to feeling a lot more upbeat about the future than is fashionable at the moment.

It would take blind optimism not to see that our democracies are in desperate need of improvement. But it would take even more blinding cynicism to believe that we have become incapable of building on the progress of the past fifty years or that our societies are condemned, whatever we do, to remain forever defined by racism and exclusion.

The road to making the great experiment succeed will be rocky. But the costs of failure are far too high to settle for a lesser destination or to give up in the middle of the journey.

PART ONE

WHEN DIVERSE SOCIETIES GO WRONG

My mother hates crowds. When I was little, we would go to great lengths to avoid them. Professional sports, with tens of thousands of supporters cheering on their own team—and heckling the opponent—made her especially uncomfortable.

Living in the center of Munich, we would sometimes see small groups of soccer fans in town to cheer their team at an upcoming match against the local favorite, Bayern, roaming the streets in search of a bar or brewery. Even when they looked harmless to me, my mother would make us cross the street as soon as she saw them.

And yet we always seemed to find ourselves in the wrong place at the wrong time. Once, at about three p.m. on a Saturday afternoon, we decided to take the subway to visit some family friends in the city's north. As soon as we got to Marienplatz, hundreds of fans on their way to a big match boarded the train, singing and jumping and egging one another on. My mother squeezed my hand very tight and told me not to worry. I knew, even then, that it was she who needed reassurance.

Her fear of crowds has something to do with her disposition; she is a private person who has always preferred the company of a few close friends to larger parties or gatherings. But it is also a matter of political conviction.

A few years before my mother was born, many members of her family were murdered in the Holocaust. When she was in her early twenties, a violent wave of anti-Semitism drove her and her parents out of Poland. Groups, to her, were intimately bound up with the tragic history of the twentieth century. When she looked at hundreds of fans chanting in unison, she did not see a bunch of people bonding over their shared love of soccer or expressing hometown pride. In some inchoate way, those chants and jeers represented the darkest side of human nature to her. It reminded her of mankind's tendency to band together in groups, to abandon individual judgment to the throes of collective passions, and, all too often, to inflict terrible suffering on outsiders.

I do not share my mother's disposition.

As a kid, I loved soccer and fanatically supported Bayern. Once I was old enough, I often went to see matches at the Olympiastadion, reveling in the collective pageantry of chants, taunts, and stadium waves. And yet my mother's assumptions about the nature of groups and the risks of tribalism deeply shaped my own view of the world.

Though I was happy to make an exception for harmless activities like professional sports, I, too, believed that the best defense against dangerous forms of tribalism was to remain resolutely individualistic. As society progresses and becomes more tolerant, I thought, the importance of group identity would gradually fade. Instead of seeing ourselves as Germans or Frenchmen, as Jews or Gentiles, as white or black, we would recognize one another as, simply, human. The age of nationalism would give way to an era of cosmopolitanism in which most of us cared as much about those whom we had never met as we did for those who have always been our neighbors.

I still believe that this is, in many ways, a noble vision. The world would be better off if people were more reluctant to favor their own group or nation and more capable of empathizing with those who are far away. Those who dare to speak up when members of their own tribe are being unjust, or to make real sacrifices for those with whom they barely share any traits, deserve our deepest admiration.

And yet I have, as I traveled the world and studied its history, also come to believe that a generalized hostility to any form of collective identity is a misguided way to build tolerant societies. If we are to keep the darkest aspects of our natures in check, the question is not whether we can overcome our "groupish" instinct; it is how we can build on its enormous potential for good while containing its terrifying capacity for evil.

Our tendency to assemble in groups is responsible not only for the darkest chapters in human history but also for our species' greatest achievements.

Chimpanzees are highly intelligent. But no matter how much they may desire to access food that they could reach by stepping on a wooden log, they are unlikely to band together to maneuver it into the right position. According to most scientists, they are simply not sufficiently sociable to pull off such a basic feat of coordination. As Michael Tomasello, a psychologist who specializes in social cognition, once said: "It is inconceivable that you would ever see two chimpanzees carrying a log together."

Humans, by contrast, are defined by sociability as much as by intelligence. By the age of three or four, human children are capable of forms of cooperation never observed in chimpanzees. Working together, we have built giant cities, created beautiful works of art, and sent a man to the moon.

Many of these feats were accomplished in the name of particular identity groups: The Romans added to the splendor of their city to contain the power of Carthage. Devout artists created beautiful paintings of Jesus Christ—or giant statues of Buddha—to exalt their own civilizations. And Americans invested giant resources in an unlikely moonshot to stick it to the Soviets.

Even my mother, that devoted individualist, spent her professional life doing an activity that social scientists often cite as a paramount example of humanity's prodigious ability to form groups that are united by a common purpose. Her job as a conductor was to forge the voices and instruments of more than a hundred musicians into a cohesive work of art.

When we talk about the challenges of building a diverse democracy today, it is tempting to focus on the present condition of our own societies, or to debate the latest wedge issues that divide opinion on social media or cable news. But before we can set out the kind of society we hope to build, and how we might be able to get there, we need to put these questions in the context of human history and psychology. For it is impossible to see the real reasons for the problems diverse democracies face—or to analyze how they might be able to do better—without an understanding of what makes humans tick, or how societies have responded when they were presented with the challenge of diversity in the past.

That is why part 1 of this book asks the big questions we need to address before we can consider the problems facing diverse democracies today. Do humans have a natural tendency to form groups? Do they necessarily favor the in-group and discriminate against the out-group? Will categories like race and religion always divide us? What are the main ways in which diverse societies have come apart? And what lessons does all this hold for how diverse democracies can do better in the future than they have in the past?

ONE

Why Everyone
Can't Just Get Along

When Henri Tajfel was born in Włocławek, a small town in the center of Poland, his parents had reason to hope that a better future might await him. World War I had just ended. Across Europe, new democracies were overthrowing royal rule and foreign domination. Poland became an independent nation for the first time in more than a century.

By the time Tajfel was a teenager, those hopes were quickly being dashed. Poland's democracy gave way to a dictatorship run by a clique of military generals. Anti-Semitism was on the rise all across Europe. Because of a local quota on the number of Jews, Tajfel was unable to enroll in a university in his own country.

In search of opportunity, Tajfel moved to Paris, where he studied chemistry at the Sorbonne. When World War II broke out, he volunteered for service in the French army, but quickly fell into German captivity, surviving some of the deadliest years in European history as a prisoner of war. Upon his liberation, he learned that the Nazis had murdered most of his family.

Trying to make sense of the fate that had befallen his parents and siblings, Tajfel resolved to study how hatred could have so consumed supposedly "civilized" nations that they slaughtered millions of people. Thanks to an essay on the nature of prejudice, he won a scholarship to study psychology at Birkbeck College, in London.

As Tajfel progressed in his studies, he learned about a series of recent experiments that showed just how easy it is to get human beings to do terrible things to one another. What happens when a scientist in a white lab coat tells you to keep administering electric shocks to a volunteer even though he is begging you to stop? If you are like most Americans— or, as later studies would show, like most Germans, Jordanians, or Australians—you keep administering the shocks even as your victim writhes in pain.

And what happens when nice middle-class boys from a peaceful American town are split into two groups, and made to compete for food and firewood? Over the course of a few days, they form a deep bond with the members of their own group—and develop a seething hatred for members of the other group.

It is, psychologists proved over and over during the 1950s and 1960s, shockingly easy to make humans hate one another when you divide them up. But as the evidence of human depravity accumulated—not just on the killing fields of the Second World War but also in the pristine laboratories of fancy universities—Tajfel grew frustrated that social scientists still didn't understand *why* groups are willing to do such dreadful things to one another. What is needed to get a group off the ground, and what about these groups makes people capable of such terrifying cruelty?

This is the intellectual puzzle that Tajfel, who had by now taken a prestigious chair for social psychology at the University of Bristol, set out to solve.

To find an answer, Tajfel came up with a brilliantly counterintuitive study. He would create groups that are so devoid of meaning that none of their members would favor their own. Then, Tajfel thought, he could slowly add more features to these groups, observing when they crossed the magical threshold that made their members willing to discriminate against outsiders.

In 1970, Tajfel assembled sixty-four teenage boys from a school in the nearby suburbs. When they had settled into a large lecture hall, he gave them the most arbitrary exercise he could think up: his assistants flashed forty clusters of dots in front of their eyes, asking them to guess how many there were on each picture.

Some people, Tajfel told the boys, tend to underestimate the number of dots. Other people tend to overestimate the number. Neither group has an advantage in approximating the right result.

In the second stage of the experiment, Tajfel split the boys up into "underestimators" and "overestimators," asking them to allocate points—which could later be redeemed for cash—to their classmates. Without knowing the exact identity of the person to whom they were giving these points, they were told to choose between giving different sets of rewards to "member No. 1 of your group" and to "member No. 1 of the other group."

Because the boys "were divided into groups defined by flimsy and unimportant criteria," Tajfel later wrote in an article that transformed vast areas of social science, he did not expect that they would discriminate in favor of their own group. Doing so would make little sense.

And yet virtually all of them did.

The difference between how the boys treated members of the underestimators and the overestimators was striking. When they had to allocate money between different members of their own group, they sought to give each of the boys the same amount. But as soon as they had a choice between allocating money to a member of their group and a member of the other group, they favored their own. "The only thing we needed to do to achieve this result," Tajfel reported, "was to associate their judgments of numbers of dots with the use of the term 'your group.'"

Bewildered by this finding, Tajfel tried to generate groups on other, equally flimsy grounds. In one iteration, he showed schoolboys paintings by Paul Klee and Wassily Kandinsky, asking them which they preferred. To his consternation, the "Klee group" promptly started to discriminate against the "Kandinsky group" (and vice versa).

Over the years, many other researchers have replicated Tajfel's findings. They have been able to get people to discriminate in favor of ingroups assembled on such silly criteria as the color of the T-shirt they were randomly assigned or their opinion as to whether a hot dog is a sandwich.

"Outgroup discrimination," Tajfel concluded, is "extraordinarily easy to trigger."

For those of us who have had the luck to grow up in comparatively peaceful and tolerant societies, it is tempting to think of tribal rivalries or ethnic hatreds as an aberration. Far from being natural, I once thought, the tendency to form groups has to be inculcated in humans.

If only we could overcome the conditioning of the past, or the cynical pundits and politicians trying to inflame our most violent passions, we would all live in harmony.

Tajfel's research gives the lie to this comforting assumption. As he demonstrates, the tendency to form in-groups and discriminate against those who are not part of them exists in all of us.

Even educated people who grow up in comfortable circumstances are hardwired to form groups. We may think of ourselves as individualists who seek to be fair toward everyone, but in reality we are willing to help the underestimators against the overestimators, or to fight for Team Klee in an altercation with Team Kandinsky.

Tajfel's "minimal group paradigm" offers an important insight. But the past hundred years are full of instances in which people murdered one another because of perceived differences that are far more meaningful than those he was able to create in his lab.

From World War I to World War II, the primary distinction in many of history's most deadly conflicts was that between one nation and another. From the violent conflicts between moderate Muslims and Islamist terrorists to the mass extermination of "class enemies" by communist governments, the primary distinction in other major conflicts has been religious or ideological. And from the killing fields of Rwanda to the murderous hills of Sarajevo, the primary distinction in others still has been racial or ethnic.

Are most deadly conflicts motivated by groups whose formation was as arbitrary as those created by Tajfel? Or are most of them driven by real differences in attributes that have persisted for a very long time?

NEITHER NATURAL NOR RANDOM

Many people believe that the groups that are most important in real life are deeply meaningful entities that track natural, biological, or long-standing historical distinctions.

French pupils learn about "our ancestors, the Gauls." The Chinese call their country the Middle Kingdom. The Mauri claim that they are the children of the earth. Virtually all these myths entail two claims about the nature of their group: They depict it as a natural unit. And they claim that its origins stretch back to the dawn of time. In the language of social science, the stories most groups tell about themselves are "primordial."

The primordial view of social groups has some basis in reality. As everyone knows, there are salient visual differences between many ethnic groups. In most cases, it only takes a split second to guess whether the ancestors of someone you see on the street originate in Europe, Asia, or Africa. If you know a culture or continent well, you may also be able to tell the difference between an Italian and a Spaniard, between a Kenyan and a Nigerian, between a Bengali and a Bihari, or between someone who hails from Japan and Korea.

In many cases, members of today's ethnic groups also share a common lineage. To the best of our knowledge, for example, Jews and Zoroastrians really are descended from the small bands of people who first took on these identities thousands of years ago. And if you send a small vial with your spit as well as a payment of $99 to the friendly folks at 23andMe, they will be able to create a pretty chart that informs you that you are, say, 75 percent West African, 10 percent South Asian, 10 percent Oceanian, and 5 percent southern European. (It will also tell you whether you are 100 percent Homo sapiens or have a little Neanderthal blood coursing through your veins.)

Genetic differences between ethnic groups can even be medically relevant. Over the decades, doctors have realized that a large number of East Asians lack an enzyme that makes alcohol more digestible. African Americans have a higher propensity to suffer from sickle cell anemia. Ashkenazi women are in greater danger of dying from breast cancer.

Much as we might like things to be otherwise, we can't wish the differences between ethnic groups out of existence. But though many ethnic groups do have a basis in history or common ancestry, there is another sense in which they really are more fluid than most people tend to recognize.

Many claims about the average differences between members of different groups are significantly overstated or altogether wrong. The ways in which we draw the boundaries between different groups strongly depends on past political battles and other historical circumstances. And because it is not always clear who should belong in which group, the way we police membership in various identity groups can be highly arbitrary—as the story of one woman who got caught in the gears of Brazil's bureaucratic apparatus for determining the boundaries between one race and another demonstrates.

Like millions of Brazilians, Maíra Mutti Araújo is of mixed ancestry.

Her forefathers likely include indigenous people who have lived on the land for centuries, enslaved Africans who were brought to the country in chains to harvest sugar or coffee, and Portuguese colonists who arrived in search of wealth and power.

Growing up, the young lawyer identified as "pardo," a Brazilian term for people whose skin color appears neither white nor black. Because she looked darker than some other members of her family, her parents lovingly called her "pretinha," a term of endearment for dark-skinned girls.

So when the state of Bahia introduced a quota system to ensure that a significant share of its public jobs would be filled by pretos* or pardos, and the city of Salvador advertised for a prestigious position as a public prosecutor, Araújo heeded the advice of her friends, and put in an application.

Araújo sat for three grueling exams, scoring third out of a thousand applicants. Her dream was within reach. Then began, as Araújo called it in an interview with the Brazilian journalist Cleuci de Oliveira, "the racial soap opera" in which she would find herself cast as the villain.

In the second round of the recruitment process, the hiring committee sought to evaluate whether promising applicants were eligible for a position reserved for brown and black Brazilians. Araújo was asked to submit photos of herself and required to answer a questionnaire about her racial identity. Did she have any black or brown idols, one asked. Was she "currently or previously dating a black or brown person," another inquired.

"I found the questions offensive," Araújo told de Oliveira. "I don't think they have any bearing on how a person defines their racial identity." But since she didn't want to throw away her shot, she dutifully submitted her answers.

After scrutinizing her photo and her questionnaire, the committee decided to disqualify Araújo. Though she had identified as pardo all

---

* "Preto" is the more official term for dark-skinned Brazilians, of which "pretinha" is the female diminutive.

her life, she supposedly lacked the requisite "Afro-descendant pheno-type."

Araújo sued to be reinstated. She won, but this only gave her an opportunity to take part in another humiliating round of the application process: an in-person verification of her racial credentials.

Like dozens of other job candidates, Araújo flew to Salvador at short notice. She made her way to a government office in which five experts were perched atop a platform, scrutinizing a parade of job candidates. She handed one of the experts her ID, and was told to sit in a chair, where she was silently inspected for three minutes.

"I felt like a zoo animal," she said.

A few weeks later, Araújo found out that the commission had definitively disqualified her. In an ironic twist that would make any writer for a soap opera proud, the prosecutor's office for which she had hoped to work began to investigate her for "racial fraud."

Compared with many other settler colonies, Brazil has always had lax rules about racial mixing. Lacking a sufficiently large number of potential spouses of their own race, male settlers frequently married enslaved or indigenous women. Rather than counting as fully black, the children of these mixed unions came to be known by a complex set of racial categories.

Over time, these categories became increasingly unwieldy. Once members of different groups had mixed for many generations, and most Brazilians came to live in big cities rather than small villages in which everyone knew everyone else, it became increasingly difficult to tell whether somebody was, say, "cafuso" or "caboclo." Increasingly, people's membership in one or another racial group began to depend, simply, on their appearance—which means that siblings who have the same parents but different skin tones are often thought to belong to separate racial groups.

In the United States, by contrast, black identity has long been governed by the "one-drop rule." Whereas a great majority of settlers in other parts of the world were men, those who set foot in North America included women and children. With no need to marry outside of their own race, American colonists developed an intricate set of laws and social conventions designed to perpetuate the inferior social status of slaves and their descendants. Because those children who did have mixed parentage threatened to upend the strict division of society into a dominant white and a subordinate black group, the colonists came up with a simple solution: children who had any known black ancestry were treated as black.

Some Americans have long ago grasped the strangeness of the one-drop rule. *The Octoroon*, one of the most successful American plays of the nineteenth century, portrays the doomed love between the owner of a slave plantation and a distant cousin of his who is one-eighth black.

But despite its troubling origins, the one-drop rule continues to shape popular perceptions of race in today's America among both white and black people. Barack Obama's skin may not be much darker than that of Maíra Mutti Araújo. But whereas, in Brazil, Araújo wound up in the crosshairs of the local prosecutor's office because she wasn't "black enough," in the United States only cranks and extremists would dare to doubt that Obama was the country's first black president.

Schemes of racial categorization that appear natural to those who were raised within one culture can seem strange and illogical to those who grew up in another. Even within any one particular country, there will be many hard cases that reveal to what extent we disagree about who should count as a member of what group.

Take the United States. Should Americans who are descended from Spain count as Latino? (The US Census answers this question in the affirmative.)

Is somebody a Native American because they have some pertinent ancestry, or do they need to be officially recognized by a relevant tribe? (Many Native Americans protested when Elizabeth Warren argued the former.)

And should the children of recent African immigrants be eligible for affirmative action programs whose goal it is, in part, to redress the lingering injustices caused by slavery? (A new activist group, the American Descendants of Slavery, believes that they shouldn't.)

There is nothing natural about the specific racial categories that animate so much of our contemporary politics. As Karen and Barbara Fields have pointed out, they are based on a kind of "racecraft": by "disguising collective social practice as inborn individual traits," they argue, we transform "racism into race."

But to say that races are, to some extent, socially constructed does not mean that they lack any grounding in reality. We love to talk about race and ethnicity as though they were either pure figments of the imagination or as though the particular racial scheme of classification each society has adopted was the only logical option that reality presents us. Both answers are too simple.

Paradoxically, ethnic identity is both very real and highly malleable. Many of the groups into which human beings invest the deepest meaning track something real that is of deep significance to their members. There is a reason why so many people care so deeply about their class or their ethnicity, their nation or their religion. Nor is it a surprise that people in the real world are more likely to risk their lives to realize the political aspirations of the proletariat, to demonstrate the superiority of the Han people, to vindicate the rightful claims of Ukraine, or to defend Hinduism than they are to go into battle to vanquish those who deny that a hot dog is a sandwich.

But for all the real grounding of the kinds of identities that most motivate humans—and make them most willing to risk their lives or impose harm on others—the role they play is deeply shaped by circumstances. There is nothing natural about which group is most salient at any one moment, or how two different groups are likely to treat each other. And that raises the question of when people with different identities are most likely to come to blows—or to coexist in peace.

FRIENDS AND FOES

The Chewas and the Tumbukas, two large tribes in southeastern Africa, have a long history of enmity. When Daniel Posner, a young doctoral student from Harvard University, traveled to Malawi to talk to members of these tribes about their attitudes toward each other, they were strikingly forthright about their complaints.

The Tumbuka, interviewees in one Chewa village told him, engage in all kinds of weird cultural practices. Their dances are all wrong. They demand a much steeper bride price. Newlywed couples have to reside close to the groom's family. A majority of his interlocutors openly told him that they would neither vote for a Tumbuka presidential candidate nor marry a Tumbuka spouse.

Did Tumbukas feel the same way about Chewas? To find out, Posner traveled a few dozen miles north. And sure enough, the complaints of his Tumbuka interlocutors mirrored those he had heard from Chewas.

The traditional dances of the Chewa, Tumbukas explained, are all wrong. They demand too small a bride price. Their newlywed couples all have to reside close to the bride's family. A majority of his interviewees unhesitatingly reported that they would neither vote for a Chewa presidential candidate nor marry a Chewa spouse.

If Posner had stopped his research after talking to people in these two villages, he may have concluded that the antipathy between Chewas and Tumbukas is primordial—one of those "ancient hatreds" about which reporters love to write when yet another civil war breaks out in Africa, the Balkans, or the Middle East. "The Chewas have always hated the Tumbukas. The Tumbukas have always hated the Chewas," he might have written. "What's there to be done?" But instead of jumping to that conclusion, Posner traveled a few miles west, crossing the border from Malawi to Zambia.

Drawn up as the result of a colonial dispute between Belgium, Germany, France, and England in 1884, the border does not reflect any important historical or geographical features. Both Chewas and Tumbukas live on either side of it, speaking the same dialects and following the same sets of customs whether their passports say they are Malawian or Zambian.

And so Posner was, at first, struck by how similar things seemed in Zambia. The roads were just as bad. The villages he saw had similar architectural styles and comparable levels of economic development.

Then he started talking to people.

When Posner asked Tumbukas on the Zambian side of the border how they felt about Chewas, their response was much more complimentary. Though he had by now come to expect the usual litany of complaints about the other group, his Tumbuka interviewees emphasized how much respect they had for Chewas. Few of them told Posner that they would refuse to marry a Chewa. Even fewer said that they would oppose a Chewa presidential candidate.

The feeling turned out to be mutual. The same spirit of tolerance was also in evidence when he spoke to residents of a nearby Chewa village.

In Malawi, Chewas and Tumbukas dislike each other. Across the arbitrarily drawn border to Zambia, Chewas and Tumbukas trust and respect each other. Why?

The reason, Posner demonstrated by painstakingly ruling out alternative explanations, is political.

In Malawi, Chewas and Tumbukas each make up a relatively large portion of the overall population. Both have real hopes of capturing the country's presidency and putting policies that favor them into place. As a result, they are political adversaries—and harbor ill will toward each other.

Zambia, on the other hand, is much more ethnically diverse. Neither Chewas nor Tumbukas make up a particularly large percentage of the overall population. Nor do either of them have a realistic chance of capturing the country's presidency on their own. In an effort to ensure that they prevail over candidates from western Zambia, whose cultural differences are even more pronounced, they often support the same candidates. Most of the time, they are political allies—and have much more positive attitudes toward each other.

What might at first seem like an ancient hatred turns out to be deeply influenced by contemporary circumstances. If Chewas and

Tumbukas are capable of being allies on one side of the border and enemies on the other, changing conditions might be able to bring about the same transformation in the relations of other groups that have historically seen each other as enemies. Strange as the story of the Chewas and Tumbukas might seem, it holds lessons about the nature of identity that are of great relevance far beyond southeastern Africa.

Over the past decades, political scientists have found dozens of similar examples. All around the world, both the salience and the impact of particular identities seem to depend on the incentives created by local conditions.

Chinese immigrants in Jamaica have, over time, changed the criteria governing membership in their group as their economic conditions evolved. Political entrepreneurs in countries like Uganda and Nigeria have exacerbated tensions between different tribal groups to maximize their chances of winning elections. And the deterioration of relationships between Serbs and Croatians was driven in part by the way in which geographic features of the decomposing federation of Yugoslavia shaped each group's security needs.

This is not to say that any of these groups are wholly arbitrary. The cultural differences between Chewas and Tumbukas, the ethnic differences between black and Chinese Jamaicans, and the religious differences between Serbs and Croatians are neither new nor immaterial. But the precise way in which these groups form—and the extent to which they see one another as allies or enemies—does depend on the particular circumstances and the incentives they create.

These kinds of incentives don't just govern how different groups relate to one another; in the many situations in which individuals have multiple identities, they also help to determine which of them is most salient.

In the United States, race is the most important marker of identity. In India, caste retains tremendous power. In sub-Saharan Africa, the bloodiest conflicts are usually carried out between members of different tribes. In much of the Middle East, the religious distinction between Sunnis and Shias is most salient. And in virtually all countries, stark differences of class and gender also help to structure the lines of political conflict to an important degree.

Even in the same country, the salience of these categories can be subject to rapid change. For much of their lives, for example, my Jewish grandparents thought of themselves as proletarians who were fighting for a more egalitarian society alongside their Gentile comrades in the Polish Communist Party. When the party's leaders decided to fan the flames of anti-Semitism in the late 1960s, my grandparents discovered that they were suddenly seen, primarily, as Jews.

Anti-Semitism was widespread in Poland before 1968. Some form of class consciousness persisted even at the height of the government's campaign to drive out the country's few remaining Jews. But the group boundary that mattered the most shifted with astounding rapidity. And for those who were sufficiently unlucky to be on the wrong side of the new dividing line, the consequences were as harsh as they were immediate. One year, my grandparents held prestigious positions and had a decent livelihood. The next year, the government considered them members of an out-group it could legitimately harass, fire from their jobs, and expel from the country.

Unlike the lab experiments undertaken by Tajfel, most real-world conflicts are rooted in distinctions that have long held deep meaning. The particular forms these conflicts take vary greatly from place to place.

But it is hardly a coincidence that the most violent conflicts around the globe usually relate to four core distinctions: class, race, religion, and nation.*

At the same time, the role that these distinctions play in particular contexts is deeply shaped by circumstances. Whether a conflict subsides or escalates depends on the choices of the powerful, the institutions with which they have to contend, and the extent to which ordinary people are able to build trusting and cooperative relationships with one another.

In some countries, people have strong incentives to double down on one overarching identity. The members of one salient group barely interact with those of other salient groups. Because they hardly know each other, they remain unaware that they may share important interests. And because they stand to gain handsomely from capturing control of the state—or to suffer greatly if they allow their nemesis to grow more powerful than them—they are always at the ready to engage in intergroup competition. Violent conflict often ensues.

In other countries, circumstances help to diffuse conflict. People who differ on one salient dimension of identity, like race, share another salient dimension of identity, like religion. They spend a lot more time together, building a greater awareness of their shared interests, and grow skeptical of fearmongers and conflict entrepreneurs who would have them believe the worst about one another. In the best cases, political institutions help to mitigate conflict by ensuring that citizens can

---

* Gender is another important source of conflict and identity. The tasks and responsibilities socially ascribed to men or women often vary significantly. Women have for many centuries been confined to a narrow "private sphere" that severely restricted their freedom to live a self-determined life. Unsurprisingly, the injustice that has been inherent in many such arrangements has increasingly become, and now remains, an important locus of political contestation.

get fair treatment even if the president or prime minister doesn't hail from their own group.

Virtually every part of the world has to contend with long-standing tensions and enmities between groups. Difference is not always benign. But whether diverse societies can sustain peace and cooperation depends not (just) on the events of the past but (also) on the actions taken today.

When I look at the many tensions and injustices that plague diverse democracies, from Brazil to Zambia, and from India to the United States, I am tempted to get impatient with them. Why can't they live up to the kinds of cosmopolitan ideals that my mother and I shared when I was growing up? Can't we all just get along?

The more I have studied history, comparative politics, and social psychology, the more naive these questions seem to me. Human beings have an extremely strong tendency toward forming groups. What's puzzling is not so much why vast societies that contain millions of extremely diverse people sometimes come to blows; it is how many of them are, much of the time, capable of sustaining peaceful cooperation on a massive scale.

This is not a prescription for quietism. All of the evidence we have points to the ever-present possibility that even diverse democracies that are comparatively peaceful will suffer from mutual mistrust, persistent oppression, or civil war.

But history and social science also teach us that we have tools for avoiding conflict. There is nothing inevitable about how people identify, or whether they choose violent means to settle their differences. All the evidence suggests that our ability to sustain peaceful and thriving democracies depends, to a large extent, on how we handle humanity's powerful instinct toward tribalism.

So what lessons can we draw from all this? Which actions and institutions are likely to prevent—or to exacerbate—conflict?

I would love to answer these questions by taking you on a tour of all the diverse democracies that have fully solved their problems and built admirably just societies. But such countries do not exist. And so the best I can do, for now, is to propose an imperfect alternative: to start thinking about how to do things right, we need to look at specific examples of how things have so often gone wrong—and what kinds of lessons those failures might offer for how to avoid the same pitfalls going forward.

TWO

Three Ways Diverse
Societies Fail

Happy families are all alike, Tolstoy famously wrote, but each unhappy family is unhappy in its own way. There is much truth to this. And yet psychologists are able to identify common patterns.

Some families are unhappy because they are extremely poor. Others are unhappy because the parents cannot stand each other. Still others are unhappy because one or more of their members inflict mental, physical, or sexual abuse on their relatives.

The same is true of diverse democracies. Hundreds of books have been written on just about every country that suffers from ethnic strife, racial subjugation, or genocide. Each has its own history and deserves to be understood in its own right. And yet we can glean a lot of insight by looking at common ways in which diverse societies have, historically, come apart.

In this chapter, I will explain the three most important: anarchy, domination, and fragmentation.

ANARCHY

Thomas Hobbes, the seventeenth-century English philosopher, was the first great theorist of the dangers posed by anarchy.

"Nature," Hobbes argued in *Leviathan*, his most important work, made men relatively "equal in the faculties of body and mind." One man may be stronger, swifter, or smarter than another. But "when all is reckoned together, the difference between man and man is not so considerable as that one man can thereupon claim to himself any benefit to which another may not pretend as well as he."

Far from taking comfort in man's equality, Hobbes insisted that its implications were terrifying. Because humans are relatively equal in ability, they are prone to seek the same goods and honors. And because even a small or weak person can use their wits to injure or kill a large and strong one, they always have reason to mistrust each other. Surrounded by potential competitors on all sides, and never sure that they could withstand an organized attack, even peace-loving people would have a strong incentive to strike preemptively.

In the absence of a central authority, Hobbes deduced from these simple premises, a "war of every man against every man" would quickly break out. Its results would be devastating. In what he called the "state of nature,"

> there is no place for industry because the fruit thereof is uncertain, and consequently no culture of the earth. No navigation nor use of the commodities that may be imported by sea. . . . No arts. No letters. No society. And, which is worst of all, continual fear and danger of violent death. And the life of man, solitary, poor, nasty, brutish, and short.

According to Hobbes, the deprivations of the state of nature retained their relevance even among people who were raised with the comforts of civilization. Writing in an age of conquests, revolutions, and civil wars, he feared that contemporary challenges to the authority of the state could, at any moment, allow the state of nature to rear its ugly head again—and that made him desperate to maintain political order at just about any cost.

The precise nature of the rules that states impose on us, Hobbes believed, is less important than that they should exist at all. Better to live under the sway of a selfish or immoral monarch than to suffer chaos and anarchy. For when there is no state, everybody suffers.

In the centuries since Hobbes published *Leviathan*, philosophers and social scientists haven't stopped arguing over whether the absence of state power would really lead to the kind of disastrous anarchy that he predicted. The evidence they have uncovered is so ambivalent that an overall verdict remains elusive.

In most societies that lack the kind of sovereign for which Hobbes advocated, life doesn't seem to be quite as dismal as he anticipated. Even in the absence of a formal state, many traditional societies manage to maintain strong norms. When the universal rules imposed by modern governments are absent, familial bonds, cultural customs, and religious rites govern who is entitled to what.

Among the Inuit of Canada's arctic coast, for example, conflicts are mitigated through "song duels." When two people have a dispute, anthropologist Jean Briggs reports, the warring parties resolve their differences by singing scornful songs about each other in front of an amused audience. The conflict is over when the community—judging the artistic merits of their songs, not simply the "righteousness of the case"—declares a winner.

Anthropologists studying tribes in far-flung places, from the mountains of Africa to the rain forests of the Amazon, have come to similar conclusions. Long before the creation of modern states, humans seem to have figured out how to avoid some of the costs of chaos. Instead of being subject to the anarchy Hobbes feared, most of our ancestors were constrained by an elaborate "cage of norms" that regulated their behavior in great detail.*

At the same time, researchers have also found plenty of evidence that suggests humans do pay a heavy price when they are unable to coordinate around a higher power that sets the rules and punishes those who break them. According to careful studies by anthropologists who have looked at human skeletons recovered in archaeological digs, for example, prehistoric societies and early human settlements suffered from enormous rates of violent death. But as rulers gradually gained the power to enforce their rules, the levels of violence fell markedly. "Between the late Middle Ages and the 20th century," Steven Pinker writes in *The Better Angels of Our Nature*, "European countries saw a tenfold-to-fiftyfold decline in their rates of homicide."

Even today, those parts of the world in which the state is weak suffer from much higher levels of violence than those parts of the world in which the state is strong. Singapore, which has a highly developed state, has a homicide rate of 0.2 per 100,000. The United States, which has always suffered an abnormally high level of violent crime for an affluent democracy, has 5 per 100,000. In El Salvador, where the state is weak and the government compromised by pervasive corruption, the rate stands at a staggering 62 per 100,000. Some of the most dangerous places in the world, from Venezuela to the Central African

---

* I will explain the cage of norms, and its implications, in greater detail in chapter 4.

Republic, are located in countries where the central government lacks effective authority over large parts of its nominal territory—or doesn't really exist in the first place.

Why do some groups manage to keep the peace without a central authority while the absence of a state condemns other societies to a proliferation of murder, violence, or even civil war?

The answer is that the human tendency to band together both helps to maintain peace *within* groups and to foster conflict *between* them.

When Hobbes wrote about the state of nature, he pictured lone individuals who are incapable of sustaining cooperation. His vision of a war of every man against every man was one of *atomized anarchy*.

In reality, humans have for hundreds of thousands of years lived in families, bands, or tribes. Within those groups, informal rules and long-standing affections usually help members to sustain some level of meaningful cooperation.

But whereas humans usually find ways of avoiding a war of all against all within small groups, they cannot rely on the cage of norms to keep the peace when one group encounters another. Members of different groups usually lack the family ties or shared culture to soften the reasons for mutual mistrust that will always exert some influence over their minds in the absence of a higher power. When two bands of hunter-gatherers meet, or two villages fight each other over access to an important source of sustenance, or two tribes compete to control the powerful machinery of the state, they do not have the tools to stop their mutual fear from working its poisonous magic.

Within groups, things were never as dismal as Hobbes predicted. Between groups, the absence of central authority often leads to wanton death and unspeakable cruelty. The danger facing humans in the absence of a strong state is not the atomized anarchy of a war of all against all; it is a destructive fight between rival groups I propose to call *structured anarchy*.

And in many parts of the world, the threat of structured anarchy remains very much alive today.

THE HEAVY TOLL OF STRUCTURED ANARCHY

On May 12, 2020, a group of young men slinging rifles and brandishing grenades forced their way into the Dasht-e-Barchi Hospital in western Kabul. Once they reached the maternity ward, they took aim at nurses, pregnant women, and newborn babies, and began to fire.

Some new mothers managed to flee their attackers. A few heavily pregnant women barricaded themselves into a room with a heavy door. One woman gave birth while in hiding, a midwife helping to deliver her with bare hands before swaddling the newborn in her headscarf.

But most were not so lucky. When government forces finally managed to beat back the attackers, some four hours after the nightmare began, the majority of women, and a great number of newborns, had been shot dead. All in all, twenty-four women and children died in the attack.

During the standoff, the hospital had the feel of a horror movie, a chaotic scene of senseless slaughter. In retrospect, it is clear that the attackers had left little up to chance.

The Sunni gunmen had likely targeted the Dasht-e-Barchi Hospital because it is located in a neighborhood populated by Hazara Shias.

Having made their way past a number of other departments, they did not alight on the maternity ward by accident. As Frederic Bonnot, a functionary at Doctors Without Borders, the organization that runs the hospital, said: "They came to kill the mothers."

In the days after the attack, there was a lot of confusion about the identity of the culprits. A spokesman for the United States declared that the Islamic State was responsible. Ashraf Ghani, then still the president of Afghanistan, appeared to blame the Taliban. Both groups denied responsibility. What is clear is that the headline-grabbing attack was yet another attempt by one of the country's many insurgent groups to showcase the weakness of the central government in Kabul, which was to collapse the following summer.

Even the most rural and remote areas of Afghanistan boast of beautiful handicrafts, a rich culinary tradition, and a deep store of traditional knowledge. Far from being engaged in a chaotic war of all against all, most areas of the country are highly hierarchical, with local elders exercising tremendous power over members of their clan. The country never resembled the "state of nature."

And yet Afghanistan has long suffered from serious problems because it lacked a central authority that could command a monopoly on legitimate violence, avoid constant bouts of intergroup conflict, and provide meaningful public goods.

The country as a whole is split up into about fourteen major ethnic groups, including the Pashtuns, Tajiks, Hazaras, and Uzbeks. Pashtuns, in turn, are divided into about four major tribes, the Bettani, the Gharghashti, the Karlani, and the Sarbani. The Bettani, in turn, are divided into more than twenty subtribes, each of which includes dozens of separate clans.

The life of an ordinary resident of a small village in rural Afghanistan is subject to these power structures to a degree that those of us who are lucky enough to live in functioning democracies find difficult to fathom. His access to arable land and his ability to defend himself from enemies, his form of religious worship and his choice of spouse are regulated in minute detail. Women, who are subject to deeply patriarchal norms, have even less agency than their fathers or husbands.

Within each of these clans, these customs and power structures help to avoid a war of all against all. But because many of these groups are deeply mistrustful of one another, the country as a whole has long been engulfed in violent conflict. Most of its citizens have at best a highly abstract allegiance to a shared Afghan identity.

This helps to explain why the democratically elected government of Afghanistan struggled to win meaningful control over its national territory. In large parts of the country, the Taliban always remained in charge. In other parts, government officials were able to exert no more than limited influence thanks to the conditional cooperation of allied warlords. Even in Kabul and the surrounding areas, they never proved capable of averting bloody attacks by an array of insurgent forces.

Because the central government was incapable of imposing its rules on much of the country, it had tremendous difficulties in raising revenues. That made it impossible to sustain public goods at any significant scale. The quality of schools in Afghanistan remains abysmal. Welfare benefits are minimal. Even before COVID-19 hit, the public health system was perpetually close to collapse. There are whole stretches of the country in which there are barely any paved roads, few functioning schools, and virtually no doctors.

The dire impact this has had on the quality of life is evident from just about every cross-national comparison. Only 43 percent of Afghanistan's population know how to read or write. Out of every one thousand children, sixty die before the age of five. In 2018, the average life expectancy was sixty-six for women and sixty-three for men, about two decades below the level in developed democracies.

In August 2021, the Taliban's conquest of Kabul temporarily united Afghanistan under their theocratic rule. But it is far from certain that this will put an end to the country's long history of ethnic and religious conflict. Warlords that are now allied with the Taliban are likely to seek generous recompense for their support and may turn on the new government if they feel inadequately renumerated. And since the traditional base of the Taliban is Pashtun, members of other ethnic groups are likely to chafe against the dominance of their historic rivals. The rule of the Taliban will not only be intolerably cruel to women and minority groups; it may also prove to be less stable than the first images of its triumph seemed to suggest.

Hobbes was wrong to imagine that most people in a country like Afghanistan would be subject to atomized anarchy. He was right that the absence of a central authority that can impose order and solve collective-action problems would exact a heavy toll. So long as many parts of the world are characterized by structured anarchy, their residents will seriously suffer on account of their inability to provide even the most basic public goods.

The costs of structured anarchy are steep. But that is not the only way in which diverse societies fail.

In some times and places, one group has long exercised domination over the others. Compared with the state failure suffered by countries like Somalia or Afghanistan, this has significant advantages. Even a deeply oppressive state can put an end to endemic conflict. And even though it may favor one group in a flagrantly unjust manner, the presence of a well-resourced central authority can help to sustain key public goods, from paved roads to running water.

Countries that suffer from structured anarchy are virtually always very poor. Plenty of countries in which one group is dominant have achieved a high standard of living. The presence of an effective state can make the difference between life and starving to death or succumbing to an infectious disease. But for members of the subjugated minority, those benefits have often proved elusive—or have come at an intolerable cost.

DOMINATION

Anthony Burns was born into chattel slavery in Stafford County, Virginia, in the late spring of 1834. Determined to win his liberty from a young age, he learned to read and write from the children of one of his masters, and set up a secret school to teach other slaves.

In his late teens, Burns was taken to Richmond to work odd jobs. Though he was obliged to pass a big portion of his wages on to his master, he enjoyed much greater control over his day-to-day movements than ever before. Realizing that a similar opportunity might not present itself to him again, he befriended some sailors in the city's harbor, and hatched an audacious plan.

On a cold morning in February 1854, a friend helped Burns sneak into a tiny compartment on a ship headed for Boston. The journey was harrowing. He could barely move, had little access to food or drink, and suffered from severe sea sickness. But when he finally walked ashore after a three-week journey, he felt like a free man for the first time in his young life.

Careful not to reveal much about his origins, Burns found work at a clothing store on Brattle Street, in the city's commercial center. But when he wrote one of his brothers to let him know about his new station in life, the letter was discovered, and his former slave master was informed of his whereabouts.

Determined to regain control of his "property," Charles F. Suttle sought a warrant for Burns's arrest. On the basis of the Fugitive Slave Act, which had passed Congress just four years earlier, a judge in Alexandria issued a warrant that obliged the United States Marshals Service to apprehend Burns and bring him back to Virginia. Within weeks, a notorious slave hunter by the name of Asa O. Butman had captured Burns in the center of Boston.

The local authorities hoped to try Burns as quickly and quietly as possible. But word about the case spread through the city and a fervent network of abolitionists sprang into action. Richard Henry Dana Jr., the scion of a patrician Massachusetts family turned crusading lawyer, offered to represent Burns. Thousands of protesters gathered outside Faneuil Hall to demand his release. Wendell Phillips, a key leader of the abolitionist movement, told a predominantly white crowd that "Anthony Burns has no master but God!"

As night fell, the swelling crowd attempted to free Burns from his cell. Guards beat them back by firing shots above their heads. President Franklin Pierce ordered a company of marines to guard the courthouse as the trial took place inside.

In the end, Judge Edward Loring ruled against Burns. "As a contingent of marines led Burns out of the courthouse to the ship waiting to take him back to Virginia and back to slavery, fifty thousand people lined the streets leading to the wharf," Joshua D. Rothman, a historian, writes. "They had hoisted American flags upside-down to signal distress [and] draped windows with the black bunting typically seen at funeral processions."

Burns was put on a ship to Virginia and returned to captivity.

Even by the cruel standards of human history, American slavery was especially brutal. And even by the brutal standards of American slavery, the story of Anthony Burns was especially tragic.

But in a sense, his story is not altogether atypical. Many—perhaps most—diverse societies have dealt with the fact of their diversity in a simple manner: they have allowed one group to dominate the others. From the monarchies of early modern South Asia to the democracies of twentieth-century Europe, diversity has often gone hand in hand with some scheme of domination.

Three have been especially important. In hard forms of domination, the majority explicitly claims the right to dominate the minority. In soft forms of domination, the majority pretends to grant equality to all citizens but effectively marginalizes or disenfranchises a large portion of the population. Finally, under minority domination, it is not the many who rule over the few, but rather the few who rule over the many.

HARD DOMINATION

Settler societies like Canada and Australia were founded on supposedly virgin lands that, in reality, contained a large number of native peoples. Meanwhile, countries from Brazil to Jamaica soon added to the diversity supplied by the native population by bringing millions of enslaved

Africans to their shores. The resulting hierarchy was usually both steep and rigid. One group openly and explicitly dominated the others.

In the eyes of many colonists, natives forfeited their claim to the land on which they lived because they were uninterested in planting grain or tilling the fields; the genocidal campaigns against them were, they thought, sanctified by a divine imperative to sow and reap. Black slaves, meanwhile, were depicted as morally and mentally inferior; their captivity was, defenders of slavery claimed, a natural state of affairs that benefited those it subjugated.

The United States combined both systems of "hard domination." In the first decades after its independence, the country rapidly expanded westward, pushing ever-greater numbers of Native Americans off their lands and killing many of them in battle. And in the four score and six years before Abraham Lincoln signed the Emancipation Proclamation, Southern states imported about three hundred thousand slaves.

In its early years, the American Republic practiced one of the most extreme forms of domination of the modern era. And yet the principles on which it was founded also gave the victims of that hierarchy—and their white allies—the tools to challenge the system.

Most sets of rules contain two key components. The first governs who is included in their purview. The second specifies the rights and duties of those to whom they apply. This helps to explain both the disastrous failure and the great triumph of America's founding documents.

The principles enshrined in the Declaration of Independence and the Bill of Rights created a moral and political framework that helped to sustain democracy and spread liberty for 250 years. The idea that "all men are created equal" remains as noble and inspiring today as it was in the eighteenth century.

But while the rights and duties set out in those founding documents retain their relevance, the country's history has been marked by the brutal exclusion of key groups from their purview. Indigenous peoples and slaves, in particular, did not figure among those who were to be treated as equals until depressingly recently.

Much of American history therefore boils down to a fight for the inclusion of those who were excluded from enjoying the liberties promised in the country's founding documents. And while the story of the past 250 years has hardly been one of steady progress, the ranks of those who can claim equal membership has greatly expanded. Slowly but surely, the moral case for emancipating slaves, for granting a form of political autonomy to Native American tribes, and for ending segregation in the country's south triumphed.

America is an extreme example of how countries can, by drawing upon their best traditions, attenuate even the most rigid racial hierarchies. In virtually every developed democracy, the kinds of explicit legal disabilities that sent Anthony Burns back into slavery in Virginia have now been abolished. It would be churlish to dismiss or understate the vast difference this has made in the lives of those who were subject to them. To claim, as is now fashionable, that a country like the United States has not made substantive progress toward equality is to insult the memory of those who fell victim to the most extreme forms of racial injustice in the past.

And yet the evidence from the United States—and many other countries—is that the victims of such schemes of domination continue to suffer from severe socioeconomic disadvantages long after the explicit disabilities to which they had once been subject are abolished. As a result, black people in the United States, the indigenous in Australia, members of lower castes in India, and numerous other groups around the world continue to be significantly poorer and less well educated than those who belong to historically favored groups.

Tragically, the problems created by a legacy of domination persist long after the original injustices have been abolished.

SOFT DOMINATION

Hard domination is especially heinous. No country that explicitly disenfranchises a large number of people living in its own territory because of the color of their skin or the origin of their parents can truly claim to be a democracy. But other forms of domination, which can be harder to recognize, are also pernicious.

Many of the democracies that were founded over the course of the twentieth century claimed, from their inception, that they granted all the people living on their territory equal rights. Proudly, they disavowed the explicit legal disabilities for disfavored minority groups that had historically characterized countries like the United States.

But in many cases, these democracies could claim to be egalitarian, in part, because a bloody history of their own had rendered them highly homogeneous. This allowed the ethnic or cultural majority to impose its preferences without explicitly needing to disenfranchise members of minority groups or bringing the roots of their dominance out into the open.

As these societies are becoming more diverse, it is becoming harder to ignore this legacy of "soft domination." For the rules that worked when they were highly homogeneous are now starting to be resented by a significant portion of the population. The major problem facing countries like the United States is how to deal with the long shadow of hard domination; the problem facing countries like Germany or Italy is how to recognize and abolish the forms of soft domination that still give unfair advantages to those of their citizens who happen to be a part of the historical majority.

To understand the challenges they face, we first need to understand how they were founded.

In medieval Europe, infidels were regularly driven into exile, and heretics burned at the stake. When Christians took control of the Iberian Peninsula during the Reconquista, they forced the country's Jews to flee or convert. As late as the seventeenth century, much of Europe operated under the motto of cuius regio, eius religio; each territory's population had to abide by the religion of their monarch.

But during the many millennia in which monarchy was the predominant form of government in much of the world, there were also a few instances of more tolerant societies. In the Baghdad of the ninth century, the Istanbul of the seventeenth century, and the Vienna of the nineteenth century, minority groups enjoyed much greater privileges than they did in other parts of the world. They were able to worship, to conduct trade without extreme impediments, and to accumulate significant wealth. The results were remarkable. Each of these societies enjoyed levels of economic prosperity uncommon for their time, saw the arts flourish, and made important scientific advances.

Then these multiethnic empires began to come apart.

For centuries, multiethnic empires had tolerated diversity without either trying to homogenize their population or granting subjects from different groups genuine equality. In an age of mass literacy and rapid industrialization, this left them vulnerable to the rapid spread of nationalist ideals. Neither Serbs and Hungarians nor Greeks and Armenians wanted to be ruled by monarchs who did not share their culture, language, and religion. They aspired to national self-determination.

Slowly and then suddenly, multiethnic empires collapsed. For the most part, they were replaced by nation-states that only managed to avoid the problem of domination to the extent that they succeeded in imposing homogeneity.

The first half of the twentieth century, in particular, amounted to a vast process of ethnic cleansing. Unspeakable violence turned territories in which people of different faiths, cultures, and religions had for centuries lived side by side into astonishingly monochrome nation-states. Especially in Western Europe, where minority groups had largely been expelled or killed, it was easy for the nearly homogeneous residents of the democracies that flourished after the defeat of fascism to fool themselves into thinking that they knew how to avoid the problem of domination.

Founded on the aspiration that cohesive cultural groups should be able to rule themselves, many European democracies were prone to marginalize those few minorities that remained within their borders—and had little facility at integrating the millions of immigrants who would flock to them over the course of the coming decades. Today, many of these democracies continue to suffer from a system of soft domination.

They were built on an assumption of homogeneity that no longer applies. Though not necessarily designed to exclude others, both their traditional self-conception about what truly makes somebody a member of the nation and the formal rules that grant newcomers citizenship bestow the status of outsider on many of those who now live within them. As a result, many immigrants and their descendants feel permanently excluded from full membership in the countries that are supposed to be their home.

The question facing these countries in the coming decades will be whether they can broaden their self-understanding enough to avoid a hardening of the informal hierarchies that have characterized them over the past decades. If they succeed in overcoming the legacy of soft domination, they will be able to treat minority groups fairly, and fully integrate the descendants of immigrants. If they don't, they will eventually fracture into nations composed of mutually hostile blocks, or even turn a system that implicitly disadvantages certain groups into one that explicitly allows the traditional majority to rule over the rest.

MINORITY DOMINATION

When we talk about the problem of domination, we usually assume that it is the majority which oppresses the minority. But in countries from Iraq to Rwanda and from Syria to Guatemala, the ruling elite has traditionally been recruited from a powerful minority.

Most of the countries in which a minority rules over the majority are not democracies. Knowing that they are almost sure to be outvoted if they accede to popular rule, the powerful stick to a long-standing monarch or support a resolute dictator. Democracy does not mix easily with domination by a minority.

There are, however, important exceptions, from the Athens of the fifth century BC to the Britain of the eighteenth century AD. Perhaps the most striking is South Africa. The Dutch settlers who colonized the southern tip of the African continent since the seventeenth century brought the aspiration to collective self-determination with them from the increasingly democratic culture of their ancestors. They also knew that they represented a small minority of the South African population. If they allowed the black majority to cast their votes, white settlers could hardly have enjoyed the benefits that their domination had allowed them to accrue.

The solution was as cruel as it was ingenious. In what the political scientist Pierre L. van den Berghe has termed "herrenvolk democracy," Dutch settlers restricted the right to vote to members of the supposedly superior white race.

This allowed the small group of so-called Afrikaners to have their bloody cake and eat it too. They maintained traditional democratic institutions like an elected parliament. They held reasonably free and fair elections. They even granted full citizens some modicum of free speech and assembly. But all these rules only applied to a small minority of the population. The great majority lacked the vote, were excluded from civic rights, and suffered from the daily indignities of racial apartheid.

Minority groups that have historically been dominant face an especially tough dilemma when their power is challenged.

When majority groups come under pressure to share their power, they can be relatively certain that the cost of acquiescence will be limited. After all, they know that their voice will always carry a large weight in any democratic system.

Minority groups cannot be sure of the same outcome. If they agree to fair democratic procedures, they are likely to be outvoted at every turn. Rather than accepting the gradual erosion of their power, these groups are thus more likely to hold on to their dominance by any means necessary. This makes them especially likely to engage in brutal measures to oppress the subjugated majority—and creates a serious danger of violent backlash if they are finally forced from power.

A failure to reckon with this dynamic was one of the many reasons why the Iraq War went so terribly wrong. For decades, the country had been ruled by a fascistic dictator who justified his cruel reign by a thin appeal to secular, left-wing values. But in truth, Saddam Hussein, a Sunni in a predominantly Shia country, had always been a sectarian as much as an ideological leader.

After the invasion of Iraq, the occupying forces were understandably keen to ensure that no members of Hussein's Baath Party should retain power. But because they were insufficiently attuned to the sectarian dimension of the country's conflict, they did not recognize that this would embolden Shias to take revenge for their long-standing oppression. Within a few months, even Sunnis who never harbored any affection for Hussein had rational reason to fear that they would now suffer from a similarly cruel subjugation.

With the central state weakened and the occupying forces incapable of creating trust between historically hostile groups, Iraq quickly fell into structured anarchy. Between Shia attempts to monopolize the state for themselves, and Sunni resistance to their loss of power, the country slid into a deadly civil war.

Whether it takes the form of hard domination, soft domination, or minority domination, domination is an ever-present danger for diverse societies. From slavery to genocide, the idea that members of one group are of superior worth has been responsible for some of the bloodiest chapters in human history.

Compared with the dangers of domination, a society in which different groups find some way to share power, sticking within their own communities and living by their own rules even though they are citizens of the same state, looks far more appealing. And so a lot of countries have, in the wake of ethnic violence or civil war, embraced schemes of power sharing that supposedly allow different groups to live peacefully in the same territory.

But on the whole, these supposed solutions have failed to live up to their promise. The societies they created suffer from the third major danger faced by diverse democracies: fragmentation.

FRAGMENTATION

At the beginning of the twentieth century, a few small countries on the northwestern tip of the Eurasian landmass governed much of the world. Never in the history of mankind had such a small part of the globe attained such enormous power.

But when the Second World War ended, even nations that nominally counted among its victors recognized that they had lost the strength to sustain their empires. Though countries from Britain to Portugal continued to fight a bloody rearguard battle for decades to come, it was obvious that the age of colonialism was coming to an end.

Nationalists like Mahatma Gandhi in India and Jomo Kenyatta in Kenya finally attained their long-awaited goal of building independent nations. But securing domestic peace would, it quickly became apparent, prove an even greater challenge than winning the anticolonial war.

Before they were ruled by colonial powers, few parts of the world had resembled modern nation-states. In some areas, emperors had commanded large expanses of land comprising highly diverse populations.

In other areas, there had barely been a centralized state, with much of the power held by local potentates and tribal chiefs. Now the founders of India and Kenya, of the Ivory Coast and Guinea-Bissau faced the difficult task of molding highly diverse populations bounded by oft-arbitrary borders into functional nation-states.

In many countries, that aspiration quickly foundered. In the 1950s and 1960s, dozens of newly independent states set out to build democratic institutions. But most soon descended into civil war or turned into authoritarian regimes led by dictators who relied on the loyalty of their own tribe or faith group to entrench themselves in power.

In Europe and the United States, a cadre of idealistic social scientists watched the process of decolonization with great hope. When countries from Asia to Africa won independence from their colonial rulers, they expected to witness the birth of thriving democracies. So when one country after another degenerated into tyranny or civil war, they naturally sought to understand how it might be possible for other diverse democracies to avoid such a sorry fate. The most influential answer to that question was given by a young political scientist named Arend Lijphart.

The Netherlands, where Lijphart was raised before immigrating to the United States, had long been a deeply divided society. Catholics, Protestants, and socialists each had their own schools, their own newspapers, and of course their own political parties. Even institutions like hospitals and welfare organizations were often split along sectarian lines.

According to most theories in political science, the country's "fragmentation" should have made it difficult to sustain democratic institutions. Because they had so little intergroup contact, Catholics, Protestants, and socialists should have found it impossible to cooperate on a functioning government. And yet the Netherlands were, as Lijphart said in a recent interview, "a very well-governed, stable country."

How, he wondered, was this possible? And might some of the new nations that were rapidly descending into dictatorship or civil war be able to emulate that success?

HOW POWER SHARING PROMISES TO SOLVE THE PROBLEM OF FRAGMENTATION

In a democracy, the majority usually gets to call the shots.

All citizens of a country have reason to agree on an impartial mechanism for choosing who gets to govern. And even though it always hurts to lose an election, it is easier to accept defeat when you know that you only need to persuade your compatriots of your ideals to win the next time around. So long as most voters can reasonably hope that their favored party will win an election once in a while, letting the majority rule is a promising way to reduce the likelihood of conflict.

But in deeply fragmented societies in which virtually everyone votes along ethnic or religious lines, the majoritarian nature of democracy instantly spells trouble. In many such countries, a large portion of the population forms a permanent minority. Even if elections are held fairly, the members of this group are likely to remain in opposition. Permanently excluded from power, they have no way to ensure that the schools in their neighborhoods are well maintained, or the streets paved.

If "the majority and minority are fixed rather than fluid, because each thinks of itself as a group defined by birth and possessing affinities and interests not shared across group lines," political scientist Donald L. Horowitz warned three decades ago, elections will largely become tribal. With each political party representing the interests of a major identity group, and little alternation in power, "the textbook case of democratic majority rule turns quickly into a case of egregious minority exclusion."

That helps to explain why ethnic and religious fragmentation often poses such a challenge to the stability of democratic institutions. Faced with the prospect that their enemies might capture the most powerful institutions of the state, many groups either refuse to cooperate in building state capacity or attempt to monopolize institutions for their own purposes. They either get stuck in structured anarchy or descend into brutal domination.

The Netherlands, Lijphart argued, could serve as a model for how to diffuse these dangers. At the time, many of the country's key decisions were made by the Social and Economic Council, which was composed of members representing three key "pillars" of Dutch society. Instead of giving the victor of an election the power to call the shots for four or five years, the country's institutions ensured that everyone—including the minority—kept a seat at the table.

A number of other European countries, including Austria and Belgium, used "power-sharing" arrangements of their own. Switzerland even invited every party that won a significant number of seats in the Federal Assembly to take part in the government. With no major party banished to the opposition benches, all their leaders shared responsibility for the country's direction.

Some countries that had a recent history of serious conflict, Lijphart then discovered to his excitement, seemed to rely on similar institutions to diffuse tensions and secure the peace. Lebanon, for example, had long been deeply divided between Christians, Sunnis, and Shias, among other groups. When the country gained its independence from France in 1943, the leaders of its most populous denominations struck a bargain to share power. Rather than letting the winner of any one election run the ship, they decided that each group would be represented in the government. The president of the republic would always be Maronite; the prime minister, Sunni; and the speaker of the parliament, Shia.

To reduce the stakes of national politics even more, the country's constitution also granted its main groups the right to govern their internal affairs. Instead of making uniform laws about marriage and divorce, education and inheritance, the Lebanese government devolved the power to rule on such matters to Shia, Sunni, and Christian clergymen. Because a lot of the most intimate laws to which they are subject depend on decisions taken within their own communities, members of these religious groups would in theory have less incentive to fight for sole control of the government.

Rather than seeking to overcome the country's divisions, Lebanon's founders decided to embrace its fragmentation. That arrangement, Lijphart wrote in the late 1960s, helped to explain why the country managed to sustain a democratic system. "A multiple balance of power," he wrote, made the key contribution "to [its] success."

Lijphart's books and articles had a big impact. What he termed "consociational democracy" seemed to give political scientists a weapon they rarely have in their armory: the ability to give practical advice that might hasten the advent of democracy or even avert the outbreak of civil war. Invoking the ever-growing list of publications by Lijphart and his followers, European and American consultants fanned out to conflict-prone countries to tell them to adopt forms of power sharing.

When Lijphart first presented his theory in 1968, only a handful of countries counted as consociational. By the 1990s, when a lot of newly founded democracies were consulting social scientists on the design of their new constitutions, and Lijphart was serving as the president of the American Political Science Association, many more had adopted some form of power sharing. (To what extent these changes were owed to Lijphart's influence, as opposed to other forces pushing countries in a similar direction, is difficult to say.)

But the results were not quite as hoped. In most countries, the new institutions led to gridlock or were ignored. Many of them quickly fell back into autocracy or civil war. Their fragmentation grew ever more dangerous.

Perhaps this should not have come as a surprise. After all, the country on which Lijphart leaned most heavily in making the case that institutions which worked so well in the Netherlands could be transplanted to other parts of the world had, in the intervening years, also gone off the rails.

Just as Lijphart was putting the finishing touches on his first major book, *Democracy in Plural Societies*, Lebanon fell into a bloody and protracted civil war. Between 1975 and 1990, more than one hundred thousand people were killed and many more injured or displaced. In the country that long served as the most central example of its promise, power sharing failed.

HOW POWER SHARING DEEPENS FRAGMENTATION

I met Abdallah Salam, an avid talker with a baby face and inquisitive eyes, about a dozen years ago during a summer school in Cortona. Along with twenty other students and professors, we spent two idyllic weeks arguing about religion and identity in an abandoned monastery overlooking the Tuscan hills. I remembered those weeks fondly, and thought back to them now and then, but mostly forgot about Abdallah—until I saw his face, looking barely more grown up, staring down at me from the pages of *The Guardian*.

In the photo, Abdallah was dressed in black tie and held the hand of a beautiful woman clad in an elaborate wedding gown. About a hundred guests applauded the newlyweds in a sumptuous garden. But despite the impression of harmony conveyed by that glamorous picture, Abdallah's marriage to Marie-Joe Abi-Nassif was causing quite a scandal in his home country.

Abdallah is a Sunni Muslim. Marie-Joe is a Christian. Even today, marriages across these religious and sectarian divides remain rare in Lebanon. When they do take place, couples face tremendous difficulty in gaining legal recognition of their bond. Because marriages are usually performed and registered by each of the country's main religious groups, interfaith couples fall right through the cracks.

Over the years, the few couples who faced this problem settled on an unsatisfactory workaround. Instead of getting married at home, they would hold their ceremony in nearby Cyprus. While they continued to face disadvantages upon their return, the civil registrar would usually acknowledge their "foreign" wedding.

That never felt like an option to Abdallah and Marie-Joe. Determined to overcome the sectarian divide that had torn the country apart within their own lifetime, they wanted to fight for real change. "We really don't exist as citizens—just members of groups. It feels like the state has completely subjugated its sovereignty," Marie-Joe said.

Their wedding, they both hoped, would make a small contribution to giving people of their generation more freedom to live in accordance with their own choices. "We want Lebanon to be a country for all people with equality before the law, free of the archaic and confessional laws and religious tribunals that apply at the moment," she said. But a few months after the wedding, the country's authorities still hadn't acknowledged their new status as husband and wife.

The challenges faced by Abdallah and Marie-Joe are representative of the ways in which consociational democracies do as much to exacerbate as to alleviate the fragmentation of deeply divided countries.

Power-sharing institutions often subvert one of the key promises of democracy: to let people decide their own fate. If all major parties are always represented in the government, elections don't have clear consequences. And so political elites are often able to rig the system in their own interests, leaving ordinary people without the tools to challenge misrule, corruption, or persistent failures by the government to deliver on basic public goods.

This democratic deficit is particularly stark for individuals who want to change the traditional ways of their own communities. In Lebanon, personal laws are subject to a wholly separate system of adjudication. If you are a Sunni who wishes to obtain a divorce, you are subject to Sunni rules and Sunni judges. If you wish to change those rules, you can of course publish op-eds or stage some kind of protest. But the decision is ultimately up to unelected religious authorities.

Consociational democracies usually rob their citizens of the ability to control the laws by which they live. In large areas of public policy, they boil down to no democracy at all.

Real solutions to the problems faced by countries like Lebanon would need to help make them less fragmented over time. Any set of institutions that actually attenuates the likelihood of future conflict would encourage greater trust and closer contact between members of different groups.

Power-sharing institutions do the opposite. By design, they put massive obstacles in the way of anybody who seeks to build close ties with members of other groups. They glorify and entrench existing identities. And in the process, they make it much harder for a shared sense of citizenship to emerge.

Consociational democracies force individuals to conceive of themselves, first and foremost, as members of the identity group into which they were born. Some people define themselves primarily as Lebanese rather than Sunni, Shia, or Christian. Others take pride in their personal attributes or professional achievements rather than a bond of blood or faith. Others still fall in love with somebody who does not belong to the same community as them. But whenever people stray outside of the predetermined communal boundaries that consociational institutions freeze into place, they face obstacles and injustices of Kafkaesque proportions.

Remarkably, Lijphart foresaw—and even praised—these shortcomings of fragmentation from the very beginning. As he wrote in his very first essay on consociationalism, the system would only work if members of different groups had very little contact with each other. "Distinct lines of cleavages between subcultures," he argued, were an important precondition for consociational democracy because "overlapping group memberships" would complicate the ability of elites to govern their own subcultures. It was, he concluded, precisely the rigid compartmentalization *between* groups that would create the "internal political cohesion" *within* groups that is necessary for the whole system to work.

The impact of such a system should, all along, have been predictable.

Trying to heal fragmented societies with the help of power-sharing institutions is a little like trying to cure an addict's withdrawal symptoms by feeding him the drug he craves. In the short run, they can help to diffuse violent convulsions. Over the long term, they only exacerbate the problem.

LESSONS FROM FAILURE

Diverse societies have suffered from at least three serious shortcomings: domination, anarchy, and fragmentation. Each of these shortcomings is emblematic of a danger that, even in some of the world's most developed democracies, remains highly relevant today.

Most developed democracies have historically been built on forms of domination. In many European countries, this domination was hidden from view. Because they were unusually homogeneous at the time of their founding, they could pretend to be tolerant without having to become truly inclusive. In other democracies, like the United States, domination was far more explicit. For the first decades or centuries of their existence, these countries were only able to reconcile their democratic aspirations with their determination to subjugate natives and African Americans by openly excluding them from the protection of noble rules like the Bill of Rights.

Over the past decades, both sets of democracies have become significantly more inclusive. Countries like Germany, Uruguay, and Japan have, for the first time, provided immigrants and their descendants with a path to citizenship. The United States finally granted minority groups full civil rights and enacted ambitious legislation to protect them from discrimination.

In virtually all diverse democracies, the majority of the population has adopted far more inclusive attitudes toward immigrants and minorities. And these groups, in turn, did not waste any time in seizing the new opportunities that became open to them. Over the past years, they have made rapid progress on key indicators of success, including income and education.*

And yet these heartening improvements have not done enough to undo the lingering effects of past domination. Even though the gap between different groups has significantly narrowed, long-dominant groups retain serious socioeconomic advantages. And while the popular understanding of who truly belongs in a country has become far more inclusive, many immigrants and members of ethnic minorities still feel that they are treated as guests or intruders.

The first great danger facing diverse democracies over the coming decades, then, is that they might fail to overcome the long shadow of domination. While formally egalitarian, their societies might in practice stratify into different castes, with members of the ethnic majority at the top, and everybody else at the bottom.

Structured anarchy is another serious pitfall for diverse societies. In many parts of the world, different groups mistrust each other so deeply that they refuse to cooperate on maintaining an effective state.

At first glance, this is not the problem most developed democracies face today. They have giant budgets, employ a huge number of civil

---

* I describe this progress in much greater detail in chapter 8.

servants, and command large standing armies. Some of them have the power to destroy the world many times over. State failure hardly seems like a realistic concern in a country like France, the United Kingdom, or the United States.

And yet recent research suggests that these powerful countries, too, could see their ability to sustain key public goods diminished over the coming years. Across North America and Western Europe, growing demographic diversity has been strongly associated with a decline in support for the welfare state. When citizens believe that their tax dollars go to "people like me," they are more likely to support generous unemployment benefits or spending on public health than when they fear that it goes to people who do not share the same identity.

The second danger facing diverse democracies, then, is that their growing diversity will undermine their ability to provide their citizens with key public goods or a sense of common destiny. If diverse democracies are to sustain the benefits of an effective state, they must ensure that members of different groups trust that their institutions are to everybody's benefit.

There is one more pitfall diverse democracies need to guard against: fragmentation. Many places around the world have—at least temporarily—solved the problem of difference by means of a kind of cease-fire. Countries like Lebanon have largely given up on the hope of fostering a shared sense of identity for their own citizens. Instead of building trust or connections between the groups they represent, political elites have brokered a deal among themselves. Detailed rules ensure that every group gets a significant share of power (and the elites stay in control).

The price the population pays for that deal has turned out to be very steep. Lacking a sense of shared citizenship, ordinary Lebanese people find it practically impossible to challenge the deep corruption of their elites. And because all their institutions encourage them to double down on their identities, the fragmentation of society shows few signs of easing up from generation to generation. Institutions that were meant to keep the peace only ended up delaying the outbreak of the country's bloody civil war.

The citizens of most developed democracies thankfully share a much stronger sense of common identity. Whites and African Americans in the United States as well as Christians and Muslims in France have a much stronger sense of shared citizenship than Shias, Sunnis, and Maronites in Lebanon.

And yet countries like France or the United States also face the danger that ethnic fragmentation might slow or undo the progress of recent years. Across much of the democratic world, conflict entrepreneurs are now encouraging dwindling ethnic majorities to rise up for their interests before it is "too late." Meanwhile, academic and activist circles that once defended the need for universalism increasingly assume that instilling a much stronger sense of ethnic or religious identity in historically disadvantaged groups (or even historically dominant groups, like whites in the United States) is the only realistic path toward equality.

These developments conspire to raise the salience of the kinds of groups that have torn diverse societies apart in many parts of the world. Even as many ordinary citizens think of identity in more fluid terms, elite institutions and new public policies are creating strong incentives for ordinary citizens to double down on their racial or religious identities.

If they are to sustain a sense of shared citizenship and mutual solidarity, diverse democracies have to find ways to address the long shadow of domination without encouraging their citizens to be more attuned to their differences than to their similarities. The third danger facing them is that they might, over the coming years, fragment into increasingly rigid and hostile groups.

THREE

How to Keep the Peace

On December 6, 1992, 150,000 Hindus from all over India staged a giant rally outside Babri Masjid, a famous mosque in the city of Ayodhya. Waving religious flags and chanting political slogans, they sought to stake their claim to a patch of land on which, they believed, a Hindu temple marking the birthplace of Lord Rama had once stood.

As the day wore on, and politicians allied with the Bharatiya Janata Party (BJP), the Hindu nationalist party now led by Prime Minister Narendra Modi, chanted inflammatory slogans, the crowd kept swelling, and so did its rage. Around noon, a young religious devotee slipped past the barricades, scaled the exterior wall of the mosque, and triumphantly waved a saffron flag.

The crowd pushed forward. Hopelessly outnumbered, most of the police abandoned the mosque to the hammers and axes of the victorious mob. It only took them a few hours to raze the centuries-old building to the ground.

In the days after the destruction of Babri Masjid, the angel of death visited many towns and cities all over India. More than two thousand people died in violent clashes and riots.

Aligarh, in the country's north, was one of the cities in which the drawn-out standoff over Babri Madjid inspired horrific violence. Even before the mosque was destroyed, local tension had risen to boiling point. When two of the city's largest newspapers falsely reported that Muslim doctors and nurses at a local hospital had murdered Hindu patients, activists vowed to take revenge. A local gang stopped a train headed for the city's central station, dragged out its Muslim passengers, and slaughtered them in broad daylight. When the killing finally subsided a few days later, more than seventy people, both Hindu and Muslim, were dead.

Many cities all across the country saw similarly bloody incidents of what Indian newspapers and politicians refer to by the rather understated name of "communal violence." But, strangely, other cities have consistently managed to avert the same fate.

Kozhikode, in the country's south, for example, has many similarities with Aligarh. Both are midsized cities. In both, a little fewer than two out of every three inhabitants are Hindu, and a little more than one out of every three are Muslim. In both, false rumors about supposed massacres by the other side made the rounds whenever tensions over the Babri Masjid ran especially high. And yet Kozhikode has so far been spared the violence that claimed so many lives in Aligarh.

"Aligarh figures in the list of [India's] eight most riot-prone cities," the political scientist Ashutosh Varshney notes. Kozhikode "has not had a single riot in [the twentieth] century."

What can possibly explain that difference? And how might that explanation help us to discover strategies that today's diverse democracies can adopt to mitigate the ongoing perils of domination, anarchy, and fragmentation? A large part of the answer to these questions lies in the work of a psychologist who was born not in India but in Indiana.

WHEN CONTACT BETWEEN HOSTILE GROUPS INSPIRES TOLERANCE (AND WHEN IT DOESN'T)

Gordon W. Allport was born just before the turn of the twentieth century in Montezuma, Indiana, a three-horse town about halfway between Decatur and Indianapolis. Raised by a devout father whose lasting claim to fame is to have been featured in *The Great American Fraud,* a bestselling exposé of infamous cheats, swindlers, and quack doctors, he founded a small printing business as a teenager and excelled at school. After attending Harvard University on a scholarship and spending a formative year studying with some of the world's preeminent psychologists in Hamburg and Berlin, he became an influential professor specializing in the new field of human personality.

Over the next years, Allport watched from afar as much of the Old World descended into barbarism. "Civilized men," he wrote after the war, "have gained notable mastery over energy, matter, and inanimate nature generally, and are rapidly learning to control physical suffering and premature death." But despite the astonishing technological progress achieved during the first half of the twentieth century, "we appear to be living in the Stone Age so far as our handling of human relationships is concerned. . . . Each corner of the earth has its own special burdens of animosity."

If humans could somehow reduce the extent of their prejudice, Allport thought, they might finally be able to make a little moral progress. And so he set out to identify social or political institutions that might help to contain this dangerous psychological instinct.

One day, his own assumptions about other people gave him a key idea for how to do that. During his free time, Allport sometimes volunteered with an organization helping refugees. At first, he was apprehensive about some of the groups he encountered. But the more time he spent with them, the more his prejudices dissipated. Perhaps, he thought, his own experience was not so unique—and increased contact between groups that had historically been ill-disposed toward one another could help them overcome their reservations?

Over the next years and decades, a vast research program confirmed his hunch. Investigating a wide variety of contexts in which members of historically hostile groups had been forced to interact, psychologists found evidence of the salutary impact of "intergroup contact" in all spheres of social and professional life.

American soldiers who had frequent contact with German civilians were much more likely to have a favorable opinion of them than those who did not. White soldiers in mixed platoons were much more likely than those in segregated ones to favor integrating combat units in the United States Army. Among civilians, whites living in integrated housing units were much more likely than those living in segregated ones to report that African Americans are "pretty much the same as the white people who live here."

Allport's insight seemed to promise a brighter future. As long as people from different groups have the opportunity to interact, the prejudices they hold about one another should gradually subside.

There may not be a single idea in the field of social psychology that researchers have spent more time trying to prove or discard over the past three quarters of a century. By and large, the evidence has vindicated what has come to be known as the "intergroup contact hypothesis."

Through painstaking work, researchers have chronicled hundreds of instances around the world in which exposure to strangers really did make people more tolerant of groups they had once mistrusted or even despised. But they also confirmed a worry that had gnawed at Allport from the very beginning: that intergroup contact wouldn't work its magic if the conditions under which different groups interact predisposed them to dislike or look down on one another.

Evidence for this wrinkle was there from the start. In one study, 64 percent of whites who had worked with African Americans performing high-skill tasks or occupying professional roles had a favorable impression of them. But among whites who had exclusively worked with African Americans occupying subordinate roles as unskilled workmen, only 5 percent did.

Drawing on other studies with similarly disappointing results, Allport formulated four broad conditions that have to be met for greater exposure to other groups to have the desired impact:

1. *Equal Status*: While the two groups might be highly unequal in society at large, they must have relatively equal status in the context in which contact between them takes place. Working alongside each other as colleagues qualifies; working together as boss and subordinate does not.

2. *Common Goals*: Members of both groups need to work together in pursuit of a shared goal. Pursuing the championship as teammates counts; participating in the same tournament as members of opposing teams does not.

3. *Intergroup Cooperation*: Members of both groups need to have an incentive to work together cooperatively. Ideally, they need to work together to solve a problem, with each member of the group making a clear contribution.

4. *Support from Authorities and Customs*: Authority figures need to favor and encourage better intergroup understanding. If a greater mutual understanding is against the law or risks angering your boss, it is far less likely to occur.

Subsequent work has mostly vindicated this view. As Allport concluded in a 1954 bestseller, prejudice "may be reduced by equal status contact between majority and minority groups in the pursuit of common goals." But these benefits will only accrue if the nature of their contact "leads to the perception of common interests and common humanity between members of the two groups."

Psychologists tend to investigate the attributes of individuals. Political scientists like to study the characteristics of larger entities like states. But without paying especially close attention to Allport's findings, they have hit upon a remarkably compatible set of insights over the past decades.

According to scholars of political science like Robert Putnam, dense associational links between citizens of a city or region help to predict better democratic institutions and faster economic growth in the following decades. The more voluntary associations, choral societies, and bowling leagues an area has, the brighter its future is likely to shine.

But just as a closer look revealed that intergroup contact only has positive effects under the right circumstances, so too the nature of this "social capital" turns out to matter for a country's ability to avoid conflict. When a locality predominantly has "bonding" social capital, which ties members of one salient group to one another, it does not do much to mitigate the risk of hostility toward other groups. But when it also has a lot of "bridging" social capital, which provides links between members of different groups, the society is much more likely to work together on key public goods like a welfare state.

If they are to help diverse democracies sustain peaceful cooperation, choirs and bowling leagues need to include a broad cross-section of society.

These are the core insights from social science on which Ashutosh Varshney drew when he set out to understand the striking contrast between Kozhikode's success in keeping the peace and Aligarh's failure to avoid communal violence.

The extent to which Hindus and Muslims encounter each other in a positive context differs strongly between the two cities. "According to survey results," Varshney reports, "nearly 83 percent of Hindus and Muslims in Kozhikode often eat together in social settings; only 54 percent in Aligarh do. About 90 percent of Hindu and Muslim families in Kozhikode report that their children play together; in Aligarh a mere 42 percent report that to be the case."

Both the residents of Aligarh and those of Kozhikode have plenty of intergroup contact. But only in Kozhikode do Hindus and Muslims encounter each other as equals.

The nature of associational life also sharply differs between the two cities. Aligarh has plenty of civic organizations, such as religious associations and welfare committees. But most of these cater to either Hindus or Muslims. The city's social capital is predominantly of the "bonding" kind.

In Kozhikode, by contrast, civic associations create a lot of opportunities for Hindus and Muslims to pursue common interests and cooperate on shared goals. There are integrated trade groups and labor unions, sports leagues and arts societies, rickshaw-pullers associations and reading clubs. "Much like Tocqueville's America," Varshney finds, Kozhikode "is a place of 'joiners.'"

In moments of crisis, like the dispute over Babri Masjid, these links between groups can make the difference between life and death. In Aligarh, where most ties run within communities, social capital helped to spread wild rumors and reinforce anger. In Kozhikode, where long-standing social links tie different communities together, they helped to dispel unfounded rumors and preserve empathy.

"Intergroup contacts" and "bridging social capital" aren't just abstract concepts concocted by psychologists and political scientists; they are concrete assets that can, even at times of extreme tension, help diverse democracies keep the peace.

THE ROAD AHEAD

When I was growing up, I thought that there was something artificial about the human tendency to form groups and discriminate against outsiders. If it weren't for history or prejudice, for hateful politicians or cynical demagogues, we would all be able to get along.

I no longer believe that this is a realistic view of the world. The tendency to favor our own comes to us naturally.

In certain times and places, this tendency has led humans to inflict terrible suffering on one another. There have been long periods of history in which some groups were brutally subjugated. There are areas of the globe in which conflict between different groups remains endemic, and most people, lacking the public goods provided by a capacious state, suffer desperate poverty. And for the foreseeable future, diverse societies will be in danger of suffering such fragmentation that people who happen to have the same citizenship lack all sense of common purpose or shared destiny.

In the long annals of history, relations between different groups have rarely been either just or harmonious. And yet it would be wrong to despair.

Though humans have a natural tendency to form groups, the nature and the attitudes of these groups strongly depends on the circumstances. Distinctions of race and religion are all too real. But despite their differences, a white Christian in Boston, a brown Hindu in Chicago, and a black Muslim in Los Angeles can cheer the same team at the Olympics.

Likewise, salient differences between groups will always raise the specter of mutual mistrust or conflict. But many groups that have been mortal enemies in some times and places have been able to get along very well in other times and places—or come to think of themselves, over time, as equal members of a larger group. Neither Germans and Frenchmen nor Chewas and Tumbukas nor Shias and Sunnis are destined to hate one another forever.

When the conditions are right, people drawn from different cultures, religions, and ethnicities are capable of sustaining amazing feats of co-operation. The question is how to put the right conditions in place, and what kind of society to aim for. That is the question to which I turn for the remainder of the book.

In part 1, I have tried to describe the world as it now is, focusing on the failings and injustices that have so often characterized diverse societies around the world; so far, the argument has primarily been "empirical." In part 2, I set out to consider how we can improve the world; my argument in the next chapters is mostly "normative." What kinds of diverse democracies, I ask, should we aim to create?

The answer to that question depends, in part, on the kinds of real-world constraints that different societies face. And because these differ especially strongly between affluent and stable democracies on the one hand, and poor or instable societies on the other hand, the geographical focus of the next parts of the book will be somewhat narrower. While the empirical analysis of the first chapters drew on examples from Afghanistan to Zambia, the next ones will primarily be directed toward citizens of developed democracies, from France to Japan to the United States.

Human nature is another important constraint. Because I don't believe that most people are capable of completely shedding their tribal loyalties, I focus on the question of how we can manage our instinct to favor the in-group in such a way that we don't all come to blows. Instead of imagining a world without groups or nations, I will ask how we can structure the relationships between groups in such a way as to engender the lowest amount of conflict and sustain the greatest extent of cooperation.

As the past chapters have taught us, this means that we need to pay close attention to the ways in which people construct their own identities, and the kinds of circumstances in which they are most likely to embrace their commonalities. To thrive, diverse democracies need to create lots of bridging social capital and sustain the right kind of intergroup contact.

PART TWO

WHAT DIVERSE
DEMOCRACIES
SHOULD BECOME

I t is far from obvious that the diverse democracies that have sprung up in every corner of the globe over the past decades will be able to endure without terrible violence or injustice.

Given how uncertain the great experiment's prospects for success are—and how terrifying the consequences would be if it should fail—some of its defenders are setting the bar very low for what we should collectively aim for. When they envisage what diverse democracies might look like in fifty or a hundred years, they imagine societies in which the balance of power may have shifted in favor of historically oppressed groups but some of the worst problems of the current moment persist. Their residents will have little in common with one another, and the major lines of battle would still pit one major identity group against another.

On this pessimistic vision, the rights and duties of members of diverse democracies will strongly depend on the subnational communities into which they were born. Most people will have a strong tie to their own ethnic or religious group but little allegiance to a common national project. Society as a whole will consist of a great variety of different groups, but the members of those groups will only have sporadic contact with one another. And the informal rules governing everyday life will be based on the assumption that a citizen's race and religion will forever remain their most important attribute.

Listening to some of the great experiment's self-declared defenders, it can be difficult to remember why anybody should hope for it to succeed in the first place.

In light of the injustices that define the present moment, and the difficulty of building diverse democracies, I understand why so many people are aiming so low. But I am nonetheless convinced that it would be a serious moral and practical mistake to give up on building a brighter future.

Aiming too low would be a moral mistake because we should build diverse democracies that are thriving, not just enduring. The world has changed dramatically over the course of the past fifty years. It would be a deep failure of imagination to think that it could not be transformed just as dramatically over the next fifty years. Difficult though it may be to make diverse democracies succeed, too much is at stake to aim for second or third best.

Aiming too low would also be a practical mistake. It seems worldly-wise to pronounce that our societies are so deeply characterized by racism or bigotry that ascriptive identities will forever determine their major battle lines—or that the best we can hope for is for those who have historically been oppressed to increase their power in a zero-sum battle for social domination. But the extensive history of diverse societies suggests that countries that are severely fragmented are usually deeply dysfunctional. All too often, they eventually fall prey to violent conflict.

This is why I suspect that a view that tells us to aim low is not so much worldly-wise as it is dangerously naive. There are good moral reasons to seek a future of diverse democracy in which citizens who stem from different ethnic or religious groups feel that they have a lot in common. But for anybody who knows how easily diverse democracies fall apart, the practical reasons to aim high are even more weighty. So long as diverse democracies consist of mutually hostile tribes, they will always remain in danger of descending into terrible injustice or terrifying violence.

So what would diverse democracies that are thriving, not just enduring, actually look like?

Because diverse democracies have embarked on an unprecedented journey over the past decades, they lack a clear road map that could guide their way. There are few accounts of previous travelers who have succeeded, and no GPS system to tell them which way to turn at every junction.

One of the key tasks for anybody who hopes for the great experiment to succeed is therefore to reflect on the basic rules and ideals that can help to provide orientation for the journey ahead. To that end, it is particularly important to answer four foundational—and highly contested—questions:

1. What role should the state play in diverse democracies?

2. Should diverse democracies embrace or eschew patriotism?

3. To what extent should immigrants and members of other minority groups be expected to "integrate" into mainstream society?

4. What kinds of informal rules should structure how people lead their daily lives?

Those are the questions I try to answer over the course of the next chapters. Diverse democracies, I argue in chapter 4, need to ensure that their citizens are free from the danger of state oppression, that they can be true to their own identities, *and* that they can (if they so choose) escape the tight embrace of their own communities. They should, I propose in chapter 5, encourage an inclusive patriotism that can sustain meaningful solidarity between members of different groups by drawing on both civic ideals and a love of everyday culture. They might, I suggest in Chapter 6, think of the future they are seeking to build through the metaphor of a public park, which allows all its visitors to do their own thing, but is more beautiful and vibrant if many of them are open to forging new friendships. And they should, I conclude in chapter 7, embrace informal rules that inspire citizens from different walks of life to cultivate true forms of mutual empathy and solidarity.

Building diverse democracies is hard. Most likely, they will, even fifty or one hundred years from now, continue to suffer from serious shortcomings. But for the great experiment to have a chance of success—and for those who are skeptical about its desirability to see why they should help to make it work—we need to insist on an attractive vision of what diverse democracies might actually look like: one in which compatriots from many different ethnic and religious backgrounds can embark on a meaningfully shared life without giving up on what makes each of them unique.

FOUR

What Role Should
the State Play?

Modern states exercise tremendous authority over their citizens. They tell millions of people what they are or are not allowed to do. They demand a hefty percentage of their earnings in tax. They regulate such minute details of their lives as what substances they can ingest or what color they may paint the exterior walls of their house. And though the enforcement mechanism for that coercion is often invisible, hard power is its ultimate guarantor. Consistently refuse to pay your tax bill and an agent of the state will knock on your door and take you to jail.

One of the fundamental questions any modern state that seeks to be legitimate in the eyes of its citizens has to answer, then, is what can possibly justify this kind of coercion. Why (if at all) is it legitimate for a bunch of politicians to determine what percentage of income you have to pay in tax, for the housing association to assess a fine if you paint your walls the wrong color, or for a cop to interrogate you about the recreational drugs you might take?

These questions become even more complicated in diverse democracies.

Homogeneous nations have a repertoire of long-standing traditions to draw on in setting their rules. Many of their citizens are likely to agree on at least some key questions of religion or morality, such as the rules governing what houses of worship can look like or whether shops are allowed to open on Sundays. Even in those kinds of societies, there will always be dissenters who disagree with the preferences of their compatriots. But they are unlikely to come from a cohesive ethnic or religious group that suffers systematic domination.

The dilemma faced by diverse democracies is tougher. In such societies, disagreements about basic questions of morality or religion are likely to go much deeper. Though they too may have long-standing traditions, those were usually created by the majority, and may not adequately reflect the needs or preferences of ethnic and religious minorities. To make things more complicated, those who contest the preferences of the majority aren't just individual dissenters who happen to have different ideas about the world; they are members of communities who can come to feel that their most cherished beliefs or their very identities are being disrespected.

All of these factors make it harder for diverse democracies to justify the power of the state. They also raise the stakes of failure. Should some groups come to the conclusion that their government is illegitimate, it is much more likely that violent conflict, attempts at secession, or even civil war will ensue.

So how should diverse democracies conceptualize the relationship between state and citizen—and earn some basic modicum of legitimacy in the eyes of their members?

In most developed democracies, the answer to this question has long been rooted in the precepts of "philosophical liberalism."

There are many different ways of expressing what lies at the core of this tradition. But it basically boils down to the idea that any legitimate state will protect the liberties of its citizens in some core ways. While the government has a right to impose rules on society and to assess taxes on residents, it has no moral authority to tell citizens what to think, who to worship, or how to lead their private lives. (Liberalism, in this philosophical sense, does *not* imply a particular position on the left-right spectrum. In the sense in which I use this term, Willy Brandt and Helmut Kohl, Margaret Thatcher and Tony Blair, Ronald Reagan and Barack Obama all count as liberal.)

The details of what this means for an array of controversial topics are far from obvious. Philosophical liberals disagree with one another about important questions like how easily parents should be allowed to homeschool their kids, under what circumstances towns can display religious symbols, or what accommodations from general rules citizens with strong religious convictions should enjoy.

Even so, the core commitment of philosophical liberalism is clear. Liberals believe that the state's authority is constrained by its obligation to respect the moral autonomy of its citizens. And that also means that—even in a country with many different religions, cultures, or ethnic groups—it is individuals, not the groups to which they belong, who are the fundamental building block of society.

Can this basic principle sustain increasingly diverse democracies? A growing number of thinkers believe that the answer is no.

Critics of liberalism like to claim that the philosophy's focus on the rights and duties of individuals makes it incapable of dealing with the challenges of diverse democracies.

Liberalism, in this view, falsely assumes that most people choose their moral ties and religious beliefs in the unconstrained way you

might pick a restaurant or buy a pair of jeans. This, its more sophisticated critics claim, makes liberals incapable of appreciating the fundamental importance that ethnic or religious communities play in the
lives of most people. For in truth, nearly all people are born into an
intricate web of relationships that creates deep ties of mutual affection.

"Individuals inherit a particular space within an interlocking set of
social relationships," the philosopher Alasdair MacIntyre argued in *After
Virtue*. "To know oneself as such a social person is . . . to find oneself
placed at a certain point on a journey with set goals; to move through life
is to make progress—or to fail to make progress—toward a given end."

The critics of liberalism are deeply split about what to put in its
place. Some hope that a cohesive ethnic or religious majority will once
again impose its will on the rest of society. For them, the right answer
to the individualism of a liberal society is the collective affirmation of
a national culture. This, for example, is what Viktor Orbán has in mind
when he explicitly defends the ideal of an "illiberal democracy" and
promises that, as Hungary's prime minister, he will ensure the preservation of the country's traditional values.

But the antiliberal tradition with the most traction in the academic
and political mainstream of most developed democracies is rooted not in
Orbán's majoritarianism, which would impose the preference of the majority group on everyone else, but rather in a form of moral relativism,
which allows each group in society to govern its own members to the
greatest possible extent. Inspired by critiques of liberalism, a wide array of
activists and academics have, over the past decades, tried to come up with
a "communitarian" conception of diverse democracies. Instead of thinking of individuals as the basic building blocks of modern states, they
suggest that we place ethnic and religious groups at their very foundation.

According to the communitarian philosopher Chandran Kukathas, for example, the rules set by the state are no more legitimate than the norms that govern the ethnic and religious communities that constitute it. Instead of thinking about individuals as possessing rights that allow them to keep an oppressive state at bay, we should think of a number of these "associations" as the real constitutive power in diverse societies. The state itself, he argues, is but an "association of associations." As such, its right to interfere in the internal affairs of various groups should be extremely limited, or perhaps nonexistent.

Can communitarian conceptions that place groups rather than individuals at the center of diverse democracies provide the grounding for a more attractive alternative to liberalism?

To answer this question, we first need an account of the different ways in which the citizens of diverse democracies should be able to lead their lives. There are, I argue, at least two sets of freedoms that need to be in place for citizens to enjoy a basic modicum of self-determination:

1. *Freedom from Persecution by the Out-group*: In a thriving diverse democracy, individuals have to be free from persecution by people outside their own identity group, whether that persecution emanates from the state or a majority of their own compatriots. This means that they must enjoy key protections against the arbitrary power of the state, such as freedom of speech and assembly. But it also means that they must know that the state will actively protect them against the wrath of an intolerant majority that might disapprove of their ethnicity, their cultural traditions, or their religious practices.

2. *Freedom from Coercion by the In-group*: In a thriving diverse democracy, individuals have to be free from the forms of coercion to which their own relatives, elders, or clerics might subject them. This means that they must have the right to violate the norms of their communities and even, if they so wish, to exit them.

In a second step, we can then compare whether liberalism or communitarianism is better able to grant citizens the twin protections they need to be true to their identity and lead a self-determined life. The answer I arrive at is clear. Diverse democracies will be better able to respect the convictions of all their citizens—including both those who give tremendous importance to their ethnic and religious ties and those who do not—if they adopt a liberal self-conception.

THE KEY FREEDOMS
(AND HOW THEY ARE THREATENED)

On August 20, 2020, at 8:06 a.m., S7 Airlines Flight 2614 took off from Tomsk Bogashevo Airport, in Siberia, en route to Moscow. The first minutes of the flight were uneventful. Then a passenger started to moan in agony, his drawn-out, high-pitched wail flooding the cabin. Disoriented, he made his way to the bathroom, and lost consciousness.

The plane made an emergency landing. Medical workers carried the sick passenger out on a stretcher. By the time Alexei Navalny, Russia's most famous opposition leader, reached Emergency Hospital No. 1 in Omsk, he was in a coma.

Over the next days, Navalny became a pull toy of political forces. Alexander Murakhovsky, the chief physician of the hospital, adamantly ruled poison out at a hastily convened press conference. When Navalny's wife, Yulia, reached the hospital, the authorities at first refused her access to Alexei because she didn't have her marriage certificate on her.

Concerned that local doctors were not doing what they could to save his life, Yulia pressed for her husband to be transported for treatment abroad. At first, the authorities refused to let Navalny depart. But thanks to immense international pressure, a chartered plane was finally permitted to fly him to the Charité Hospital in Berlin.

Navalny's new doctors quickly ascertained that he had been poisoned "with a substance from the group of cholinesterase inhibitors." Treated with drugs that counteract nerve agents, he made a strong recovery. Less than a month after his collapse, Navalny announced that he and his wife intended to return to Russia despite the evident risk to his life.

When Navalny was finally ready to return, in January of 2021, half of the plane consisted of journalists chronicling his act of foolhardy bravery. Quoting a cult movie from the early 2000s, Yulia turned to a flight attendant and said: "Bring us some vodka. We're going home."

As expected, the couple's joy at being back in Russia did not last long. The plane was diverted to stop a throng of Navalny's supporters from cheering his return. As soon as he stepped onto Russian soil, he was arrested.

A few weeks later, a court in Moscow sentenced Navalny to more than two years in prison. By leaving Russia to be treated in Germany, the judge explained in a ruling whose perversity ranks high in the long annals of oppressive regimes, Navalny had violated the conditions of his probation for a previous punishment on equally dubious charges.

"This is happening to intimidate large numbers of people," Navalny said in a defiant speech to the court. "They're imprisoning one person to frighten millions." His experience, Navalny insisted, was the essence of dictatorship. Though the naked power of the Kremlin occasionally likes to play dress-up in the robes of judges, a determination to jail or kill opponents "is what happens when lawlessness and tyranny become the essence of a political system."

FREEDOM FROM PERSECUTION

The story of Alexei Navalny is no aberration. At the darkest moments in human history, the angel of death often wore official robes. In large parts of the world—in the Germany of the 1930s and the Soviet Union of the 1950s, in the China of the 1960s and the Brazil of the 1970s—the story of the twentieth century was the story of state persecution.

Even today, oppressive regimes in totalitarian countries like North Korea control the lives of their citizens in their most intimate details. A cautious word of dissent, uttered to your wife or husband within the walls of your own home, can get you jailed or executed. Even failing to express your loyalty loudly enough can provoke the most unspeakable punishments. Some unfortunate souls have been sent to labor camps whose horrors defy description because they did not cheer the regime with sufficient abandon or failed to cry with appropriate despair when the death of the "dear leader" was announced.

Thankfully, totalitarian states are now rare. In the twenty-first century, most dictators have learned that they do not need to politicize every aspect of their subjects' lives. Unlike North Koreans, the citizens of "run-of-the-mill dictatorships" in Russia and Nicaragua, in Turkey and Zimbabwe, are mostly able to stay out of politics. If they go about their lives without complaining about the regime, investigating corruption, or aiding the opposition, they can largely do what they want.

But the moment they start to speak out of turn, to voice an unorthodox opinion, or to upset the business dealings of political insiders, the state can bring the full brunt of its force to bear on them. If, for reasons rational or not so rational, it decides that somebody is a threat, they will quickly become acquainted with its awesome machinery for subjugation. Perhaps they will suddenly prove unable to secure a loan or get an exit visa. Perhaps they will lose a job or an apartment. Perhaps they will be interrogated, jailed, executed, or assassinated in the street.

Even countries whose citizens have, until recently, prided themselves on their freedom are now sliding back into absolutism. As Larry Diamond has chronicled, we are now in the midst of a serious "democratic recession." During each of the past fifteen years, more countries have moved away from free political institutions than have moved toward them. According to Freedom House, the share of the world's people who live in free countries had, by the end of 2020, fallen to the lowest levels in a quarter century. Fewer than one in five people now live in countries where they can stand up to their government without fear of serious retribution.

Any democracy deserving its name must keep the arbitrary power of the state at bay. Its citizens need to know that they won't be targeted for criticizing the powerful or rallying the opposition. But, especially in diverse societies, protections for individual citizens must go further than that: to lead a dignified and self-determined life, they must also know that neither the state nor their own compatriots will persecute them on the basis of their identity.

From local sheriffs tasked with ensuring the smooth operation of a slave auction to soldiers ethnically "cleansing" local villages, and from Gestapo agents hunting for hiding Jews to uniformed Hutus massacring defenseless Tutsis, the murder and maltreatment of minorities has often enjoyed the sanction of the state.

Even in supposedly consolidated democracies, members of ethnic and religious minority groups now remain at greater risk than their compatriots. Across the Western world, far-right populists who promise to defend the country against the urgent danger supposedly posed by outsiders have won tremendous power. In many cases, they have incited hatred against members of minority groups or instructed the agents of the state to violate their basic civil rights.

Nor does the threat of persecution always have to come directly from the state. In many countries in Eastern Europe, for example, large parts of the population harbor strong prejudices against gays and lesbians. Because state authorities often fail to protect them in an adequate manner, citizens who are publicly recognizable as homosexual or dare to show up for a pride parade have to fear grievous bodily harm. A state can facilitate the persecution of minority groups simply by turning a blind eye to the tyranny of the majority.

It is therefore not enough for the state to refrain from persecuting its own citizens on the basis of their political views, their religious convictions or their sexual orientation; it must take active steps to protect minority communities from oppression by nonstate actors. In a free society, members of all groups must be able to be true to their own identity without fear of persecution by either the state or their fellow citizens.

But there is also a rather different freedom that citizens of diverse democracies need to enjoy. If they are to lead a self-determined life, it is not enough that they be protected against persecution by an out-group; they must, at the same time, be protected from the terrible forms of coercion to which members of their own in-group might subject them.

FREEDOM FROM COERCION

Sometime in late 2017 or early 2018, Saif Ali Khan, a twenty-two-year-old fruit vendor who made his living in the markets of Bikaner, in the picturesque northwest of India, met a young woman who lived in a nearby neighborhood. They fell in love, met up whenever they could, and resolved to get married. Then the family of the would-be bride found out about the young couple.

Horrified that their daughter, a Hindu, would start a relationship with Khan, a Muslim, the bride's parents hastily arranged a more "suitable" match, and sent her to stay with family in Rampura Basti, about two miles from her own home. But Khan was not willing to give up so easily on the woman he loved. When he found out where her family had hidden her, he went in search of his lover. If all went according to plan, the couple would elope before she was married off against her will.

All did not go according to plan. As soon as Khan arrived at the house, six men set upon him. After beating him bloody and unconscious, his lover's relatives—including her father, brothers, and cousin—drove him to Karni Industrial Area, at the edge of Bikaner, and dumped him in a pool of wastewater. "They hit him mercilessly and broke his legs," Khan's brother, Asmal, would later tell a local journalist. "They drove their car over his legs and left him in the drain."

When factory workers noticed Khan's body hours later, he was still alive. By the time the sun next rose over Bikaner, he had succumbed to his injuries.

The bloody history of the twentieth century has focused the minds of philosophers and social scientists on the oppressive powers of modern states. But this threatens to elide a more long-standing, and equally potent, danger to individual liberty: the so-called cage of norms.

As Daron Acemoglu and James A. Robinson have chronicled in *The Narrow Corridor*, the absence of a state need not result in a life of anarchy that is "nasty, brutish, and short." To maintain some semblance of social order "in societies without centralized authority," unwritten rules often exercise "a different but no less disempowering sort of dominance on people." They tell people how they ought to worship and what they can wear, whether they may speak and what they should say, when they can have sex and whom they must marry.

In most traditional societies, priests and parents, elders and neighbors severely punish people who seek to strike out on their own path or fraternize with members of an outside group. This minutely regulated cage of norms may be more stable and peaceful than the war of all against all which so terrified Hobbes. But it is deeply claustrophobic, highly hierarchical—and at times just as nasty.

Developed democracies have thankfully abolished many of the practices that Acemoglu and Robinson describe. But even today, members of tight-knit ethnic or religious communities can, like Saif Ali Khan and his beloved, be subject to the power of their elders in horrific ways. From fundamentalist Christians in Topeka who are forced to attend "conversion therapies" to suppress their homosexual urges to Orthodox Jews in Brooklyn who lose the right to see their children if they leave their community, and from Somali women in northern Sweden who suffer genital mutilation to Turkish women in Berlin who fear being murdered in an "honor killing," the cage of norms persists—often unseen and sometimes violent—in diverse democracies around the world.

A free society must protect its citizens against persecution by the state or an intolerant majority. But it must also push open the heavy doors that have historically enclosed most of humanity in a claustrophobic cage of norms. To lead a life free of humiliating coercion, the citizens of diverse democracies must be able to disregard the rules of the groups into which they were born and even, if they so wish, to exit them altogether.

Can diverse democracies succeed in protecting their citizens both from persecution by outsiders and from coercion by members of their own groups? And does liberalism or its communitarian competitor offer a more realistic account of how they can do so?

KEEPING PERSECUTION AT BAY

Thankfully, the long and bloody history of humanity gives us plenty of information about how to keep the worst forms of persecution at bay.

For millennia, large swathes of Europe and Asia were ruled by monarchs who enjoyed plenipotentiary powers. And as long as one man or woman enjoyed a monopoly on power, injustice and oppression were rampant. As Lord Acton put it in 1887, summarizing centuries of European history in four simple words, "absolute power corrupts absolutely."

Because absolute power corrupts absolutely, the history of liberty is, in good part, the history of imposing creative limits on the state. Over the course of centuries, three kinds of limits on state power evolved: limits on the ability of the powerful to stay in office without their subjects' consent; limits on the kinds of decisions these leaders can make without the cooperation of rival institutions; and limits on the range of affairs with which the state properly concerns itself.

Over time, these core features of liberal democracy have become so central to free societies around the world that it would be tempting to take their existence for granted. But it is worth taking a moment to remember what their core purpose is, and why it is that all three of them need to be in place at the same time for the danger of persecution—both to individuals like Alexei Navalny and to whole communities like the Rohingya—to be contained.

1. *Regular Elections*: In most societies in human history, there was no way to remove the powerful from office without immense violence and upheaval. If most people resented the behavior of their king or tribal chief, they had but two choices. They could wait until he died, hoping against hope that his successor would prove to be more benevolent. Or they could, in the words of John Locke, resort to an "appeal to heaven," staging a revolt that was unlikely to succeed yet almost certain to cause immense bloodshed.

   Thankfully, there is now a better alternative. Over many centuries, some states have invented and refined mechanisms that allow us to remove those who abuse their power from office. That is the core purpose of holding regular elections.

Elections give citizens a way to influence the decisions of their governments. But as any citizen of a democracy knows, politicians often fail to keep the promises they made to get elected. If elections were onetime events, which turned their victors into monarchs for life, democracy would barely constitute an improvement over autocracy.

This is why the powerful only get to occupy the most important offices in the land for a limited period of time. After a set number of years—two for US representatives, four for US presidents, an unusually long six for US senators—the individuals who occupy key roles in the state have to seek a renewal of their powers. If the electorate is no longer convinced that they are working in its interests, it can send them packing.

2. *Separation of Powers*: There is one obvious problem with regular elections: What if an incumbent president or prime minister refuses to leave office after losing an election—or even rigs the vote to ensure victory?

This is hardly an abstract fear. From Robert Mugabe in Zimbabwe to Hugo Chávez in Venezuela, a huge number of leaders moved to concentrate vast powers in their own hands soon after winning democratic elections. They quashed the freedom of the press, placed their loyalists in courts or electoral commissions, and jailed opposition leaders.

Once they succeeded, it quickly became impossible to throw these democratically elected leaders out of office by democratic means. Though Mugabe, Chávez, and dozens of other dictators kept up the charade of sustaining democratic institutions—staging regular elections that lent them a superficial veneer of popular legitimacy—they effectively turned themselves into monarchs for life.

A second innovation is therefore needed to guarantee that citizens retain the ability to remove oppressive leaders from office: the executive needs to be constrained by competing institutions. Opposition parties need to be allowed to do their work even if it displeases the government. Journalists need to be able to criticize presidents even if they threaten to throw them in jail. And judges need to retain their political independence, telling presidents when they overstep the boundaries of their rightful authority.

This is the purpose of the seemingly paradoxical set of rules and norms that political scientists know as the "separation of powers" or, alternatively, "checks and balances." A president or prime minister is in charge of the executive, directing the cabinet, leading diplomatic efforts, and overseeing the delivery of government services. But her powers are not limitless. For the laws are written by the legislature, which can disagree with the executive or (in many countries) even remove the president or prime minister from office. And disputes about the interpretation of existing laws, or the extent of the president's rightful powers, are adjudicated by the judiciary, with independent judges safeguarding the constitution.

3. *Individual Rights*: Regular elections allow citizens to remove leaders from office when they grow unpopular. The separation of powers helps to make sure that elections will actually

be free and fair. But on their own, these institutional innovations are not enough to ensure that citizens get to lead lives that are meaningfully free. For if a majority of citizens should *want* the state to intrude into the lives of their compatriots, even freely elected governments could grow to be oppressive.

The danger that the majority will turn tyrannical is especially acute in ethnically or religiously divided democracies. Even when countries hold regular elections and have a real separation of powers, they can ban religious minorities from worshipping as they please, stop ethnic minorities from cultivating their own cultures or languages, or stand by as fanatical mobs persecute minority groups. Something else is needed to protect such groups from both the state and the tyranny of the majority.

Thankfully, a third institutional innovation goes a long way toward giving all citizens the ability to lead their lives in accordance with their values: the recognition that there is a sphere of life in which everybody should be able to do what they like without having to worry about anyone else's opinion.

Both America's Bill of Rights and France's Declaration of the Rights of Man recognize that there are many essential decisions that citizens should get to take for themselves. The majority may deeply dislike the words you choose to publish, the people you invite for dinner, or the religious practices in which you engage. But as long as the state adopts core liberal principles like free speech, free assembly, and the free exercise of religion—and energetically punishes anybody who seeks to

undermine them by threatening unpopular minority groups—
all citizens should be safe from persecution.

In conjunction, regular elections, the separation of powers, and individual rights grant the citizens of diverse democracies key protections
against persecution. But do the core institutions of liberal democracy
allow them to orient their lives around the deep ties many of them have
to their own communities? Or do alternatives to liberalism, like communitarianism, do a better job of balancing between individual freedom and the great importance that so many people invest in their own
cultural and religious groups?

PROTECTING CITIZENS AGAINST COERCION
BY THEIR OWN GROUP

Communitarians believe that they are in a better position than liberals
to respect the deep importance that cultural ties play in the lives of
many people. Rather than thinking of diverse democracies as composed
of individual citizens, thinkers like Kukathas propose, we should conceptualize them as lose federations of ethnic or religious communities.

A diverse democracy that embraces communitarianism would
seemingly do well at upholding one plausible goal of diverse democracies: ensuring that cultural or religious communities can thrive. In recognizing, say, the Catholic Church, the Southern Baptist Convention,
and the Council on American-Islamic Relations as basic building
blocks of society, it would grant them far-reaching rights and privileges.

These should, in principle, ensure that members of these communities can live a life that is true to their identity.

But there are a lot of serious problems with this proposal. One has to do with the difficulty of giving official recognition to various groups and drawing boundaries between them. How should a diverse democracy go about determining which groups should enjoy official recognition and which are too new or too small or too "frivolous" to count as one of its basic building blocks? How can they ensure that the leaders of these groups actually speak for their members? And what happens to the many people who don't neatly fit into any recognized group?

An even bigger problem is that such a communitarian conception would, even as it seemingly protects people from persecution and allows them to be true to their inherited identity, make it impossible for them to chart their own course through life. Individuals who do not agree with the customs of the communities into which they were born would, on the model of diverse democracy advocated by Kukathas and his allies, be left at the mercy of an oppressive cage of norms.

States that conceive of themselves as a mere "association of associations" have no apparent justification for interfering in the "internal" affairs of these groups. This means that they would have to stand aside when groups fail to tolerate internal dissent, render their children incapable of living a self-determined life, or stop those who want to strike out on their own from exiting the group. If you are a gay man born into a Christian cult that believes homosexuality to be evil, or an intellectually curious child born into a Hasidic sect that discourages you from pursuing a secular education, you will have to get used to living within the cage constructed by "your" association.

Communitarians fail to grant citizens of diverse democracy a sufficient modicum of freedom from the coercion that the groups into which they were born might try to impose on them. This makes communitarianism an unappealing account of the future we should build. But can liberals do any better at reconciling the desire of many citizens to be true to their identity with their need to be free from the cage of norms?

The answer is yes.

On the liberal view, diverse democracies are constituted by a broad variety of individuals, not a set of groups. They should be committed to protecting the core freedoms of these individuals. And so it seems straightforward that a just democracy has a legitimate reason, and even an obligation, to step in when ethnic or religious groups attempt to coerce their own members.

But while liberals are much better able to uphold citizens' freedom from the cage of norms, it is less obvious how they can ensure that people who give great importance to their cultural or religious ties can be true to their own identity. Isn't it a mistake, as Alasdair MacIntyre warned, to talk about the deep religious faith with which many citizens of diverse democracies are raised—and which many of them might never shed—as a mere "choice"?

This objection misunderstands the nature of the liberal project. It is often said that liberals' emphasis on individuals makes us incapable of appreciating the importance that groups play in the lives of so many people. But we are deeply aware of the overriding significance with which many people imbue the groups to which they belong and even that most people never step back from these relationships. People don't freely "choose" to maintain or abandon their cultural or religious ties as though they were picking between different dinner options on their food delivery app.

Philosophical liberals do, then, have deep respect for the importance of family, religion, and tradition in contemporary societies. We are fully aware that a large number of citizens lead their lives in accordance with norms they consider dictates of conscience. In fact, this is precisely why we are so concerned with protecting the kinds of guarantees of personal liberty, such as freedom of speech and worship, that ensure that citizens won't be forced to abdicate their innermost beliefs.

This is also why liberal states across the world should—and do—allow their citizens to structure their lives around their cultural and religious commitments in ways that the majority might at times feel to be extreme. So long as they provide pupils with enough secular education to give them genuine choices for how to lead their lives once they become adults, religious communities can found schools that instruct children in the traditions of their faith. Citizens who genuinely feel that serving in the army would violate their conscience enjoy exemptions from compulsory military service. And when communities like the Amish decide to live in great isolation from the customs of mainstream society, nobody forces them to use modern technology or mingle with their neighbors.

But for liberals, this deep respect for particular cultural or religious communities ultimately derives from the commitments of their members. If we respect Baptist churches or the Muslim faith or the Humanist Union, it is not because we regard these groups as the founding units of our society; it is because they hold tremendous significance to millions of people.

To be truly free, citizens of diverse democracies must know that they will not experience hostility or discrimination based on the color of their skin; that they can worship as they please; and that they are, if they so wish, free to spend most of their lives within the ethnic or religious communities into which they were born. Guaranteeing their citizens' freedom from oppression by an out-group is a key task of a liberal state. But citizens of diverse democracies must also know that they will be free to leave the group into which they were born; to violate its norms without fear of suffering destitution, violence, or death at the hands of their own elders; and to define themselves by the identities and associations they themselves choose. Any state that neglects its citizens' freedom from coercion by their own group neglects a second, equally important, task.

To live up to their promise, diverse democracies must actively protect their members against the double dangers they face, then. Citizens need to benefit from all the institutional innovations that have historically proved capable of keeping a tyrannical state at bay and know that the communities to which they belong will be able to practice their customs in peace. And they must also be able to call upon the assistance of the state to defend them against any private groups that might, against their will, enclose them in a cage of norms. Only a diverse democracy built on the principles of philosophical liberalism is capable of protecting both of these core values at the same time.

Only states that are powerful enough to protect individuals from the groups that seek to oppress them yet sufficiently constrained that they do not themselves grow oppressive can guarantee the twin liberties everyone deserves.

A society in which all citizens enjoy such a double freedom helps to protect them from oppression and defuses some of the most obvious sources of intergroup conflict. But as a basis for a thriving diverse democracy, it does not suffice. For if citizens from different races and religions are to be truly committed to living together as part of the same state, they also have to have some sentiment they share.

Traditionally, patriotism or nationalism has provided citizens of most democracies with that glue, giving them a concern for the common good, and making them care about the well-being of people they have never met. But many people are now, for good reason, skeptical of these sentiments. Is it possible, they wonder, to encourage a healthy form of patriotism without opening the door to ethnic exclusion, racial discrimination, and deadly international conflicts?

That is the question to which I now turn.

FIVE

Can Patriotism Be a
Force for Good?

In the most despairing months of World War II, when the planes of the Wehrmacht were raining bombs upon London and the Nazis seemed destined to rule vast swathes of Europe, George Orwell set out to write about a surprising subject: the virtues of patriotism.

Orwell was as aware of the destructive potential of nationalism as any of his compatriots. A few years earlier, he had joined an international band of idealists to defend the Spanish Republic against its fascist enemies. "The energy that actually shapes the world," Orwell warned those who still dismissed Adolf Hitler as too absurd to pose a real threat, "springs from emotions—racial pride, leader worship, religious belief, love of war—which liberal intellectuals mechanically write off as anachronisms."

But it is precisely because Orwell knew how powerfully such emotions drive politics, and how destructive they can become when they are allowed to fester into a fervid nationalism, that he defended the need for a constructive form of patriotism.

"What has kept England on its feet during the past year?" he asked during World War II. In the main, he answered, it was "the atavistic emotion of patriotism [. . .] For the last twenty years, the main object of English left-wing intellectuals has been to break this feeling down. And if they had succeeded, we might be watching the SS men patrolling the London streets at this moment."

For Orwell, the implication was clear. Many activists and intellectuals had managed to destroy their own sense of patriotism "so completely in themselves as to have lost all power of action." But the right way to fight back against murderous nationalism was not to insist on a purely rational politics that proudly dismissed all local attachments; it was to foster and embrace a healthy patriotism that might provide a bulwark against the worst manifestations of national sentiment.

In the first half of the twentieth century, nationalism was the most powerful political force in the world. During the comparatively peaceful period that followed, many writers and academics quickly fell back into the trap Orwell identified. That is the intellectual atmosphere in which I was raised.

Growing up in Germany, my friends and I referred to right-wing nationalists as Ewiggestrige, those who are "forever of yesteryear." The future would lie in greater tolerance, more international cooperation, and European integration. Nationalism, we believed, was but an anachronism—a form of collective prejudice befitting scoundrels and demagogues, and headed for the dustbin of history.

Then far-right nationalists like Narendra Modi in India, Jair Bolsonaro in Brazil, and Donald Trump in the United States started to win elections. To anyone who took an unflinching look at these changes, it became obvious that our contempt had amounted to yet another bout of wishful thinking. While we were writing high-minded essays about a postnational future, political leaders animated by bellicose nationalism had conquered the world.

Nationalism is back, and it is likely to remain as influential in this century as it was in the last. How should defenders of diverse democracy respond?

One answer would be to double down on attempts to leave all forms of national sentiment behind. Perhaps the rise of noxious nationalists is all the more reason for decent people to turn themselves into "cosmopolitans," setting out to care equally about people whether they happen to be neighbors or live at the other end of the earth. After all, philosophers have a point when they ask why anyone should give special consideration to people who happen to be their fellow citizens when those in distant places might be in much more urgent need of help.

There's some truth to this. We do have serious moral obligations to people with whom we don't share ties of culture, ethnicity, or citizenship. If more people took these obligations seriously, the world would likely become a better place. The few people who are capable of such boundless empathy have my full admiration.

But over time I have also (as I explained in part 1) grown deeply skeptical about whether most people are capable of sustaining this kind of altruism. Humans are groupish. Our tendency to form in-groups, and to discriminate against those who do not belong to them, goes deep.

Given those facts, I fear that it is naive to assume that a society that discourages its citizens from feeling any form of national sentiment would thereby encourage them to care about those who are more distant. In practice, a society without patriotism is less likely to consist of altruistic cosmopolitans who donate all their money to starving children in distant countries than of mutually hostile tribes that ruthlessly fight for their own interests.

This is of special relevance in diverse democracies. For them to thrive, citizens drawn from many different ethnic and religious groups will need to sustain a real sense of solidarity with one another. A shared devotion to their country might just help to attenuate intergroup conflicts and instill a sense of care for the common good.

That is why I have long thought of patriotism as a half-wild beast. If the worst people are left to stoke its most violent instincts, it is capable of wreaking terrible havoc. But when decent people succeed in domesticating patriotism, it can be of tremendous use in allowing the citizens of modern states to care for one another's fate.

So how can diverse democracies domesticate this half-wild beast, making patriotism useful rather than dangerous? And what might serve as the basis for an inclusive patriotism in societies that are highly diverse, and therefore lack common touchpoints like shared religious practices?

There are three basic answers.

According to the first, democracies should hold on to an ethnic sense of nationalism. Rooted in the history of particular peoples, countries like Japan or Italy should continue to recognize those who descend from its original inhabitants as having special standing.

This kind of ethnic notion cannot work as the basis for diverse democracies that treat all their members fairly. While there is nothing wrong with honoring the special historical role that particular groups have played in shaping their nations, immigrants and their descendants must be given equal place in them going forward.

According to the second answer about what form patriotism should take, democracies should define themselves by their civic cultures or constitutional values. Founded on the basis of ideals like political liberty, countries like India and the United States have long emphasized their countries' founding documents as sources of shared identity. Even countries like Germany, which had once defined themselves in more explicitly ethnic terms, are now following suit.

Civic patriotism can help highly diverse nations operate on the basis of shared ideals and aspirations. It has an important role to play. And yet I believe that it is an incomplete description of the sense of patriotism that most citizens of contemporary democracies actually do share.

This leaves a third answer. A core reason why most citizens of modern democracies have a deep attachment to their countries is, simply, that they love its culture. Though they may be deeply disturbed by some of their country's problems, and revile many of its injustices, they feel an attachment to the things that help to define it in the everyday: its language and its cities, its celebrities and its television shows, its instinctual habits and its social conventions.

To resonate, this kind of cultural patriotism needs to look to the future rather than obsess about the past. And to be inclusive, it needs to make space for all of a country's residents rather than put one group on an undeserved pedestal. But understood in the right way, it can make a key contribution to inspiring the sense of common purpose diverse democracies need to thrive.*

---

* Some writers like to distinguish carefully between nationalism and patriotism. Nationalism, they believe, is bad because it necessarily implies that one country is superior to all others. Patriotism, by contrast, is said to consist in a love of country that is not jealous of other nations. I fear that this is too simple. Even at its worst, nationalism can inspire common purpose. And even at its best, patriotism is susceptible to being weaponized. Though I agree much more strongly with the goals and aspirations of those thinkers who have historically called themselves patriots than with those who have historically called themselves nationalists, I worry that an overly clean distinction between these two concepts blinds us to an important empirical reality: rather than being wholly separate, patriotism and nationalism are but the pretty and the ugly side of the same coin. Since the distinction between patriotism and nationalism is

THE POWER AND PERIL OF ETHNIC NATIONALISM

In 451 BC, the most famous orator in all of Athens rose from his seat to address his compatriots. His beloved city, Pericles argued, faced an urgent crisis. Immigrants and their descendants could meddle in affairs that should rightfully be reserved for those whose ancestors hail from the polis. It was high time to limit citizenship to real Athenians.

Even before Pericles's proposed reform, the laws governing Athenian citizenship were highly restrictive. In order to speak in the assembly, vote on a law, sit on a jury, or own property, a resident of Athens had to trace his father's heritage all the way back to the city's original founders.

After the assembly passed the law Pericles championed, the city guarded the "purity" of its citizens even more jealously. Only residents who descended from the city's founders on both their father's and their mother's side now enjoyed full civic standing. Some of the writers, scientists, and philosophers most closely associated with the glories of Athens—Aristotle, Diogenes, Democritus, and Protagoras—remained relegated to second-class status throughout their lives.

In the long history of democracy, Athens is closer to the rule than the exception. For the past three thousand years, the citizens of the world's most celebrated democracies prided themselves on their ethnic purity.

The Roman Republic, for example, quickly took on vast dimensions. By the time of Julius Caesar's birth, its borders were located thousands of miles from the city's seven hills, and more than a million

---

widely accepted, though, I follow the usual convention of describing forms of collective pride that I support as "patriotism" and those that I find worrisome as "nationalism" in the following pages.

people enjoyed the privileges of Roman citizenship. Casting about for a model that could inspire their own grand experiment in self-governance, America's Founding Fathers would, nearly two thousand years later, look more to Rome than to Athens.

But though the vast Roman Republic was much more diverse than the tiny Athenian polis, it, too, stipulated ethnic criteria for membership. Inhabitants of conquered territories that were located on the Italian peninsula and were thought to belong to the same extended tribe could win the right to call themselves Romans. The inhabitants of more distant territories, who were seen as ethnically distinct, remained relegated to an inferior status.

In the modern era, the democratic obsession with ethnic purity intensified. In the eighteenth and nineteenth centuries, Europe's nationalist movements courageously opposed the sclerotic monarchies that held millions of peasants captive in feudal servitude and denied meaningful political participation to virtually everyone else. But even in the heyday of progressive nationalism, democracy remained closely linked to ethnicity. When German or Italian patriots fought to forge disparate kingdoms and principalities into unified nations, they assumed that their inhabitants would share one language, history, and heritage.

Nationalist movements that hoped to gain independence from large multiethnic kingdoms put even more emphasis on common descent. The Czech, Slovak, and Romanian patriots who sought to cast off the domination of the Austro-Hungarian Empire, for example, hoped to create new states that would be limited to those who shared their culture and custom. Over the following century, they achieved their goal in good part by expelling or curbing the rights of the ethnic minorities that happened to live within the territories of their newly independent nations.

Asian and African states that won their independence from European colonists over the course of the twentieth century look like a possible exception. Because their borders had usually been drawn with little regard for culture or geography, most of them contained too many different groups to create one state for each ethnic group. Even so, their leaders quickly identified supposed outsiders they could blame for the problems of their newly independent nations. From Hindus in today's Bangladesh to South Asians in today's Uganda, the birth of postcolonial states often went hand in hand with a violent purge of minority groups.

Any credible account of what patriotism might mean today needs to take the ethnic roots of modern nations seriously.

From ancient Athens to contemporary Uganda, ethnic criteria have long played a strong role in determining who is in and who is out. And so it is, even today, impossible to understand the nature of modern-day Denmark, Thailand, or Rwanda without referencing the ways in which these countries were formed by one or multiple specific ethnocultural groups. Anybody who loves these countries must also harbor some appreciation for the peoples who have shaped them over centuries.

And yet the changes of the past half century have, especially in developed democracies that have experienced a high level of immigration, made a purely or predominantly ethnic conception of nationalism unfit for purpose.

A lot of the people who now live in and love Denmark, for example, do not descend from the Vikings who dominated that area during the Middle Ages. Just as ancient Athens condemned Aristotle and Protagoras to the status of "Metics," unable to encounter their contemporaries as equals, so too an ethnic conception of Danish patriotism would forever condemn nearly one out of five people who live in the country to second-class status.

Ethnic nationalism would also bear less and less resemblance to the lived reality of most modern democracies. Forever hailing the achievements of one part of the population, it would be unable to acknowledge to what extent they have, in the last fifty years, been shaped by immigrants and their descendants. Members of modern democracies who belong to minority groups would never get full credit for their contributions, and would be all the more likely to grow bitter or resentful.

To build thriving democracies that value all citizens fairly, diverse countries need to forge a new conception of patriotism. A nationalism based on shared descent is not fit for purpose. So what other form of common identity could help to bind compatriots of a big, diverse country to one another?

TWO CHEERS FOR CIVIC PATRIOTISM

On a beautiful morning in the spring of 2017, I walked into the John F. Kennedy Presidential Library in South Boston wearing a navy suit, a white shirt, and a blue-red-and-white handkerchief. Along with two hundred people from all over the world, I filed into a light-filled auditorium to listen to a succession of official speeches.

The director of the Kennedy Library told us about the immigrant roots of the thirty-fifth president of the United States, whose great-grandparents had arrived in Boston Harbor from Ireland. A judge teared up as he talked about the time he presided over a naturalization ceremony that included his own daughter-in-law. A man by the name of Mohamad Ali—the CEO of a tech company, not the famous boxer—recalled how he and his parents arrived in the country with only a few dollars to their name.

Then the judge asked us all to rise from our seats. Standing between a middle-aged man who was born in China and a young woman who grew up in Morocco, I pledged that I would "support and defend the Constitution and laws of the United States of America against all enemies, foreign and domestic." When we finished the oath, we were American citizens.

The naturalization ceremony encapsulates a key feature of America's self-conception. Most countries have long defined themselves along ethnic lines; George Washington and Thomas Jefferson and Alexander Hamilton claimed that the American Republic was founded on an idea. What set the Founding Fathers apart from the British monarchs whose rule they could no longer tolerate was neither language nor heritage; it was a commitment—however imperfect—to moral liberty, political self-determination, and the principles enshrined in the Declaration of Independence.

Many philosophers are skeptical of all forms of national sentiment. But if you must defend what many of them consider a base and misguided sentiment, there is a kind of consensus about how to go about it. Drawing on the particular story of the founding, they say, you should make the case for "civic patriotism." To be proud to be an American, for example, is to love the ideals to which the country committed itself in the Constitution.

The modern roots of this conception lie in the United States. But, over time, it has planted offshoots around the world.

When the founders of India tried to figure out how they could give an identity to a vast new country that had a Hindu majority but also included a large number of Muslims, Christians, Sikhs, and Parsis, Mahatma Gandhi championed an Indian version of civic patriotism. "When the Republic of India was created in 1950, its citizens sought to be united on a set of ideals," the Indian historian Ramachandra Guha writes. "The basis of citizenship was adherence to these values, not to [. . .] a shared faith or a common enemy."

Even some countries that long defined themselves on ethnic grounds have, of late, attempted to reconceive of themselves in civic terms. How, German intellectuals asked themselves after World War II, could their compatriots develop a healthy affection for their country without reverting to the kind of racial politics that had led it terribly astray? Citizens who feel pride in the democratic institutions of postwar Germany, thinkers like Jürgen Habermas argued, should make the country's basic law the object of their devotion. The Grundgesetz should become for Germans what the Constitution has long been for Americans.

The advantages of civic patriotism are significant. Unlike ethnic nationalism, it allows anybody who is willing to embrace a set of shared political values to become a full member of the community. So long as a German Jew, a young woman from Morocco, and a middle-aged man from China agree to abide by the Constitution, they should be able to live together in peace—and become as American as a white Anglo-Saxon Protestant whose forefathers arrived on these shores hundreds of years ago.

There is also some reason to think that civic patriotism is less likely to draw countries into international conflict than ethnic forms of nationalism. A love of country that is based in a belief in the inherent superiority of one's own ethnic or racial group provides an easy excuse for those who want to dismiss the legitimate interests of other nations. But a nation that is founded on the importance of self-determination should be able to recognize that other countries also have a legitimate interest in ruling themselves.

Civic patriotism should be better able than ethnic nationalism to welcome newcomers into the fold and sustain meaningful international cooperation.*

The idea of civic patriotism strongly appeals to me. It defines nations by their highest ideals rather than their basest instincts. It gives citizens a way to be proud of their country without indulging in bigotry or chauvinism. If I didn't hesitate to swear the oath of citizenship on that morning in March 2017, it is, in part, because I love the United States Constitution and the inspiration it has provided for civic patriotism, both at home and abroad.

And yet I fear that civic patriotism may, on its own, be an insufficient answer to the question of how diverse democracies can sustain a common national identity.

Most Germans now accept that somebody called Ali or Mustafa can be a true member of their nation, for example. But when they think of what they love about their country, they are less likely to point to the Grundgesetz than they are to insist on cultural and linguistic markers, from the German language to currywurst.

In India, civic patriotism is in even greater danger. For Narendra Modi, the country's powerful prime minister, India is a Hindu nation— and he is passing a raft of discriminatory policies that will go a long way toward turning it into one.

Even in the countries where civic patriotism has its deepest roots,

---

* Reality, as ever, is a little more complicated than theory. Over the course of American history, millions of people have been excluded from full citizenship in the country on the basis of their sex or ethnic origin. And even countries that are founded upon civic patriotism have often violated the rights of other nations or picked unjustifiable wars.

like the United States, many people don't take sufficient interest in history or politics to feel a deep attachment to their constitution or to recognize when a politician poses a threat to it. Most Americans know who won last year's Super Bowl and have an opinion about Meghan Thee Stallion. A lot of Americans have a strong liking for one political party—or at least a pronounced disdain for the other one. But few Americans can explain the three branches of government or recall the meaning of the First Amendment.

Patriotism is one of the most universal sentiments in the modern world. Most citizens of democracies feel it at least to some extent. But an interest in civic documents like the United States Constitution remains the preserve of a politically minded minority. Noble though the idea may be, civic patriotism will never fully describe what most people actually feel when they think of their country with love or affection.

Another reason why civic patriotism does not adequately describe what gives many citizens a special affection for their country may be that national pride is, by its very nature, an attachment to a *particular* place. Though French patriots need not hate or disrespect other countries, they feel a special tug of affection for their own nation. Any account of patriotism that does justice to the nature of their feelings thus needs to explain how France is different from Germany or the United States.

Civic patriotism has trouble doing that. The values that animate the constitutions of France, Germany, and the United States are very similar. Though these documents do of course have some notable differences, they can't explain why most French citizens feel deeper affection for France than they do for Germany or the United States.

The notion of civic patriotism puts abstract political principles at the center of our collective sentiments. This runs the danger of mischaracterizing a sentiment that is, at least as much, about our emotional attachment to real people and places. It simply does not capture what most people talk about when they say that they love their country.

This is no reason to discard civic patriotism. Insofar as it goes, a shared commitment to a country's most basic political values really can help to sustain diverse democracies. But to develop an account of inclusive patriotism that fully expresses the devotion that most citizens feel for their nations, we need to add another dimension: cultural patriotism.

THE CASE FOR CULTURAL PATRIOTISM

On April 22, 1993, John Major, the prime minister of the United Kingdom and Northern Ireland, was trying to reassure the country that a closer relationship with Europe would not alter its essential character. Even if parliament ratified the Maastricht Treaty, which established the European Union, he said, Britain would "still be the country of long shadows on county grounds, warm beer, invincible green suburbs, dog lovers and pools fillers."

The speech was widely mocked. Major, an editorial in *The Independent* complained, was "confusing Britain with certain parts of England." The idea that warm beer or pools fillers (whatever those might be) would forever define Britain seemed silly to many of his compatriots.

Major's failure is no aberration. Whenever politicians try to define the nature of their country, they end up sounding cheesy, antiquated, or both. It would be easy to conclude that these smart politicians and their well-paid speechwriters keep failing because they are trying to give voice to something that doesn't exist. "National characteristics,"

Orwell wrote in 1941, "are not easy to pin down, and when pinned down they often turn out to be trivialities." Have so many people failed to put the essence of their nations into words because modern countries, with their vast territories and millions of diverse inhabitants, don't share any real cultural commonalities?

I don't think so. For as someone who has lived in five different countries, and spent long stretches of time in ten or so others, I am daily struck by the extent to which national cultures continue to differ from one another. Though they may be difficult to put into words, these particularities, as anybody who has lived abroad will be able to recall, are fundamental features of everyday life.

A few years ago, I boarded a train in the northern German city of Hamburg, spent a few hours walking around the southern German city of Offenburg on a layover, and finally arrived in the French city of Strasbourg.

Hamburg and Offenburg differ from each other in important ways. One is a big city, the other a small town. One has historical links to the Netherlands, Sweden, Russia, and the Baltic states. The other has long been influenced and even occupied by France. More than four hundred miles separate Hamburg from Offenburg.

But upon arriving in Offenburg, I was immediately struck by the many things that were exactly the same as they had been in Hamburg. The buildings in both cities have a remarkably similar style. The streets around the station feature many of the same shops. When I entered a bakery in Offenburg, it offered the same Butterbrezeln and Mohnschnecken I had bought when I stocked up on supplies at the beginning of my journey.

Offenburg and Strasbourg should, by comparison, be much more similar to each other. Fewer than fifty miles separate the two cities. They have much greater commonalities of size, climate, and geography. Though Strasbourg is now in France, it had, for long decades, been part of the German Empire.

And yet I was, upon my arrival, immediately struck by how different Strasbourg looks from both Hamburg and Offenburg. The predominant architectural style is not at all the same. A different set of stores dominates the high street. And the bakery I entered offers all the same delicious goods—from pain au chocolat to tarte au citron—I knew from my favorite patisserie in Paris.

Germany and France are both members of the European Union. The border between the two countries barely exists anymore. And yet the national cultures of France and Germany remain remarkably distinct.

The influence of modern nations also shapes the habits, assumptions, and mannerisms that structure everyday life. They help to determine the "cultural scripts" that, as the sociologists Cliff Goddard and Anna Wierzbicka put it, set "background norms, templates, guidelines or models for ways of thinking, acting, feeling, and speaking."

These cultural scripts need not be uniform across a nation. They change significantly over time. And they aren't necessarily welcomed or embraced by all members of a country. But as Goddard and Wierzbicka point out, "even those who do not personally identify with the content of a script are familiar with it. . . . It forms part of the interpretative backdrop to discourse and social behavior in a particular cultural context."

All of this suggests that a third kind of patriotism plays a much bigger role in how citizens of diverse democracies feel about their countries than most philosophers and social scientists have recognized. When they say that they love their country, most people need not be celebrating the ethnic links that unite members of the majority group. Nor need they be thinking about politics or the constitution. They may, rather, be expressing affection for the things that make up modern nations in the everyday: their fields and their cities, their dishes and their customs, their buildings and their cultural scripts.

Skeptics are likely to worry that a celebration of these similarities would amount to a kind of cultural imperialism. Even if most people in diverse democracies do have something in common, they claim, those commonalities reflect the experience of dominant groups. Cultural patriotism, they say, is bound to focus on stereotypical aspects of a culture, such as historical costumes or past military victories. In doing so, it privileges historically dominant groups over more recent immigrants. It will, they fear, always be static, exclusionary, or backward.

This is a danger that deserves to be taken seriously. For nationalists who think of culture in an exclusive way, Italy would cease being Italy if a greater number of Italians chose not to celebrate Christmas, and India would cease being India if most Indians started to celebrate Halloween. There is a way for nationalists to invoke culture that puts the dead over the living, continuity over change, and purity over inclusion.

But that is not what lends cultural patriotism its power in practice. While politicians might, for a lack of words, invoke a lot of clichés or historical symbols when making patriotic speeches, most people arrive at their cultural patriotism by a more direct and unpretentious route. Their love of country is deeply imbued with their appreciation of its everyday sights and smells and sounds and tastes. And in a diverse democracy, these bear the mark of many different groups.

When asked about their favorite foods, Germans are now more

likely to mention a "foreign" dish like spaghetti Bolognese or Döner kebab than they are to go on about a "local" dish like Schweinshaxe. And when Americans think about dishes they love, they are as likely to list pizza and tacos as they are to talk about meat loaf or apple pie.

Nor is this living, breathing, ever-changing everyday culture somehow alien to immigrants and ethnic minorities. Though minority groups often retain pride in elements of their ancestral culture, the vast majority of them are, simultaneously, perfectly comfortable with the cultural mainstream.

In most diverse democracies, members of ethnic or religious minorities are among the most fervent fans of local sports teams and celebrities. They keenly celebrate nondenominational holidays like Thanksgiving and New Year's Eve. In some places, they are even appropriating the most traditional and stereotypical aspects of national culture for themselves: Scots of Indian extraction have taken to the kilt in considerable numbers, for example, while Bavarians with Turkish roots are increasingly likely to don lederhosen when they go to the Oktoberfest.

I love New York City.

Nobody is particularly puzzled by this. And yet it is hard to explain what is so special about this place. Sure, New York has a lot of wonderful food—but so do Paris and Tokyo. And sure, New York is one of the most energetic places I have ever been—but so are Beijing and Mexico City.

We all instinctively understand that a city's culture can hold a special place in our hearts even though it shares many of its attributes with other cities. The fact that New York is not the only city in the world that has amazing pizza or soaring skyscrapers does not make it strange that I have a special affection for this particular place, with its specific spirit, history, architecture, and mixture of cultural influences.

What seems obvious in the case of cities is often dismissed as strange or puzzling in the case of countries. How can you love the culture of a particular modern nation-state when all nations increasingly resemble one another, contain a lot of variety within their own borders, and suffer from serious injustices?

But this is to misunderstand the nature of the attachment that many people have to their own countries. When someone says that they love Brazil or Indonesia or the United States, they don't mean that their attributes are unique, that there is nothing wrong with them, or that other countries are terrible. They are simply expressing a special affection for what is theirs.

"Are there really such things as nations?" Orwell asked in his defense of patriotism. The answer he gave was unambiguous:

> When you come back to England from any foreign country, you have immediately the sensation of breathing a different air. Even in the first few minutes dozens of small things conspire to give you this feeling. The beer is bitterer, the coins are heavier, the grass is greener, the advertisements are more blatant. The crowds in the big towns, with their mild knobby faces, their bad teeth and gentle manners, are different from a European crowd.

Orwell is well aware that there is nothing objectively better about bad teeth or blatant advertisements. He did not think that the national culture of England was superior to that of Spain. And yet he loved it dearly, because it was his.

This cultural patriotism, I have come to believe, is an important and widely overlooked part of what it means to love your country. Diverse democracies that desperately need their citizens to sustain a real sense of solidarity for one another should—without imposing it from above, or allowing it to become exclusionary—make unapologetic use of it.

———

Patriotism and nationalism have often served the very worst of purposes. They were enlisted in the cause of exclusion and discrimination, of war and ethnic cleansing. As a result, many well-meaning advocates of diverse democracy have come to believe that we should give up on this kind of collective identity altogether. For them, the obvious solution to the dangers posed by the abuse of nationalism is to be on guard against patriotism in all its forms.

As a German Jew whose ancestors perished in the Holocaust, I have a lot of sympathy for this position. To put it mildly, neither patriotism nor nationalism came to me naturally. But as a political scientist who is trying to understand how we can keep the worst instincts of humanity in check, I have gradually come to revise my initial instincts. If we are to make the great experiment succeed, we need to enlist patriotism in its cause.

Patriotism can never be wholly cleansed of its attendant dangers. But just as important, it is the strongest foundation for solidarity between people who might otherwise have few things in common. Historically, it has played a significant role in extending the circle of our sympathy beyond our own family, our own village, and our own tribe. Today, it can be the glue that binds the citizens of hugely diverse nations to one another. At its best, it can inspire a white Christian living in rural Tennessee to feel special concern for a Hispanic atheist living in Los Angeles—and vice versa.

For diverse democracies to thrive, their citizens need to share a common identity. Without some sense of inclusive patriotism, they are condemned forever to regard one another as strangers or adversaries.

But many of the open questions about how citizens live alongside one another go beyond whether they are willing to call themselves patriots. The members of different groups might live door by door or be confined to separate neighborhoods. They might have many friends from different walks of life or fastidiously stick to their own. It is possible to imagine a country in which a lot of citizens are quite patriotic—but members of different groups barely ever encounter one another.

A thriving diverse democracy would, then, be defined not only by what is in the hearts of its people but also by how they relate to one another in their daily lives. So is there some way to allow citizens of diverse democracies to be truly and authentically themselves without giving up on the hope that many of them will choose to cooperate and engage with one another in deep and meaningful ways?

That is the next question to which I now turn.

SIX

Must the Many
Become One?

Virtually every developed democracy has become much more diverse over the course of the past fifty years, and is likely to include an even greater variety of ethnic and religious groups fifty years hence. But while the fact that most democracies will be highly diverse seems reasonably certain, big questions remain about what that diversity will look and feel like in daily life.

Will these societies impose a dominant culture on their members, with the children of immigrants and minorities casting aside many of the characteristics that now make them stand out? Will diverse democracies splinter into a series of parallel societies, with the members of different groups rarely encountering one another or embarking on common projects? Or might there be a third possibility—one that allows citizens to remain true to their identities without depriving diverse democracies of a shared culture or a strong sense of the common good?

Over the past decades, these questions have often been answered through the prism of metaphors like the "melting pot" and the "salad bowl." Discussions about which of these to aim for can sometimes feel academic in the pejorative sense: a bunch of professors debating the pros and cons of an abstract ideal that only has a loose relationship to lived reality. But getting the ideal that diverse democracies should aim for right is nevertheless important. For these metaphors help to set the vision of the future that diverse democracies strive for, the goals that influential organizations like schools, universities, and foundations pursue, and the expectations that many citizens have of their compatriots.

That makes it especially concerning that the two most prominent metaphors of the past decades have, each in their own way, led diverse democracies astray. According to the "melting pot" metaphor, immigrants and members of other minority groups should assimilate into their societies without holding on to their original cultures. But this is an unduly homogenizing ideal that does not sufficiently respect the cultural traditions of citizens who hail from different parts of the world. It helped to create a world in which some members of ethnic, cultural, or religious minorities felt that they needed to hide their real selves in order to gain full acceptance.

According to the "salad bowl" metaphor, meanwhile, citizens drawn from different backgrounds should live side by side, preserving the integrity of their groups. But advocates of the salad bowl often give up on the aspiration that the members of diverse democracies could ever come to have anything important in common. As a result, the concrete practices this ideal encouraged often helped to fragment, rather than to unify, diverse societies.

Neither the melting pot nor the salad bowl paint an attractive vision of the future. If diverse democracies are to thrive, they can and must do better—and in this chapter, I suggest an idea for how that might be possible.

THE MELTING POT: A VISION TOO NOBLE

David Quixano, the fictional protagonist of a famous play that was to have an outsized influence on ideas about immigration and integration, fled the terrible pogroms that were taking place in Russia at the beginning of the twentieth century and took refuge in New York.

David was a neurotic boy given to frequent flights of fancy and the occasional nervous breakdown. At the slightest provocation, he would be seized by terrifying visions of the "butcher's face" that had murdered his parents and siblings during the infamous massacre of Kishineff. But now that he had found safety in America, David was determined to use his prodigious musical talents to pay homage to his new homeland. His ambition was nothing less than to write the Great American Symphony.

This symphony, David explained to anyone who would listen, was to express the spirit of the New American. When immigrants arrived at Ellis Island, they consisted of "fifty groups, with your fifty languages and histories, and your fifty blood hatreds and rivalries." But, he hoped, they "won't be long like that." The crucible of America would prove "a fig for [their] feuds and vendettas! Germans and Frenchmen, Irishmen and Englishmen, Jews and Russians—into the Crucible with you all! God is making the American." David's symphony was to express the sound of that new man for the very first time.

Only one person recognized David's talent. A political radical who had left behind the comforts of her aristocratic family in Russia to make her way to America, Vera Revendal devoted herself to the care of poor immigrants. Inspired by David's vision, she found an orchestra that could perform his symphony. Inevitably—and impossibly—they fell in love.

"He will not separate us?" David asked Vera when he first learned that her father was a baron.

"Nothing can separate us," she assured him.

The next month was bliss. Then Baron Revendal crossed the Atlantic to stop his daughter from marrying a Jew. Vera persuaded him to meet her beloved. But as soon as David took one glance at the Baron's face, he realized that it was he who had supervised the slaughter of his family and now haunted his waking nightmares.

Vera pledged to cut all ties with her father. But when she tried to embrace David, he pushed her away. "You cannot come to me," he told her. "There is a river of blood between us."

He broke off the engagement.

Four months passed. On the Fourth of July, David's symphony saw its world premiere in front of an audience composed mostly of immigrants. It was the first triumph of what promised to be an exceptional career. But David was miserable. Unable to bear the well-wishers congratulating him on his success, he fled to the roof of the concert hall.

"How can I endure them when I know what a terrible failure I have been," he told Vera when, with strained formality, she approached him on the roof.

"Failure?" she asked.

"I preached of God's Crucible, this great new continent that could melt up all race-differences and vendettas," David explained. But then

God tried me with his supreme test. He gave me a heritage from the Old World, hate and vengeance and blood, and said, "Cast it all into my Crucible." And I said, "Even thy Crucible cannot melt this hate, cannot drink up this blood."

And so I sat crooning over the dead past, gloating over the old blood-stains—I, the apostle of America, the prophet of the God of our children. Oh—how my music mocked me!

Disoriented, Vera made a start for the exit. "What else can I do?" she asked him, when he seemed to suggest a reconciliation. "Shall the shadow of Kishineff hang over all your years to come? Shall I kiss you and leave blood upon your lips, cling to you and be pushed away by all those cold, dead hands?"

"Yes," David responded, "cling to me, despite them all, cling to me till all these ghosts are exorcised, cling to me till our love triumphs over death."

Embracing for the first time since they broke off their engagement, the newly reconciled lovers watched the sun set over New York City. As the curtain fell, David marveled "how the great Alchemist melts and fuses" the city's residents—Celt and Latin, Greek and Syrian, Black and Asian—"with his purging flame."

Israel Zangwill's play *The Melting Pot* opened to instant success at the Columbia Theatre in Washington, DC, in 1908. The vision of America it expressed was both moving and noble, all the more so at a time when the reality of the country hardly lived up to its protagonist's idealism. At its inception, the ideal of the melting pot was rooted in a keen sense of history's tragedies and a deep awareness of the injustices from which many people have suffered on account of their race or religion. Far from denying the dark shadow this cast over attempts to build diverse societies, it was an exhortation to transcend them, even if doing so came at immense personal cost. For his portrayal of David Quixano and Vera Revendal, Israel Zangwill deserves our lasting admiration.

The moral power of this vision helps to explain why the melting pot became the paradigmatic metaphor for American life for much of the twentieth century. Especially after World War II brought millions of Americans from different ethnic and cultural backgrounds into prox-imity to one another in barracks and battlefields, it felt as though Da-vid's ravings had proved to be prophetic. Distinctions that had once been of momentous significance—between Irish and Italian, Catholic and Protestant, Jew and Gentile—started to recede in importance. At the height of the Cold War, the melting pot seemed like an accurate description of what was happening on the ground as well as a natural goal for American institutions to pursue.

Perhaps because—despite their many derisive references to it—they haven't actually read Zangwill's play, many academics and activists who now talk about the melting pot seem blind to its appeal. Its ideal, they claim, ignored the deep conflicts between different cultures and religions. Worse, it presumed that immigrants would uncritically "as-similate" into a preexisting American culture. They would come to embrace existing norms and values, turning themselves into imperfect imitations of the white Anglo-Saxon Protestants who had long formed the country's informal aristocracy.

This is an uncharitable caricature that willfully ignores why the idea of the melting pot once held such a powerful hold over the American imagination. David's symphony was to express the sound of the New American, not that of the longtime inhabitants of Boston's Beacon Hill. But for all its exaggerations, the criticism that the melting pot is too homogenizing does help to explain why it should not serve as the principal prism through which defenders of the great experiment envis-age the future of diverse democracies.

The metaphor of the melting pot does to some extent seem to imply that individuals should abandon their ancestral cultures to become true Americans (or true Italians or Australians). Zangwill's play, for example, went beyond condemning those, like Baron Revendal, who seek to stop their relatives from marrying the partners of their choice; it presumed that the cultures of the Old World needed to melt away, creating a wholly new yet largely homogeneous substitute, if America was to realize its true purpose. That is to ask too much of most people—and really does risk impoverishing the culture that would result.

And while the ideal of the melting pot can seem abstract, this really is, to some extent, what started to happen in America after World War II. Because of the restrictive immigration policies passed in the early twentieth century, the proportion of foreign-born residents had, by the 1960s, fallen to record lows. The spread of television sets was providing Americans with a common set of reference points. The country's culture was more homogeneous than it had been at any point since its founding. And even though the American mainstream had already embraced kung pao chicken and spaghetti with meatballs, the children and grandchildren of Chinese or Italian immigrants were often mocked if they brought more adventurous or "exotic" foods to school in their lunch boxes.

In those years, millions of Americans grew ashamed of their cultural heritage. Many abandoned the food of their ancestors for burgers and TV dinners. And some contemporary observers really did start to use the metaphor of the "melting pot" as a cudgel that could be used to beat on immigrants who refused to assimilate into the mainstream. That was clearly wrong.

The right guiding ideal for immigrant societies should retain something of Zangwill's insight. Part of their beauty is the ability of people who are drawn from different cultures, and whose ancestors once felt deep animosity toward one another, to forge a common spirit as compatriots. The question is whether diverse democracies can accomplish that noble goal without asking their citizens to abandon their original cultures and identities to the extent implied by the metaphor of the melting pot.

THE SALAD BOWL: A FUTURE TOO FRAGMENTED

The perceived pressure to assimilate into a homogeneous mainstream soon provoked a countermovement. A new generation of academics and activists believed that it had been a big mistake to insinuate that immigrants and their descendants needed to subsume their cultures in a melting pot that would require them to give up many hallmarks of their ancestral cultures. Instead, they now embraced a vision of diverse democracies that centered around the sustenance and celebration of distinct communities.

This rejection of assimilation soon spawned a series of artistic or culinary metaphors of its own. Some said that we should reconceptualize diverse societies as a "mosaic"; their beauty would derive from each constitutive element remaining separate. Others argued that we should think of the appropriate guiding ideal as a salad bowl; a dish whose constitutive ingredients are allowed to remain integral, they maintained, is much tastier than one that has been ground down into a uniform liquid.

Both the mosaic and the salad bowl capture something important about many of the cities and countries to which I am most drawn. One of the wonderful things about New York City, for example, is that you can experience so many cultures in the same day. You could, to stick with the culinary theme, have brunch at a soul food restaurant in Harlem, take coffee in El Barrio, go for a late lunch in Chinatown, stop off for an afternoon coffee at a Georgian café in Bay Ridge, and end the evening with a Russian dinner and plenty of vodka in Brighton Beach.

The aspiration to build a "multicultural" society inspired by metaphors like the mosaic or the salad bowl also helped to pave the way for a much greater willingness to celebrate the heritage of immigrant groups. Especially in Europe, most countries had long pretended that immigrants were but temporary visitors. Even once that self-serving myth became untenable, some of the leading politicians of the 1970s and 1980s really did insist that they should assimilate without holding on to their own cultural inheritance. Over the course of the 1980s and 1990s, this finally started to change.

Town councils all over Europe put on cultural festivals that highlighted Turkish dances, Algerian dishes, and African clothing designs. In Germany, the Green Party celebrated what it called Multikulti, a vision of the country's future that emphasized the contributions that different cultures could make to the country's everyday life. In the United Kingdom, the imperial nostalgia of "Rule, Britannia!" gave way to the joyous celebration of cultural heterogeneity at the heart of "Cool Britannia."

The ideal of the salad bowl remedied the principal shortcomings of its predecessor, and helped to inspire a greater appreciation for cultural diversity in the real world. There is a lot to like about it. But for all these virtues, both the ideal and the practices it inspired also suffer from serious shortcomings of their own.

Advocates of the salad bowl have changed the popular imagination of what the culture of an immigrant society might look like. Insofar as "multicultural" societies simply celebrate the multiplicity of cultures that now flourish on their territory, they constitute a significant improvement on the ideal of a melting pot.

But in both theory and in practice, the salad bowl has gone a good step further than that. Like the communitarians who favor an "association of associations," some of its advocates explicitly endorse the vision of a society in which members of different groups have very little contact with one another or are subject to the unchecked authority of their elders. An uncritical embrace of that kind of multiculturalism runs the risk of deepening the fragmentation of diverse democracies.

In Great Britain, for example, the last Labour government encouraged the formation of faith-based state schools—public institutions, funded by the taxpayer, in which Jewish, Sikh, Hindu, and Muslim children would be educated in isolation from one another and society at large. Within ten years of the formation of these schools, educators started to raise grave concerns about the impact they were having on society. "I worry that many young people are being educated in faith-based schools, with little appreciation of their wider responsibilities and obligations to British society," David Bell, then the chief inspector of schools at England's Office for Standards in Education, wrote in 2005.

"Unless there are crucial changes in the way many faith schools run we fear divisions in society will be exacerbated," Mary Bousted, the general secretary of the country's Association of Teachers and Lecturers, echoed in 2008. "Why should state-funded schools be allowed to promote a particular faith rather than educate children to understand and respect all faiths so they are well able to live in our diverse, multicultural society?" But although a majority of the population has long opposed the existence of state-sponsored faith schools, English taxpayers continue to fund them against their will.

A liberal state should, of course, allow for private schools to select their students on religious grounds. And if some of its citizens have a strong desire to stick among members of their own community, it mostly has to respect their choices. But when the state actively encourages and funds the creation of schools that minimize the amount of contact that children born within religious communities have with the outside world, this shows how easily the logic of the salad bowl can end up promoting counterproductive forms of cultural separatism.

In some developed democracies, respect for the cultural autonomy of constituent groups has had even more pernicious results—both for society as a whole and for those born into these communities.

In the United Kingdom, for example, Mohammad Lutfur Rahman served as the mayor of the London borough of Tower Hamlets. Over more than a decade, he built up a remarkable system of corruption and intimidation. In April 2015, he was finally found guilty of rigging the vote, giving community organizations grants in exchange for ballots, and using "undue spiritual influence" by recruiting local imams to his electoral cause. Local critics who dared to speak out against him had their shop windows broken or were accused of being "a slave of the British."

National politicians and the mainstream press were long reluctant to put an end to Rahman's abuses of power. Though many of his victims were fellow immigrants from Bangladesh, they feared accusations of being hostile toward an ethnic minority group. Playing to that reluctance, Rahman himself slandered the white politician who ultimately unseated him as a "racist."

Out of a misguided reluctance to meddle in the cultural affairs of minority communities, authorities across a number of countries have, over the past decades, even turned a blind eye to the practice of female genital mutilation. In 2014, for example, Anissa Mohammed Hassan, a Somali immigrant and feminist activist in Sweden, discovered that a significant proportion of girls at a school in Norrköping had been subjected to the practice.

And yet some academics have argued that multiculturalism requires respect for such cruel rituals. Others seemed more worried about negative headlines concerning minority communities than about the underlying injustice done to immigrant girls. As one Swedish anthropologist, Sara Johnsdotter, told *The Guardian* in the aftermath of Hassan's revelations: "I've worked in this field for the past 15 years and every few years there is a new drive from the government to end it, and there is an accompanying report in a newspaper to give it more attention. Personally, I think it is dangerous."

The attractive version of the salad bowl is the kind of cultural festival to which I would often go as a child in Germany. On a beautiful summer day, an affluent neighborhood in a nice town would put on a kind of block party. Alongside the food stalls and clothing stores, there was a stage that featured the different groups now living in the new Germany: Kurdish bands, African dances, and a little klezmer music.

But there is also a darker version of that same vision. It is one in which residential segregation is the norm, friendships between members of different groups are rare, kids who hail from different countries and cultures go to separate schools, communities barely tolerate the idea that their children might marry an outsider, and many of their members are unfree to make their own choices.

The salad bowl remedied some of the problems of the melting pot. But it also raises the specter of a society whose members have little contact with, or sympathy for, one another. Each ingredient of the new multicultural dish, the metaphor implies, would just about tolerate the proximity of the others—but never take pride in the common whole.

We are, then, in need of a better guiding metaphor for what a successful diverse democracy should look like. It would need to encapsulate the most attractive aspects of each. Like the salad bowl, it should preserve the idea that a multiethnic society will be far from homogeneous. And like the melting pot, it must recognize that the compatriots of a successful democracy should embark on a life that is, to some meaningful extent, shared.

What might a diverse democracy that lives up to these values look like? And what kind of metaphor can help to express the destination we should strive for?

A NEW VISION: THE PUBLIC PARK

When I lived in New York, I would, once a week, pack my cleats, take the subway all the way to the Seventh Avenue stop in Park Slope, walk across a few blocks lined by stately brownstones, and enter Prospect Park to play soccer.

I loved this ritual because it allowed me to see old friends, meet new people, and play my favorite sport. I also loved it because every trip, in some way, showcased the sheer vibrance and diversity of the city—and the country.

As I made my way to our improvised soccer pitch, I would pass teenagers taking selfies on their brand-new smartphones; hipsters in their twenties discussing the latest album by their favorite band; large Puerto Rican families celebrating a child's birthday; groups of African Americans enjoying a cookout; and Italian American old-timers playing cards.

Often, each of these groups did its own thing. But sometimes, I saw them enter into conversation with each other—with Italians and Dominicans swapping food and their children playing catch together.

Once, when I was cutting through a wooded section of the park, a startled teenage couple drew away from each other, then looked at me with evident concern. For a second, I was puzzled. It didn't look to me as though they had been doing anything more scandalous than exchanging a few lingering kisses.

Then it hit me: The girl, who was wearing dark red lipstick and a crop top that revealed her midriff, looked Puerto Rican. The boy, who had taken off his dark hat and jacket, carefully folding them over a tree branch, sported a shining white shirt and long brown locks: he was evidently a Hasidic Jew.

As I mumbled an apology for disturbing this modern-day David Quixano and his Juliet, and hurried along to meet my friends, I caught myself thinking that it wouldn't be the worst thing in the world if the whole country began to resemble Prospect Park.

No single metaphor can perfectly encapsulate the ideal of a diverse democracy. But to be helpful, it must, unlike the melting pot, recognize that different citizens have a right to lead their lives in accordance with the dictates of their own tastes. At the same time, it should, unlike the salad bowl, inspire the creation of a common space in which people from different walks of life have meaningful opportunities to interact and cooperate. Simple though it might be, the image of a public park accomplishes both of those things—and three of its features are especially useful in thinking through what kind of society diverse democracies should build.

1. *A public park is open to everyone.* Parks allow visitors to do things on their own, to congregate in likeminded groups, or to pursue joint activities with complete strangers. And though the presumption isn't that everyone who uses them shares a common purpose, they provide a wonderful venue for those who do to meet one another and persuade strangers to join their group.

   Similarly, diverse democracies must ensure that nobody suffers from pervasive discrimination or enmity on the basis of their ascriptive identity. This also means that they must allow all their members to use public spaces—or build private structures—on the same terms. Just as a park is for everyone, so a diverse society needs to treat members of every race and religion with equal respect and dignity.

2. *A public park gives its visitors options.* Visitors pursue a huge variety of legitimate activities in parks. They run or walk, read or talk, play sports or share food.

   That great variety is a very good thing. But for a park to remain safe and attractive, its visitors need to afford one another the same rights and freedoms they themselves wish to enjoy. You cannot rob somebody, force them to play baseball because you happen to dislike soccer, or tell them what food they must consume. And if somebody breaks those rules, everybody needs to know that they can quickly count on assistance.

Similarly, in diverse democracies, all citizens should be free to lead their lives in accordance with their own views and values. They can be religious or secular, prioritize family or business, and watch TV or go to the gym.

But diverse democracies must also ensure that some citizens don't start to harm others, to intimidate people they dislike on account of their opinion or their identity, or to control those who happen to be born into their own communities. Just as a park needs to have rules to ensure that its patrons can choose whether to interact or do their own thing, so liberal democracies need to offer their citizens freedom from both the oppression of the state and the coercion that might be imposed on them by their elders.

3. *A public park creates a vibrant space for encounter.* When I visited Prospect Park, it always felt vibrant, beautiful, and astoundingly safe. But there are lots of parks in the world that are dangerous, poorly maintained, or eerily empty.

As is the case with most aesthetic judgments, we won't always agree about which park is better or what kinds of attributes it should have. Some people like wide open spaces; others prefer wooded areas that look a little wild. Some love the hustle and bustle of a lawn that attracts hundreds of revelers on a hot summer day; others prefer winding paths that allow them to get lost in solitude.

These aesthetic judgments will, in turn, drive our views on important matters concerning the park. It should be beyond dispute that it is wrong to exclude some citizens from public parks on the basis of the color of their skin. But other questions are subject to legitimate disagreement. Based on our different values and preferences, we might argue for a more manicured or a more natural layout and seek to impose stricter or more lenient limits on how much noise each person is allowed to make.

Just as there are legitimate disagreements over what kinds of rules or architectural features make a park especially attractive, so too there are legitimate differences over what kinds of norms and habits are likely to create the most thriving diverse democracies.

Some people want to impose one strict set of rules and cultural norms on all citizens. Others are seemingly giving up on the hope that members of different groups could ever see one another as friends and allies rather than competitors or even enemies. I disagree with both. My own hope for the future of diverse democracies is that they will have many of the features that made me fall in love with Prospect Park. They should be bustling yet peaceful and heterogeneous without being fragmented.

Most important, I hope that they will create lots of space for the kinds of chance encounters that public spaces can, at their best, facilitate. While each person will retain the liberty to stay within the confines of their own group or community, many people would, on that vision, recognize how much they have in common with those compatriots of theirs who do not, at first blush, look or sound anything like them.

The best kinds of public spaces allow each person to do their own thing while facilitating unexpected encounters that could lead to lasting connections. Similarly, the kind of diverse democracy we should build must maintain respect for communities that prefer to stay among themselves yet encourage a majority of citizens to embark on a life that is, to some meaningful extent, shared.

————

Neither the melting pot nor the salad bowl can point the way toward how to build a thriving diverse democracy. For in that kind of society, people would not have to face a choice between becoming a member of the nation at the expense of their specific culture or cultivating their specific culture to such an extent that something like the nation barely exists. At their best, diverse democracies can have both a real feel of cohesion and boast of a huge variety of subcultures. We should aim for nothing less.

Thus the picture of the kind of diverse democracies we should build begins to emerge. Their citizens would enjoy a double liberty, free to express their whole selves without fear, and protected from undue constraints imposed by either the state or the cage of norms. They would embrace an inclusive patriotism that is rooted in both civic tradition and everyday culture. And they would cultivate their societies like a vibrant public park—a place whose visitors can do their own thing, but often choose to encounter strangers with openness and curiosity.

But to gain a fuller picture of what kind of diverse democracies we are trying to build, there is one last set of questions we need to answer. For, like public parks, societies are not just defined by the formal rules that assign rights and duties to citizens, by the way in which they think of their collective identity, or by the extent to which they spend time with one another in the day-to-day. They are also shaped by social and political norms that influence or constrain the choices of individuals without the force of law.

So to what extent do democracies need to change long-standing national narratives to accommodate newcomers? How can they sustain political solidarity between members of different identity groups? Is it good or bad when they influence one another's cultures? And should key social institutions—from public schools to major foundations—encourage them to emphasize their commonalities or stress their differences?

These are the questions, as important as they are contested, to which I turn to round off the vision that diverse democracies should embrace if they are to thrive.

SEVEN

Can We Build a Meaningfully Shared Life?

In virtually every corner of the democratic world, fierce fights over seemingly small social or cultural controversies have consumed an astounding amount of public attention over the course of the past few years. In the United Kingdom, for example, activists have been engaged in a passionate disagreement over the extent to which members of privileged groups should defer to members of disadvantaged ones, surrendering their political judgment of how to redress injustices to that of the most oppressed. Meanwhile, in the United States, food writers engaged in a bruising battle over whether it constitutes a dangerous form of cultural appropriation for white chefs to run a taco truck.

These debates can come across as overwrought. It would be easy to write them off as part of a culture war in which the principal combatants are desperately looking to identify emotive issues that can keep their supporters as angry as possible. But though it is undoubtedly true that some participants in these debates operate in bad faith, it would be a mistake to ignore these questions. For the sides people take in answering them are often proxies for deep and important disagreements about the way democratic societies should deal with the challenge of diversity.

Roughly speaking, the positions that participants in these debates tend to take are rooted in three different approaches to the informal rules that should govern diverse democracies. One school of thought seeks to abandon the great experiment in order to recover a supposedly better past in which most democracies were highly homogeneous or had a clear ethnic and religious pecking order. But the hope to "turn back the clock," which is finding expression in increasingly powerful political movements on the far right, is neither realistic nor desirable.

Another school of thought claims that diverse democracies can accommodate newcomers without making any serious adjustments to the rules that govern their societies or the stories they tell about their own histories. But those who "refuse to change" fail to see how formally neutral rules can disadvantage members of ethnic or religious minorities who were absent or marginalized at the time of their creation.

A final school of thought argues that diverse democracies must abandon the liberal principles and individualistic assumptions on which they were founded, remaking society from scratch with a focus on the rights of oppressed groups. But those who seek to "double down on identity" run the risk of throwing the baby out with the bathwater, abandoning many ideas that can help to sustain diverse democracies, and essentializing the identity of minority groups in a way that is likely to harm the cause of true equality.

There is no humane or realistic way to abandon the great experiment. Building fair societies will require real change. And giving up on the philosophically liberal principles that underpin diverse democracies would only serve to deepen the injustices that now characterize them.

If the great experiment is to succeed, we need to embrace a new vision for the informal rules that should govern diverse democracies in the future—one that is far more sanguine about our ability to build a meaningfully shared life.

TURN BACK THE CLOCK

While he was growing up in Chemnitz, an industrial city in Germany's east, Benjamin Jahn Zschocke joined an antifascist group. "That's the kind of person I am," he told me in the dining room of a fading grand hotel located along the Avenue of the Nations. "When someone gets beaten up, I come to his defense."

Then Zschocke's politics began to shift. He came to see immigration as the most urgent threat to his hometown. His worries were supercharged when, starting in the summer of 2015, more than a million refugees arrived in Germany. Zschocke drifted right, becoming a key leader of the local ultranationalist scene.

According to Zschocke, who was impeccably dressed and unfailingly polite, big cities in the west of Germany are doomed because a majority of their residents will soon be descended from immigrants. "If their inhabitants took to the streets, clans of Arabs would tyrannize their children the next day," he claimed. "For those who like their own culture, the west is already lost."

Thankfully, Zschocke said, whites still constitute a clear majority in cities in the east of the country. "For those who don't want a multiethnic society, the east is becoming a kind of refuge."

After about an hour of conversation, police sirens cut through the genteel calm inside the hotel. A few days before I arrived in Chemnitz, a Syrian asylum seeker had fatally stabbed Daniel Hibbing, a German-Cuban carpenter, in a late-night brawl, provoking spontaneous protests by far-right extremists. Since then, Zschocke had helped organize daily rallies to protest Angela Merkel's leniency toward asylum seekers. Another was set to begin at any moment.

I asked Zschocke when he would head over to the rally he had helped organize. Flashing a sly smile, he shook his head. "I'm far too sensitive for that," he said. "The huge crowds, all that intense emotion—I'm going home to listen to classical music."

Most democracies in the world are in the midst of a disorienting transformation. The attempt to build polities that are diverse, democratic, and genuinely equal is without precedent. This is likely to bring about significant cultural and political changes, and cost groups that have long stood at the top of their countries' ethnic and religious hierarchy some of their unearned advantages.

Over the past decade, a new generation of activists and politicians has risen to prominence by exploiting the fears that that transformation has inspired in parts of the population. If given the chance, they vow, they will take their countries back to what they see as a better past.

Matteo Salvini, the leader of Italy's far-right Lega, for example, wrote that he would allow Italians "to return to the joy of being able to have children without resorting to the horror of population change by means of out-of-control immigration." Donald Trump's campaign slogan put it more pithily. He would, he vowed, "Make America Great Again."

What the promise to turn back the clock amounts to in practice varies widely. Right-wing politicians in those few democracies that remain comparatively homogeneous want to ensure that their countries never become heterogeneous in the first place. By opposing most forms of immigration, some leaders in central European and East Asian democracies hope that they can sidestep the problems now plaguing so many diverse democracies.

But that option is not open to right-wing activists in the much more numerous democracies that already are highly diverse. Some of them insist on accomplishing the same goal and commit to doing so by much more cruel means. They dream of "restoring" their countries' homogeneity by expelling members of minority groups or pushing them to leave. Zschocke, the far-right activist I met in Chemnitz, for example, hopes that he and his comrades will be able to create a sufficiently hostile atmosphere for most immigrants to leave the city "of their own volition."

For the most part, far-right leaders like Trump and Salvini recognize that this is an unrealistic goal. Their countries, they know, are likely to remain diverse. Instead of trying to turn them into homogeneous entities, they seek to reestablish the clear hierarchies of yore.

Some democracies have even adopted concrete policies that are designed to stop the cultures of minority groups from finding recognition in the mainstream. In Switzerland, for example, a majority of citizens voted to prohibit the building of minarets in a 2009 referendum. A number of other democracies ban ritual slaughter in a thinly veiled attempt to make it harder for devout Jews and Muslims to make a home for themselves there.

The problems with these "solutions" are stark.

Countries like Japan or Bulgaria can, if they are willing to live with the adverse consequences of rapid depopulation, choose to remain comparatively homogeneous. But most democracies already are highly diverse. Even if they radically cut down on immigration, they will continue to grow more so over the coming years.

Plans to prevent these changes without massive violence are unlikely to be effective. The kinds of rhetorical provocations in which populist politicians love to indulge may help to feed the anger and resentment of one section of the population; but though big on bluster, they are low on impact. It is telling, for example, that the population of the United States grew more diverse, and voters' views about immigration more permissive, during Trump's tenure.

The only realistic way to reverse the demographic transformations now taking place would, then, involve unspeakable cruelty. Diverse democracies would need to remove people who now have a legal right to live in them by force or drive members of minority groups out through the kind of hostile atmosphere Zschocke hopes to create.

In the history of humanity, there have been many instances of ethnic cleansing. Even today, these extreme ideas enjoy some measure of support. No one should be so rash as to rule this outcome out as impossible. But it is a future to be feared, not desired.

The upshot is clear. Democracies can have legitimate debates about how open they should be to further immigration. But in countries that are already highly diverse, attempts to turn back the clock are likely to be cruel, futile, or both. For while humane ways to put a stop to the great experiment would likely fail to be effective, effective ways to halt the great experiment are virtually certain to be morally intolerable.

REFUSE TO CHANGE

Thankfully, most citizens of diverse democracies are not all that tempted by the promise of turning back the clock. They regard many of their new compatriots with affection or admiration and are adamantly opposed to the cruel measures it would take to halt, much less reverse, demographic change. Though they may have real concerns about the great experiment, they recognize that a return to the 1950s—or, for that matter, the 1980s—is a fool's fantasy.

At the same time, many of those same people remain invested in aspects of their cultures and countries that have their roots in a more homogeneous past and are difficult to justify in an increasingly heterogeneous present. Though they proudly reject the explicit scheme of domination championed by those who seek to turn back the clock, their view of the world unwittingly perpetuates an implicit scheme of domination that divides societies into a group of insiders who fully belong and various groups of outsiders who remain marginal.

One manifestation of this approach is a reluctance to make the kinds of accommodations that are necessary for immigrants and other minority groups to feel like full members of the community. There is, in principle, nothing wrong with the aspiration to build or retain a shared public culture that can serve as a foundation on which citizens from different walks of life can encounter one another. A society that lacks any sense of common culture or identity is likely to fragment in dangerous ways.

But in practice, advocates of what Germans sometimes call Leitkultur, or guiding culture, often assume that the norms and expectations that would provide a common basis for social interactions between members of different groups would have been set in stone long before democracies became as diverse as they are now. They may not aim to exclude newcomers by their insistence on perpetuating old habits, like forbidding stores from opening on Sundays or displaying Christian symbols in classrooms of public schools. But their refusal to change—or even to acknowledge that, far from being neutral, these traditions are designed to accord with the preferences of the majority—will likely have the effect of alienating members of minority groups.

Another manifestation of the refusal to change is a reluctance to think about the role that race and other ascriptive identities now play in diverse democracies. The aspiration to be "race blind" is based on an important moral insight: human beings are not worth more or less—and nor are they more or less capable of becoming upstanding citizens—because of their ethnic heritage. The determination to treat people in accord with their actions or their character, not the color of their skin, is a noble one.

But at times, the aspiration to be race blind can turn into a reality of being racism blind. Though it is good to wish for a society in which a citizen's ascriptive identity matters as little as possible, racism and bigotry still persist. These injustices need to be studied, acknowledged, and remedied.

A refusal to recognize that an increasingly diverse society needs to break with some of its old habits will make it harder to build democracies that are truly inclusive.

Even when they are in principle committed to welcoming newcomers, many nations define themselves in terms of the historical achievements or cultural traditions of the majority group. They think of the United States as created by the passengers of the Mayflower and the participants in the Boston Tea Party, and of France as synonymous with the revolutionaries who stormed the Bastille or the pretty churches that grace so many of its village squares.

Insofar as it goes, there is nothing wrong with that. Diverse democracies will forever be shaped by their origin stories and long-standing historical narratives. America wouldn't be America without the Founding Fathers and France wouldn't be France without the French Revolution. But it becomes a problem when a focus on those aspects of national identity starts to obscure the ways in which diverse democracies have changed over time. This makes it easy to overlook the significant contribution that newcomers are now making, and neglects the importance that today's everyday culture has in shaping a cohesive national identity.

This problem is aggravated when diverse democracies also hold on to a whitewashed view of their own history. Most countries have dark chapters in their past. It would be inappropriate to let these consume their entire identity; groups should no more be reduced to their worst crimes than they should be lionized with an exclusive focus on their most heroic achievements.

And yet it is important that they deal with that history in an honest manner. Many members of diverse democracies now refuse to do so. Denying or downplaying the extent of past misdeeds, they cling to a partial or downright dishonest account of their own countries.

When members of minority groups have suffered at the hands of their compatriots, any attempt to create a sense of shared destiny between them needs to be premised on an acknowledgment of historical wrongs and a sincere apology for them. When neither that acknowledgment nor that apology is forthcoming, it is unsurprising that many people will refuse to buy into the airbrushed story their country tells about itself—and feel reluctant to embrace a shared identity.

The project of building diverse democracies that truly thrive will involve some difficult changes to long-standing habits, narratives, and self-perceptions. Those who refuse to change old ways are not necessarily motivated by malice. And yet they need to recognize that the preservation of values they deeply care about—like the maintenance of social peace and the cultivation of mutual affection between compatriots—requires them to adapt to the more diverse nature of their societies.

DOUBLE DOWN ON IDENTITY

A third model for how to build diverse democracies is motivated by the shortcomings of the previous ones. It is rooted in frustration at the inadequate imagination of those who refuse to accept the changes that are necessary to accommodate all citizens of diverse democracies. And it is energized by righteous anger at those who seek to turn back the clock, trying to recover the hierarchies of yore by the use of unspeakable cruelty.

Variously identified as "woke," as an applied form of "critical race theory," or as a likely "successor ideology" to liberalism, this movement vows to remake society in a radical manner. To do so, many of its most vocal advocates are willing to rethink fundamental principles, like the focus on individuals over groups, on which liberal democracies have traditionally been built.

As is true of any political or intellectual movement, the adherents of what I propose to call "challenger ideology" do not necessarily agree with each of the claims that are commonly associated with it.* And yet three interlocking ideas are central to its vision for the future of diverse democracies: a set of claims about the role that ascriptive identities like race should play in them; a set of claims about the extent to which members of different groups are able to understand one another and what this means for the kind of political solidarity to which they should aspire; and a set of claims about what the culture they collectively build should look like.

1. *Strategic Essentialism*: In the 1970s and 1980s, many social scientists began to argue that racial categories were "socially constructed." Labels like white or black, they argued, did not track biological reality; rather, they were artificial constructs that had been invented for political purposes. And in nearly every case, the goal of that invention had been simple: to find a justification for elevating members of some groups while subjugating those of others.

   This theoretical emphasis on the ways in which most categories of identity are socially constructed could imply two very different courses of action for those who oppose the racism they had long underwritten. According to the first, it seemed to suggest that they should de-emphasize the importance of race. If categories like white or black are artificial, and have always been used to nefarious ends, scholars like

---

* None of the existing terms to describe this movement are satisfactory. "Woke" is too loaded. "Critical race theory" is overly focused on its academic origins and fails to capture that it is also deeply concerned with related topics like gender or religion. What Wesley Yang has called the "successor ideology" is the most promising: It has the virtue of being morally neutral and calling attention to the ways in which the theory aims to supplant many of the principles that have traditionally governed western democracies. But since it falsely implies that the fight is already over, with the new movement sure to win, I will instead use a term of my own: "challenger ideology."

Karen and Barbara Fields argued, then it would be for the best if people made as little hay of them as possible. A true emancipation from racism would also require an emancipation from the concept of race.

Especially on the left, this interpretation once held significant appeal. But in most parts of the academy, a diametrically opposed way of interpreting the political implications of social construction has since gained the upper hand.

Many people suffer severe disadvantage because they are widely seen to belong to a subordinate group. If categories like Latino or African American have real-life consequences for how their members are treated, scholars like Gayatri Chakravorty Spivak argued, then they have every reason to band together to fight for justice. For all intents and purposes, those to whom these artificial labels have traditionally been applied should act as though they were grounded in objective reality. In the language of social science, their strategy should consist in acting as though essentialist accounts of race and identity were true.

Over the course of the past decades, this form of strategic essentialism has won a resounding victory on the Anglo-Saxon left. It is now making rapid inroads in the social and political mainstream of countries from Australia to the United Kingdom.

The result has been a remarkable reemphasis on race and identity. Whereas leftist politicians once preferred to cast their goals in class terms, they now tend to emphasize the need for racial equity. Whereas leftist policy makers once favored a universal vision for the welfare state that would offer key benefits to all citizens, they increasingly favor the introduction of "race-conscious" policies that make the receipt of specific forms of aid conditional on membership in a particular ethnic group. And whereas leftist writers and artists once tended to emphasize the universality of the human condition, they now think it more important to represent the "lived experiences" of the identity groups to which they belong.

2. *The Impossibility of Mutual Comprehension*: From the great works of literature to the most viral posts on Instagram, a lot of art insists on the universality of the human experience. In the most famous monologue from Shakespeare's *Merchant of Venice*, Shylock, the Jewish protagonist, insists that he is as capable of joy and suffering as his Christian contemporaries. ("If you prick us, do we not bleed? If you tickle us, do we not laugh?") And in the stories posted by Humans of New York, residents of the city who hail from every corner of the world tell stories of love and loss, of adversity and unlikely triumph that resonate with millions of readers of every faith and color.

For many writers, this kind of mutual comprehension is a core goal of literature. As Salman Rushdie once put it, fiction comes to life when it sets out an "idiosyncratic vision of one human being, in which, to our delight and great surprise, we may find our own vision reflected." Some scientists have even tried to prove the benefits of literature by demonstrating that people who read fiction become more capable of empathizing with people who are very different from them.

But many proponents of the challenger ideology are deeply skeptical of such universalist claims. They don't, of course, deny the importance of compassion or the existence of shared human traits. But the differences between groups, they claim, ultimately go deeper than these commonalities. Those who have a comparatively privileged position, they contend, will never understand the harrowing experiences to which members of underprivileged groups are subjected. Men do not understand what it is like for women to go through life fearing sexual harassment. And white Americans do not recognize what it is like to worry that a cop may target them for unfair treatment due to the color of their skin.

Insofar as it goes, this observation is—or should be—uncontroversial. Clearly, people who haven't experienced a particular form of injustice are more likely to be ignorant about it, and may never fully "get" what it is like to do so.

But many advocates of the challenger ideology go on to draw a more radical inference from this observation. If members of comparatively privileged groups do not have any direct exposure to certain forms of injustice, then they are—even if they carefully listen to stories about them—supposedly incapable of relating to the lived experiences of underprivileged groups. And if they are incapable of relating to the lived experiences of underprivileged groups, then they cannot judge what is needed to remedy those injustices. Instead of forming their own opinion, they should simply defer to demands made by the more oppressed.

In this way, a highly plausible account of what people can see or understand based on their own experiences often culminates in a far more controversial set of claims about what political solidarity should look like in diverse democracies. To be a good ally, on this vision, goes beyond listening to one another or trying to find common ground. For members of advantaged groups, true political solidarity demands nothing short of "decentering" themselves, giving up their insistence on making their own judgments, and "privileging" the demands of the oppressed.

3. *The Danger of Cultural Appropriation*: In decades past, the humanist left used to celebrate the idea of different cultures mixing and influencing one another. From hippies who loved to don Indian saris to aid workers whose apartments were (as one satirical poem put it) "full of carvings, curios and draped with batik," an engagement with the fashion, music, and food of other cultures was seen as an indication of openness to the world.

Today, this demonstrative cosmopolitanism is increasingly giving way to concerns about the ways in which mutual cultural influence can lead to all manners of injustice. Understandably worried about the history of white artists stealing the work of black singers or the way in which some people have donned the clothing of minority cultures in order to mock them, advocates of the challenger ideology have increasingly embraced a blanket prohibition on "cultural appropriation."

In many progressive milieus, it is now seen as a serious faux pas for members of the majority group to wear clothing that is typically associated with the historically disadvantaged. And while it remains acceptable to cook another country's cuisine at home, white restaurateurs from Portland to Toronto have gotten into serious trouble for "appropriating" the cuisine of Asian or Latin American countries. Far from being a sign that diverse democracies are building a more inclusive everyday culture, the incorporation of cultural influences from minority groups is increasingly seen as inherently suspect.

The challenger ideology can be understood, in part, as an attempt to redress serious blind spots in the ways that alternative models for how to deal with the great experiment go wrong. Its force derives from the fact that many of the shortcomings to which it points are real. Many citizens of diverse democracies *do* remain willfully blind to the obstacles faced by members of minority groups. And it really *is* naive for the most idealistic members of society to refuse to think in terms of race so long as some of the most reactionary ones continue to discriminate against anybody who, according to them, belongs to an "inferior" group.

And yet I worry that many of the substantive answers and prescriptions offered by the challenger ideology fail to advance the values of its proponents. Instead of helping to make the great experiment succeed, they run the risk of emboldening and empowering its most devoted detractors.

Encouraging members of historically dominant groups to defer to the views and demands of members of historically oppressed groups, for example, is unlikely to build the kind of political solidarity that is needed to root out actual injustices. Those members of diverse democracies who are comfortable with the status quo or who dream of turning back the clock are simply going to ignore such injunctions; as a tool to broaden concern for the fate of the most disadvantaged, it is a nonstarter. But even those who are highly motivated to make their societies fairer will in practice find it hard to follow this precept in any meaningful way.

Because Latinos and African Americans have a wide range of political views, for example, it is not clear to whom white Americans who seek to defer to members of those groups should actually listen. In the end, this leaves two possibilities. Either they will defer to comparatively powerful members of those groups who have managed to turn themselves into its spokespeople—likely with the aid of media outlets or political parties that are mostly controlled by members of the white majority—even though their views may hardly be representative of those held by less privileged members of the same group. Or they will determine whom they regard as an appropriate spokesperson on the basis of their own political predilections, pointing to those with whom they agree as an authentic voice and dismissing everyone else as "inauthentic." Either way, it is far from clear that the demand to "defer" to the views of a more oppressed group actually helps to serve the interests of those who are most in need of solidarity.

The problems with strategic essentialism go even deeper. Proponents of the challenger ideology are right that an embrace of a pure form of race abolitionism is naive. In countries in which some political parties hope to make it more difficult for members of minority groups to vote, for example, it may be necessary for activists to organize with the goal of raising political awareness and electoral participation among its members. For better or worse, the injustices that have always characterized diverse democracies do, to some extent, necessitate thinking in terms of race.

But to encourage members of diverse democracies to think of

themselves *primarily* as members of their ethnic or religious groups is just as naive. Entitlement programs that are explicitly targeted at members of particular ethnic groups, for example, provide a strong incentive for members of all ethnicities, including whites, to identity with their racial groups and organize along sectarian lines—thus deepening the kind of racial consciousness that has historically underwritten serious forms of injustice and discrimination.

These problems become particularly acute when the essentialist emphasis on race sheds its supposedly strategic character and starts to constitute a long-term vision. Many adherents of the challenger ideology now seem to take a rather pessimistic view of the prospects of the great experiment. The history of diverse societies, they believe, has always revolved around conflict between different racial and religious groups. In the future, groups that have been oppressed may be in a better position to fight for a fair share. Perhaps they will even predominate. But race will, even twenty-five or fifty years from now, remain the most important social and political category in diverse democracies around the world.

On this vision, race isn't just an important part of today's social reality. Rather, it is an inescapable part of our collective destiny. Rooted in an attack on essentialism, the challenger ideology has, oddly, begun to champion the essentialist view that race has always been, and will forever remain, the most important attribute of every human being.

That, I fear, is neither an attractive nor a constructive vision for how the great experiment might play out. Thankfully, there is a way to do better.

A BETTER MODEL

The three dominant ways to respond to the cultural battles that are now consuming so many diverse democracies all turn out to be flawed.

Any hope of turning back the clock on the changes of the past decades is a dangerous chimera. It would be a mistake for diverse democracies to resist the kinds of cultural or political changes that are necessary to give minority groups equal recognition. And they must also avoid doubling down on identity, embracing the deeply pessimistic vision of what the diverse democracies of the future might look like that is now being championed by defenders of the challenger ideology.

People drawn from different identity groups are capable of coming to understand one another's problems and priorities, of sustaining real political solidarity, and of building a meaningfully shared national culture. Those who want the great experiment to succeed must offer a vision that is both realistic about today's challenges and sanguine about the possibility of a tomorrow worth fighting for.

The way to do all this is to follow three core principles. Diverse democracies should aspire to a form of political solidarity that is based on greater empathy between its citizens. They should celebrate when the cultures of their members influence one another. And, most important, they should try to build a future in which race and religion matter less—not because more people will deny the role they now play in the real world but because fewer people will suffer disadvantage on the basis of their ascriptive identity.

1. *More Empathy and Deeper Solidarity*: It is naive to think that humans naturally understand one another's experiences. If

you have never gone hungry, you will find it hard to imagine what it is like to live without reliable access to food. And if you are part of a dominant majority group, you may be oblivious to what it is like to fear that others will treat you with derision or hostility because of the color of your skin. Advocates of the challenger ideology are right to say that there are serious barriers to mutual understanding in a diverse democracy—and that many of their compatriots are naive about the difficulties this raises.

But though a member of one group may never be able to perceive the world in exactly the same way as a member of another group, it is a mistake to give up on the promise of effective communication. A man need not have experienced sexual harassment to recognize its injustice. Nor does someone who is white need to have "lived experience" with racism to recognize how vile it is.

This is why, far from giving up on the idea of mutual understanding, diverse democracies should double down on inspiring empathy. The citizens of diverse democracies should be highly attuned to the ever-present possibility that they might be ignorant about one another's experiences, or mistrustful of one another's motives. But they should insist that they can, if they do the hard work of actually listening to one another, come to feel a deep compassion.

That also implies a different vision of political solidarity than the one that has, of late, been embraced by many activists. Men are capable of fighting for a society that treats women fairly because they believe that anything else would violate their own moral standards. Similarly, many whites want to make their democracies better for members of ethnic minorities because of their own aspirations for the kind of country in which they seek to live.

Citizens are unlikely to stand up for the interests of an out-group because they have been told to defer to its views. But they are capable of acts of real courage and altruism when they believe that their own ideas about what is just are being violated. And that is precisely why diverse democracies must insist on an ambitious model of political solidarity.

2. *The Virtue of Mutual Influence*: It is a long tradition for writers and politicians to denounce the ways in which their nations change because of immigration or other forms of contact with the outside world. In the late nineteenth century, Richard Wagner inveighed against the deleterious effect that French culture was supposedly having on his home country. In the early twentieth century, many Americans grew concerned that the influx of Catholic immigrants from countries like Italy would change the country for the worse. And today, politicians like India's Narendra Modi are lambasting outside influences, from Halloween to Valentine's Day, as dangerous attacks on the cultural integrity of their nations.

If the great experiment is to succeed, diverse democracies have to reject this form of cultural purism. Cultures are fluid constructs that reflect the ever-changing choices and predilections of their members, not static entities that, like a butterfly display at New York's Museum of Natural History, must be preserved with chloral hydrate. Newcomers can't be expected to integrate into existing cultural practices without having a chance to make their own contributions. Diverse democracies will not, and should not, turn into homogeneous societies in which every citizen has come to embrace the same set of tastes and preferences.

The left has long defended the value of these forms of mutual influence. But recently a different kind of anxiety about cultural exchange has gained prominence in activist and artistic circles. Critics of "cultural appropriation" worry about the hurt caused when members of the majority group mockingly don the clothes of a minority group; the exploitation that many artists from underprivileged communities suffer when those who are more affluent steal their intellectual property; and the anger that children in middle school feel when their classmates make fun of them for the unaccustomed dishes in their lunch boxes.

These are real injustices. Children should not bully one another for the contents of their lunch boxes. Artists who steal the work of others should have to pay hefty penalties. And people who mock minority groups should be shamed. But what makes these cases wrong is not the presence of mutual cultural influence between members of a diverse democracy; it is the way in which some members of the dominant group have either exploited or mocked their fellow citizens. A generalized suspicion of mutual cultural influence would do little to remedy these problems—while mistakenly "problematizing" the kinds of free cultural exchange that can help diverse societies embark on a meaningfully shared life.

Human cultures have always influenced one another. Identity groups don't enjoy collective property rights over particular ideas, dishes, or cultural practices (and nor should they). Modern democracies cannot possibly be successful if their members are forever fearful about the ways in which they might inspire one another. For all these reasons, mutual cultural influence is not a worrisome sin but rather one of the principal joys of thriving diverse democracies.

When African Americans enjoy Chinese takeout before going to dance salsa, Korean Americans sell French patisserie to tourists from Latin America, or a group of friends drawn from every racial and religious group gets drunk at a Tex-Mex restaurant while "Old Town Road" blares from the speakers, we see a first glimpse of the kind of future we should seek to build. Those who want the great experiment to succeed should proudly defend the joys of mutual influence and inspiration against the advocates of cultural purism.

3. *An Emphasis on What We Share*: Even in a diverse democracy with a meaningfully shared culture, many citizens will strongly identify with their own subnational groups. For the most part, they are likely to continue practicing the cultural rites of their ancestors or to worship the gods of their parents. A liberal society that recognizes what sociologists call the "meaning-making" role that cultural and religious communities play in the lives of most people should celebrate, not oppose, that pluralism.

Similarly, categories of ascriptive identity like race are likely to retain real significance for the foreseeable future. In countries that have a long history of domination, a racial lens will remain important for examining to what extent present conditions perpetuate these injustices. And even once the conditions that brought them into existence no longer persist, groups that have long been discriminated against on the basis of their race are likely to retain forms of political solidarity and cultural cohesion.

And yet diverse democracies should never waver from a vision of the future in which ascriptive identities play a smaller, not a larger, role than they do now. They should aim to construct societies in which people of different groups have sufficient contact to understand one another's concerns and care about one another's fate. And they should try to remedy historical injustices to such an extent that a racial lens becomes less important—not because people ignore its continued relevance, but because it really does structure reality to a lesser degree.

There are many problems with the (metaphorical) park we inhabit.

Its rules were written long ago and are in urgent need of an update. Some people feel welcome on its lawns and walkways while others still have reason to worry about being seen as intruders. And while its visitors sometimes strike up conversation, they remain likely to eye one another with skepticism or hostility.

All these problems make it tempting to lower our collective aspirations for the future. Perhaps the best we can do is negotiate an uneasy truce by giving up on the hope of fostering a meaningfully shared space. Should each group be given some corner of the park where it can stay among those who are alike in outlook or origin? Or even have access to it at separate times to avoid coming to blows?

That would be a serious mistake. Everyone should feel welcome in the space we share. It is possible to update the park's rules to allow everyone to go about their favorite activities at the same time. And over time, groups that now eye one another skeptically may come to see one another as compatriots or even friends.

The future of the park we share can look brighter than its present.

Skeptics are likely to scoff at this sentiment.

There is no sign that the injustices that have always characterized diverse democracies are disappearing, they will say. Members of minority groups are making little progress toward true equality. The politics of many countries remain deeply split among racial and religious lines. And policy makers are not doing enough to remedy these shortcomings.

This is the argument I take on in the final part of the book. While diverse democracies remain imperfect, I argue, minority groups are making much more rapid progress than either the proponents or the opponents of the great experiment now tend to believe. While many countries do remain politically polarized along demographic lines, there are first signs that their political systems are beginning to integrate in meaningful ways. And while the power of public policy to change the world is limited, there are many sensible steps that diverse democracies can take to hasten a better future.

In part 1, I set out why it is so difficult for diverse democracies to endure. In part 2, I developed an ambitious vision for what the diverse democracies of the future should look like. Finally, in part 3, I try to show why achieving diverse democracies that truly thrive will be hard—but is nevertheless possible.

PART THREE

HOW DIVERSE DEMOCRACIES CAN SUCCEED

For the great experiment to succeed, we must build diverse democracies that actually attract the wholehearted support of their members: societies whose residents feel pride in their collective accomplishments, encounter strangers with an open mind, and are capable of sustaining real solidarity with each other.

Few readers will disagree that it would be wonderful if we could build diverse democracies that sustain such a spirit of mutual care. But many may doubt how realistic that goal is. Is it possible for the great experiment to turn into a real success? And, if so, what can we do to make it work?

Anybody who surveys the state of diverse democracies from Sweden to the United States will discover plenty of reasons to grow depressed about their current reality and fearful for their future prospects. Some of their members continue to face significant discrimination. Long-standing conflicts between different ethnic and religious groups loom large. And some societies are regularly rocked by violent hate crimes or bloody terrorist attacks. It is natural to feel deep concern.

But in recent years, concerns grounded in an unflinching look at reality have at times mutated into a fashionable pessimism that distorts reality. And, oddly enough, that fashionable pessimism is now shared by people whose political views otherwise have little in common—including both committed champions and devoted detractors of the great experiment.

According to that motley crew of cynics, most diverse democracies have barely made progress in recent decades. Immigrants and members of other minority groups are doing very poorly in economic terms and remain marginal to the societal mainstream. The conflict which pits members of the historic majority against ethnic and religious minorities is intensifying by the day.

This pessimistic description of the present often goes hand in hand with a defeatist prescription for the future. According to this narrative, diverse democracies will most likely fail to make any meaningful progress. And if they are to have any chance of overcoming the horrors of the present, they will need to take a radical departure from the basic principles on which they were founded.

If the past decades have brought no meaningful improvements, why hold out hope?

I believe that this pessimism is overstated. Most diverse democracies *have* made meaningful progress over the past decades.

As I show in chapter 8, many societies are succeeding in integrating newcomers, broadening their conception of membership, and offering real economic opportunity to historically underprivileged groups. Though serious problems persist, there is reason to think that developments on the ground bode well for the future.

The boundaries and alliances between different demographic groups, I argue in chapter 9, are much more fluid than many pundits and politicians now like to assume. With the right choices, it is possible to avoid a future that pits members of the historic majority against a coalition of minority groups.

This, I explain in chapter 10, suggests that a number of principles and public policies can help to make the great experiment a success. Though they will hardly prove to be a panacea, concrete actions taken by politicians or ordinary citizens can help diverse democracies thrive.

Many developments on the ground are positive. Faith in a better future need not be premised on the unlikely prospect that politicians will pursue a brilliant strategy that turns a terrible situation around. It is as much a matter of reinforcing positive trends and avoiding bad mistakes.

To build diverse democracies that are worth living in, we need to insist on a vision with which members of both minority and majority groups can get on board, and double down on policies that attenuate rather than deepen their fragmentation. If the great experiment should succeed, it will not be because of a single politician or activist group. It certainly won't be because of the smart policy ideas made up by some solitary writer typing away at his standing desk. It will, rather, be because millions of people prefer to cooperate than discriminate, listen than shout, and make friends or fall in love than hate or kill.

EIGHT

Reasons for Optimism

This is a time of deep pessimism about the current state and the likely future of the great experiment.

Even as developed democracies have grown more polarized than they have been in half a century, a lot of people who barely see eye to eye on any political issue agree on one conclusion. For a wide variety of reasons, they all believe that developed democracies around the globe are failing to deal with their growing heterogeneity.

On the right, many writers blame immigrants and ethnic minorities for these problems. From France to Japan and from Germany to the United States, surprise bestsellers have argued that these groups are more poorly educated than members of the native majority, earn a lot less money, and commit crime at higher rates.

Of late, right-wing populists have won a lot of political power on the back of similar attacks. Jair Bolsonaro in Brazil and Viktor Orbán in Hungary, Marine Le Pen in France and Donald Trump in the United States all thrived on scapegoating outsiders for the perceived problems of their countries.

Much of the left passionately disagrees with both these diagnoses and these prescriptions. Like me, it rejects the idea that most immigrants or members of ethnic minorities pose a threat; that they are incapable of success; or that their very presence is bound to undermine the stability of developed nations. Instead, their goal, like mine, is to make diverse democracies thrive.

And yet growing parts of the left have, over the past decade, taken a similarly pessimistic turn.

They, too, tend to emphasize how poorly minority groups like Hispanics in the United States and North Africans in France are doing. And while they blame the injustices of the system rather than the supposed failings of those groups, they, too, seem to think that the future is unlikely to get much better.

In this chapter, I seek to take the case for pessimism seriously. To that end, I will give a fair hearing to the most commonly cited reasons—including both those to which I am naturally sympathetic, and those of which I am instinctively skeptical—that have driven so many people to despair of the likely future of diverse democracies.

Three concerns, I show, are central to today's prevailing mood of pessimism. There is the sense that immigrants and minority groups are not fully accepted into the social mainstream, and will forever remain second-class citizens. There are worries that they are underperforming in schools, universities, and the job market, and will forever constitute a kind of socioeconomic underclass. And then there are fears that they are responsible for crimes or terrorist attacks, and will forever remain a fundamental threat to the core values of developed democracies.*

The conclusion I reach after considering these three sources of pessimism is unfashionably optimistic. To understand what is happening

---

* Pessimists on the left and the right both express some version of the first two claims, though they blame different factors for these failures. The third claim is mostly advanced by the right.

on the ground, we need to acknowledge that there are real dangers and injustices. But we must not allow our unflinching attention to the serious challenges facing diverse democracies to blind us to the fact that most diverse democracies have made big strides toward a better future—and can, if we fight for the right principles and adopt the right policies, continue to do so in the years to come.

EXCLUSION AND INTEGRATION

A few years ago, I visited a Muslim religion class at a middle school in Dinslaken, a drab town in Germany's northwest that borders Europe's largest sewage treatment plant. Lamya Kaddor, the teacher who had invited me to sit in on the lesson, is a staunch defender of a liberal interpretation of Islam. A frequent guest on the country's political talk shows, she now represents the Green Party in the Bundestag.

As soon as I set foot in the classroom, I realized that something about her direct language, delivered in the singsongy cadence of Germany's northwest, made her students trust her blindly. Her sixth graders asked for advice on everything from how to handle a devout grandmother who pressured girls to cover their heads to how to deal with a man on a social networking site who claimed to be killing a woman live on camera.

Kaddor, whose round face is framed by long black hair, answered their questions with imperturbable patience. ("You should only wear a headscarf if that's what you want to do." "No, I don't think he really was killing her.") When one student nervously told the class that his mother didn't want him to reveal that he was Shia, Kaddor used the occasion to emphasize that all religious beliefs deserve the same respect. "It doesn't matter whether you are Shia, Sunni, Alawi, or something else. A human being is a human being. It doesn't matter one bit whether he is a Muslim or not."

"That's right," Federico, a big-eyed, overenthusiastic boy who kept interrupting class to share his thoughts, shouted. "I have a German friend!"

"Do you think the other people around us are worth less?" Kaddor asked. "Or do you think that Yascha Mounk—I don't know his religion, but I suspect he's Jewish—do you think that he's worth less than us?"

"No," everyone muttered.

"A human being is a human being," one of the children added.

"That's right," Kaddor said. "We judge people by their actions. By how they treat us."

As she expounded on the theme of religious tolerance, Federico turned around to me. "That's cool," he stage-whispered, and gave me a big thumbs-up.

In the moment, I found the lesson inspiring—a testament to both the entrepreneurial spirit of many immigrants, like Kaddor, who are transforming the face of public education in the country and to the tolerance of a younger generation, like Federico, who see the world in a more inclusive manner. But then I started to reflect on small details, the significance of which had, at first, passed me by.

How strongly does Federico feel that he belongs in his native country if he considers it noteworthy that he has "a German friend"? Federico was born and raised in Germany. And yet "Germans," to him, seemed to be those few classmates of his who are white and Christian.

And didn't even Kaddor mention far-reaching limits on her religious freedom as though they were facts of nature? At one point, an earnest boy named Kheder told her, with a mix of pride and embarrassment, that he got up to pray at five in the morning on summer weekends. "Whoa, Kheder! At five in the morning?" Kaddor asked. She gently explained that, on religious grounds, it was perfectly acceptable to make up for a missed prayer later in the day. As for herself, she told the class, she generally prayed five times a day. "But of course," she said offhandedly, "I can't pray in school."

"Why not?" a student asked.

"I don't want to pray in front of all my colleagues. Perhaps they wouldn't understand. They'd think I'm a fundamentalist or something like that. They might start to be afraid of me."

Most developed democracies were founded with a monoethnic, monocultural conception of themselves. If, in 1950 or 1970, you asked the first person you met in Rome or Berlin or Stockholm to tell you who truly counted as Italian or German or Swedish, the answer would likely have been straightforward: someone whose parents and grandparents and great-grandparents had also lived in the country.

Over the past half century, these societies have become increasingly diverse. The share of citizens who have, as authorities in Germany like to put it in typically long-winded fashion, "a background of migration" has rapidly risen. But while the reality of these democracies has become much more diverse, some of its ideas and practices continue to be shaped by a founding ideology that defines membership in more restrictive and exclusionary terms.

From Italy to Switzerland, members of ethnic and religious minorities report that they still encounter people who refuse to regard them as true compatriots. In the minds of some Europeans, somebody named Ali or Mohammed will forever seem like he isn't "one of us."

Survey data also indicates some ongoing resistance to changing notions of membership. A significant minority of Europeans continue to believe that it is shared descent, not linguistic facility or a passport, that makes somebody a "true" Pole or Spaniard or Italian. In their minds, anyone whose parents migrated to the country doesn't and shouldn't count as a true compatriot.

Even in countries that have long emphasized their immigrant origins, like Canada and the United States, a strong link between ethnicity and exclusion persists. Asian Americans, for example, often report fielding insistent questions about their origins. "Where are you from," an acquaintance of mine described the opening gambit of one such interaction to me. "From Iowa City," she responded. "No," her interlocutor replied. "Where are you *really* from?"

Even when stereotypes about immigrant groups appear to be positive, they often have a hard edge to them. Latinos, for example, may have a reputation for being hard workers. But for some Americans, this implies that they are more naturally suited to menial than to professional jobs. (Something similar holds true for Poles in the United Kingdom or for Albanians in Italy.)

Taken together, these forms of marginalization can add up to a strong sense of second-class citizenship. Some descendants of immigrants are made to feel that their membership in the only club they have ever known will forever remain conditional.

All of this helps to make sense of the world in which Federico grew up. To him, classmates with names like Thomas or Susanne are German. Those with names like Kheder or Lamya are—like him— "foreigners."

Will that ever change?

Even for some defenders of the great experiment, the answer to that question appears to be a clear no. Pointing at the ways in which some members of minority groups continue to be excluded in most developed democracies, they conclude that things are unlikely to get any better. Members of minority groups will, even decades from now, continue to be defined by the fact that their ancestors come from elsewhere, that the color of their skin is different, or that they follow a different faith.

Oddly enough, the pessimism about the future among those who see themselves as proud defenders of the great experiment is at times echoed by people who openly oppose it. But whereas those who would in principle like diverse democracies to succeed tend to emphasize the ways in which members of the majority perpetuate unjust forms of marginalization, those who oppose the great experiment tend to blame minority groups for their own exclusion.

Immigrants and other minority groups, according to these depictions, reject democratic values, are religiously intolerant, and have no interest in adapting to local customs. They live in "ethnic enclaves" that constitute "parallel worlds" and will never integrate into the cultural mainstream.

One key concern that is often expressed by authors who take this view is the supposed slowness with which newcomers learn the local language. Thilo Sarrazin, a former member of Germany's Social Democratic Party, for example, has warned that the children and grandchildren of Turkish immigrants might never acquire fluent German. In one fictional scenario he develops in his bestselling book, *Germany*

Abolishes Itself, he imagines that the descendants of immigrants will one day win the right to be taught in their ancestral language, and effectively stop their children from learning German. "By 2045, there will still be 48 percent . . . of first graders who choose to be taught in German," Sarrazin speculates. By the turn of the next century, only one in five schoolchildren will do so.

In the United States, some prominent writers have expressed similar fears about Hispanics. As the eminent political scientist Samuel Huntington wrote in 2009, "Unlike past immigrant groups, Mexicans and other Latinos have not assimilated into mainstream US culture, forming instead their own political and linguistic enclaves—from Los Angeles to Miami—and rejecting the Anglo-Protestant values that built the American dream."

Is there something to these fears? Will immigrants and members of other minority groups—whether because of unjust forms of exclusion or because of their own supposed failings—forever remain shut off from the cultural mainstream, living in a kind of parallel world?

Thankfully, the evidence strongly contradicts such fears.

Across a large number of diverse democracies, majority attitudes toward those who "truly" belong in their countries are rapidly liberalizing. Meanwhile, members of minority groups are integrating into a broadening social mainstream.

The evidence that attitudes about who belong in their nations is becoming more inclusive among members of the historic majority, for example, is quite clear. According to recent polls, most Europeans still believe that being "truly" French or British or Italian necessitates speaking the local language. About half think it requires sharing in some national customs and traditions. But, especially in Western Europe, only a very small fraction of the population now believes that being born in the country, having common ancestors, or sharing the local religion is a prerequisite.

Even in America, it has in recent years become much more obvious than before that Latinos and Asian Americans are a natural part of the country's social fabric. No doubt some prejudices against Latinos still persist, and Asian Americans are still at times treated as though they aren't "true" Americans. But over the past years, the visibility of both groups has, in just about every realm of the country's everyday culture, vastly increased. The number of people who believe that Eva Longoria and Alex Rodriguez or Ali Wong and Andrew Yang aren't "true" Americans simply isn't that large.

The claim that most members of immigrant or minority groups reject the values and customs of the countries in which they live is even more spurious.

Their strong support for democratic values is a case in point. Compared with the native-born, immigrants to the United States are more likely to express trust in institutions like the Congress, the presidency, and the Supreme Court. In fact, the most striking characteristic of many immigrants is just how patriotic and optimistic they are. In the United States, for example, more than two out of every three new citizens are proud to be American and believe that their adopted home is "better than most other countries."

The evidence that, belying projections by alarmists like Thilo Sarrazin, immigrants are rapidly integrating is even more stark when it comes to easily observed behavior like language acquisition. It is true that poorer immigrants tend to arrive in their new country with little or no command of its language. If they settle in communities with a lot of coethnics—like the Chinatowns that remain prevalent in many of America's major metropoles or the banlieues that now surround France's biggest cities—they may go to their graves without ever learning it. So long as new waves of immigrants keep arriving, it will always be easy to find plenty of people who don't speak the local language.

But it would be a big mistake to conclude that immigrants and their descendants fail to pick up the local language as they spend more time in their new countries. While the children of immigrants to the United States usually speak their ancestral language reasonably well, since many of them need it to communicate with their parents, nearly all of them prefer to speak English when spending time with their peers. Even within the home, second-generation immigrants have an ambivalent relationship to their parents' language. A great many households have two operating languages, with parents speaking to their children in their native tongue, and children responding to their parents in English.

By the third generation, English usually wins a decisive victory. As a 2015 study by Pew shows, the grandchildren of Latino immigrants barely know any Spanish. While a clear majority of first-generation Hispanic immigrants predominantly speak their ancestral language, that remains true for fewer than one in a hundred descendants of immigrants by the third generation.

While both cultural and linguistic integration tends to proceed a little more slowly in many European countries than it does in North America, the basic trend appears to be similar. There are some real examples of second- or even third-generation immigrants who speak the local language imperfectly. But on the whole, the children and grandchildren of immigrants who are born in Italy or France, in

Sweden or Greece speak the local language much more confidently than that of their ancestors.*

Across the world's diverse democracies, members of minority groups continue to suffer real forms of exclusion. And yet it would be a mistake to conclude that they will forever remain marginalized—or, for that matter, that they lack the ability or interest to join the societal mainstream.

The rapid progress of many minority groups contradicts both those pessimists who believe that they are somehow unwilling to integrate into their new environment and those who fear that diverse democracies put such obstacles in their path that they will never be able to do so.

THE GAP IN JOBS AND EDUCATION

There is a second area in which pessimists about the current state of diverse democracy tend to focus whether they are sympathetic or hostile to the great experiment: the large socioeconomic gap that now persists between members of the historically dominant majority and many minority groups.

According to this narrative, minority groups tend to have much worse educational attainments, lesser participation in the job market, and lower wages. While some immigrants have thrived, their descendants, on

---

* To be clear, it is by no means an unalloyed good that many immigrants lose command of their ancestral language in later generations. Whereas many educators advised immigrants not to speak with their children in their native tongue as recently as a few decades ago, the pedagogical consensus has thankfully swung in favor of multilingual education. My point here is, simply, that one of the core concerns voiced by opponents of the great experiment—that descendants of immigrants will never integrate or learn the local language—is strongly contradicted by the evidence.

average, remain far less likely to have a high income or gain an advanced degree than those whose ancestors already lived in the same territory.

A look at the aggregate numbers suggests that there is at least some truth to this pessimistic view. Across most developed democracies, the members of minority groups do, on average, tend to have a significantly lower socioeconomic status than those whose ancestors belong to the dominant group. The United States, for example, suffers from large wage and wealth gaps between different ethnicities. The average white American earns significantly more than the average Latino or African American, and the wealth gap is even more significant.

Meanwhile, the Organisation for Economic Co-operation and Development (OECD) has found "accumulating evidence that, in Europe, young natives with immigrant parents are overrepresented in disadvantaged positions in the labor market." Residents of the European Union who were born outside of its territory, another study finds, are twice as likely to be at risk of "poverty and social exclusion" than those Europeans who live in their country of birth.

Even countries that have long strived to be highly egalitarian and provide all their residents with generous welfare benefits are seeing the fates of different demographic groups diverge to a striking extent. In Sweden, for example, students with an immigrant background significantly lag behind their native-born peers in school and are much less likely to go on to university.

Both pessimists who support the great experiment and pessimists who oppose it agree that the earnings and education gap between the majority and the minority remains large. But as was the case with questions concerning integration and exclusion, they give very different explanations for why that might be.

Supporters of the great experiment tend to locate the principal reason in past and present discrimination. Minority groups whose ancestors arrived in their countries centuries ago still suffer from the long shadow of hard domination; it is, for example, impossible to understand the special challenges faced by African Americans without reference to their long history of enslavement and exclusion. But even immigrants whose ancestors arrived more recently, many supporters of the great experiment argue, are marginalized in the educational system and discriminated against in corporate hiring.

A series of clever studies suggests that ongoing discrimination really does continue to play a significant role. When researchers sent fake CVs to the human resources departments of large corporations in the United Kingdom, for example, candidates that bore typically English names were twice as likely to be invited to a first-round interview as those—otherwise identical ones—who bore names that suggested that they had roots outside the country. Around the world, studies have found similarly disheartening results in Japan, Switzerland, the Netherlands, and the United States.

But that account is nevertheless rejected by many pessimistic authors—such as America's Ann Coulter, France's Éric Zemmour, and Japan's Ko Bunyu—who are openly inimical to the great experiment. They put the blame squarely on the shoulders of immigrants and minorities. The reason for the persistent gaps in jobs and education, they claim, is immigrants' lack of work ethic, their disinterest in adopting local customs, or even their supposedly lower IQ.

These factors, ethnonationalist pessimists about the great experiment believe, are unlikely to change. To them, the socioeconomic disadvantage of minority groups is not a temporary problem that might be solved by the right policies or a multigenerational process of social mobility. Rather, they see it as a permanent state that can only be remedied by cutting down on the number of newcomers or deporting a great number of people.

Are things really that bad?

No.

In the most pessimistic narrative, the gap in jobs and education is vast and shows no signs of improving. But this is misleading in a number of key ways. For one, the actual differences in earnings between groups are, especially if you correct for factors like age or size of household, often significantly smaller than the most viral statistics suggest. For another, some immigrant groups actually outearn natives by a significant margin. On average, for example, Indian immigrants to the United Kingdom as well as Chinese, Lebanese, and Nigerian immigrants to the United States make more money than members of the white majority. But by far the biggest problem is that the pessimistic narrative fails to account for the significant upward mobility that most immigrant groups achieve in virtually every diverse democracy.

Most rich countries now attract quite a lot of highly skilled immigrants: doctors, entrepreneurs, and software engineers who speak the local language fluently, have excellent educational credentials or a significant track record of professional achievement, and are able to command high salaries from the day they arrive. But they remain the exceptions. For the most part, a majority of immigrants have had comparatively little formal education, do not speak the local language very well, and remain poor.

This makes it completely unsurprising that a lot of immigrants achieve significantly lower wages than the native-born—and makes many of the statistics that are trotted out to emphasize the persistent gap in jobs and education meaningless. Aggregate measures that average over first-generation immigrants who have just arrived from much poorer parts of the world and those whose ancestors have been in the country for one or two generations tell us very little about what to expect in the future. Instead, anybody who is genuinely curious about the current state of diverse democracies should be looking at metrics that show whether immigrants improve their condition once they have been in their new countries for a considerable length of time.

Do the children and grandchildren of immigrants do significantly better than their ancestors? And how do they fare relative to peers who are part of the historically dominant group?

The answers to both questions, it turns out, are surprisingly upbeat.

Looking at Europe, for example, two economists recently studied how descendants of immigrants fared relative to native-born peers whose parents had similar levels of education. In virtually all the countries Doris Oberdabernig and Alyssa Schneebaum looked at, the children of immigrants were much more likely to climb up the educational ladder. Their conclusion was unambiguous: their analysis, they wrote, "provides clear evidence of a narrowing gap in educational attainment levels between natives and immigrants across the two most recent generations [. . .] If this process persists over future generations, people with a migration background might soon have comparable education levels to the native population."

We should expect that immigrants who attain higher levels of education can also command higher wages; what is surprising is just how quickly this process seems to take place, according to recent studies. In one of the most ambitious attempts to investigate the economic mobility of newcomers to the United States, for example, four top economists analyzed a million data points representing immigrants who came to the country over the past century. What they found was heartening on just about every front.

Immigrants fared very well, rapidly boosting their incomes from one generation to the next. And, interestingly, the rate of their success barely depended on their country of origin. "Children of immigrants from nearly every sending country," the economists write, "have higher rates of upward mobility than the children of the US-born."

What's more, immigrants rise in the economic ranks about as quickly now as earlier generations of newcomers did fifty or a hundred years ago. This should be especially heartening to those who fear that earlier immigrants, who were mostly white, were given opportunities from which today's immigrants, who are mostly nonwhite, might find themselves barred because of structural racism.

A lot of observers, the economists conclude, "underestimate the long-run success of immigrants." In reality, even those "who come to the United States with few resources and little skills have a real chance at improving their children's prospects."

As long as diverse democracies allow high levels of immigration, some gap in jobs and education will likely persist at any one moment. But this focus on aggregate numbers conceals the extent to which most immigrants benefit from intergenerational mobility that allows the second and third generation to make rapid progress. Even those who arrive in diverse democracies from poor countries today have good reason to hope that their children and grandchildren will do very well.

———

The experience of African Americans presents the most serious challenge to an optimistic account of the future of diverse democracies.

This group not only suffered one of the most extreme and violent forms of domination in the past; it also continues to face one of the worst forms of compounded disadvantage in the present. Even so, an accurate picture leaves significant room for hope.

African Americans suffer the long-term impact of past domination more strongly than just about any other group. On average, African Americans earn 75 percent of what whites earn in median hourly earnings. The wealth disparity between white and black Americans is even more striking: the net worth of a typical white family is $171,000, nearly ten times the net worth of a typical black family.

This disparity is even evident in comparison with other ethnic minorities. For example, the median income for a black household in 2018 was $46,073, while the median income for a Hispanic household was $56,113. For Asian households, who significantly outearn whites, it was $98,174.

These yawning economic disparities go hand in hand with equally shocking discrepancies in other metrics. According to data compiled by the NAACP, a majority of Americans killed by the police are white. But on a per capita basis, African Americans are much more likely to suffer that tragic fate. While 13 percent of the US population is black, African Americans make up 22 percent of all fatal shootings by the police. They are also much more likely to be incarcerated than whites; in 2014, for example, they constituted about a third of the total correctional population.

But none of this justifies the apocalyptic language that politicians like Donald Trump have used to describe the state of African Americans. In his speeches, it often sounded as though most of them live in "inner-city" neighborhoods that offer virtually no opportunities and suffer from enormous crime rates. Making his electoral pitch to black voters in 2016, Trump repeatedly asked: "What do you have to lose?"

But for most African Americans, the answer to that question is quite a lot.

A significant minority of African Americans really do live in terrible conditions. The obstacles facing anyone who is born in the poorest parts of Detroit or Baltimore are enormous. But by and large, the condition of black America has significantly improved over the past sixty years.

Commentators often talk as though a majority of African Americans who grow up in poverty are likely to stay there. And as Raj Chetty's important research demonstrates, both race and class do powerfully shape an individual's prospects in life. But even his charts, which went viral in part because they were presented as proof of the pessimistic narrative about the state of black America, show that most African Americans who grow up in poverty experience significant upward mobility over the course of their lifetimes.

Of every one hundred black Americans who grew up with parents whose earnings put them in the lowest quintile of the income distribution, twenty-eight remained poor. But thirty-three reached the fourth quintile, becoming members of what Chetty calls the lower middle class. Another twenty-one became middle class; eleven, upper middle class; and six, rich. And while black boys experience less social mobility than white boys, black girls have a higher chance of moving up the socioeconomic ranks to lower middle class or middle class than white girls.

Data on absolute income paints a similar picture. According to the United States Census Bureau, the inflation-adjusted income of African

Americans has, with brief interruptions during recessions, increased for every quintile of the income distribution. Despite the Great Recession and the global pandemic, this progress has continued over the past two decades. The income of an African American household at the twentieth percentile of the distribution has increased from about $11,000 to $17,000 since 2002; that of the fortieth percentile from $22,000 to $35,000; that of the sixtieth percentile from $36,000 to $60,000; and that of the eightieth percentile from $60,000 to $100,000. (African American households in the ninety-fifth percentile, meanwhile, can now expect to make about $200,000 per year.)

The progress of black America shows up even more starkly on non-economic metrics. The gap in life expectancy, for example, is finally closing. At the beginning of the twentieth century, a white newborn could expect to live a staggering sixteen years longer than a black newborn. By 1950, the gap had fallen to under ten years. By 2016, it was down to fewer than four.

African Americans are also starting to earn higher degrees in much greater numbers. As *The New York Times* recently reported, "from 2000 to 2019, the percentage of African Americans with at least a bachelor's degree rose from 15 to 23 percent, as the share with a master's degree or higher nearly doubled from 5 to 9 percent." Over the same period, "the share of African Americans without a high school degree was cut by more than half."

As a result of these changes, the great majority of African Americans have, by now, entered the middle class. Today, in 2021, typical African Americans live in the suburbs of large metropolitan centers or in small towns rather than either the urban core or the countryside. They have completed high school, and if they are below the age of forty, have spent some time at a community college or research university. They work in white-collar jobs as nurses or schoolteachers rather than as construction workers or employees of fast-food chains. They get their health insurance from their employers rather than purchasing it on an open marketplace or being uninsured.

Consequently, the views of the median black American are much more upbeat than you might expect from listening to Donald Trump—or, for that matter, reading the pages of mainstream newspapers. They are proud of their country and say that they love America. And they are actually more likely than their white fellow citizens to "believe in the American Dream" or to say that the country's best days still lie ahead.

CRIME AND TERROR

On a cold morning in November 2019, Learning Together, a Cambridge University program that aims to rehabilitate prisoners by creating "transformative learning communities," celebrated its fifth anniversary in the elegant rooms of London's Fishmongers' Hall. Surrounded by historical artifacts, from narwhal tusks to golden chandeliers, participants lambasted the British criminal justice system. After speeches by an assortment of academics and activists, Usman Khan, one of the program's vaunted "success stories," recited a poem about his traumatic experiences.

Then Khan, who had until recently been in jail for plotting to blow up the London Stock Exchange, steadied his nerves, revealed the two kitchen knives he had concealed underneath his long sleeves, and charged his fellow delegates. Over the next ten minutes, he stabbed five of the organizers, killing two of them.

In the eyes of many who are hostile to the great experiment, the story of Khan and Learning Together illustrates urgent lessons about politics that its well-intentioned defenders would prefer to ignore. Immigration and cultural diversity, they insist, are fraught with deadly dangers. Over the past few decades, homegrown terrorists have staged attacks in France and Germany, in the United Kingdom and the United States, and in scores of other democracies around the world. Somebody like Khan is not a victim of the criminal justice system but rather a dangerous ideologue who seeks to impose his fundamentalist views on the world by any means necessary.

To make things worse, they believe, much of the cultural and political mainstream has remained willfully blind to this reality. To the fancy students and professors at Cambridge University, Khan was a misunderstood victim waiting for them to save him. The adulation they directed at somebody who was, quite literally, plotting to kill them demonstrates the extent to which their obsession with the rottenness of their own societies distorts their view of the world.

For many decades, opponents of diverse democracy mostly focused on the supposed tendency of immigrants and their descendants to commit crimes. When I was growing up in Germany, for example, one of the most common slogans on the billboards of far-right political parties was KRIMINELLE AUSLÄNDER RAUS! (DEPORT CRIMINAL FOREIGNERS!).

These concerns are often exacerbated by the existence of heavily immigrant areas in which crime really is rampant and ethnically based gangs really do thrive. Though Sweden as a whole has extremely low levels of crime, for example, there were eighty-one shootings and fifty-eight bomb explosions in the midsized southern city of Malmö in 2017. In the years since then, these bombings have spread to immigrant neighborhoods in other major cities, such as Gothenburg and Stockholm.

Because European countries welcomed millions of refugees from Africa and the Middle East—many of them young men unaccompanied by their families—in the summer of 2015, the latest newcomers have become the focal point for similar concerns. After a refugee from Afghanistan in his twenties murdered his fifteen-year-old ex-girlfriend in the small southwestern town of Kandel, and was only sentenced to eight and a half years in juvenile detention, far-right movements protested the leniency of the German judicial system. "What do all these men in the best age for fighting and procreating even want here?" Christiane Christen, one of the organizers of a protest outside the courthouse in nearby Landau on which I reported, asked. "They are leading a war," she answered her own question.

But the biggest concern is now, understandably, occasioned by the series of terrorist attacks that have rocked developed democracies over the past two decades. From the murder of the journalists at *Charlie Hebdo* to the siege of the Bataclan concert hall, and from the bombing of the Boston Marathon to the shooting at the Pulse nightclub, terrorists—many of them homegrown—have claimed hundreds of lives over the past decade. This has led some prominent far-right politicians to conclude that Islam is incompatible with Western civilization. As Beatrix von Storch, the deputy leader of the Alternative for Germany, put the point: "Islam is in itself a political ideology that is not compatible with the constitution."

The pessimists are right to point to Usman Khan's story as a serious warning about the consequences diverse democracies are likely to face if the great experiment goes wrong. Some immigrants really are deeply hostile to the most basic rules we need to be able to live together peacefully. Academics and intellectuals who refuse to recognize this are doing a disservice to the causes they purport to care about.

And yet there is a telling detail that opponents of the great experiment usually leave out of the story of the Fishmongers' Hall terror attack. For, thankfully, another immigrant was working in the venue's kitchen that day.

Łukasz Koczocik, a Polish citizen, is one of many millions who came to the United Kingdom over the past two decades. When he heard calls for help, he sprang to action without a moment's hesitation.

Desperate for any kind of weapon that might help him contain Khan, Koczocik snatched a decorative spear off a wall and charged the attacker. Khan fought back, stabbing Koczocik's hands and shoulders. Despite his injuries, Koczocik pursued Khan into the street. With the help of other men—including Darryn Frost, a South African immigrant wielding a narwhal tusk—he managed to immobilize Khan until the police finally arrived on the scene.

Few people, immigrant or native, are likely to match Koczocik's courage. But a dispassionate look at the evidence suggests that his commitment to the society in which he now lives is far more representative of the attitude of most immigrants than Khan's determination to inflict pain and suffering.

Most immigrants embrace the core values of the societies in which they live.

As I have shown in this chapter, they want to be integrated into the social mainstream (and are making rapid progress to that end). They believe in the fundamental values of democracy. In some countries, they are even more likely to be patriotic than the native-born.

At the same time, it is undoubtedly true that a minority of immigrants reject those values. Some may be religious fanatics. Others may turn to a life of crime due to poverty, a lack of opportunity, or a personal psychological predisposition. Others may have joined criminal gangs or networks even before they arrived in the countries in which they now live. Does this provide opponents of diverse democracies with a definitive objection to the great experiment?

I think not. In many diverse democracies, there is a genuine problem with ethnically based criminal gangs or networks. In some of them, the evidence suggests that immigrants commit crime in similar proportions to other members of their socioeconomic class but at somewhat higher levels than the general population. In still others, including the United States, the evidence strongly suggests that they are actually less likely to commit crimes than the native-born.

All of this gives diverse democracies good reason to control those who attempt to enter their territory and turn away at the border those who would pose a danger to their citizens. But the fact that a fraction of newcomers will commit crimes is no reason for barring all would-be immigrants from the country. And it certainly is no excuse for violating the rights of the many people who are already living within their borders and have a legal right to do so.

Similarly, it is worth noting that gangs formed by immigrant youths from poor countries are nothing new. Over the past 150 years, New York has seen the rise of Irish, Italian, Puerto Rican, Chinese, and now El Salvadoran criminal clans. The fact that they have existed before should not detract from the danger they pose in their latest iteration. MS-13, for example, is undoubtedly capable of terrifying cruelty.

And yet the fact that other ethnically based gangs associated with significant immigrant waves have faded in the past should give us confidence that they are likely to do so again. Irish and Italian gangs, for example, became far less powerful as law enforcement took robust action against their leaders and the larger community from which its members were being recruited integrated into an expanded American mainstream. For similar reasons, diverse democracies will, over time, succeed in defeating the ethnically based gangs that are now operating in cities from New York to Malmö to Berlin.

Finally, terrorism is the hardest worry to assuage because it is an area in which such a small number of people can cause such terrible damage.

The great majority of Muslims in Europe and North America practice a tolerant form of Islam, and disdain the way in which extremists invoke their religion as a justification for violent murder. As Mohammed Moussaoui, the president of the French Council for Muslim Worship, wrote after yet another terrorist attack in the country: "Muslims in France are horrified by this abject crime."

Moussaoui is right. Claims that Islam is somehow incompatible with democracy are belied by the great majority of Muslims who are deeply supportive of the democratic states in which they live, and reject violent forms of political action at about the same rate as citizens of other faiths.

And yet this argument is unlikely to convince those who are worried that the next homegrown terrorist is, somewhere in Europe or North America, lying in wait for an opportunity to kill his fellow citizens. How can defenders of diverse democracies respond to that fear in an honest manner?

The first step is to be forthright about the seriousness of the problem and our inability to solve it completely. It may, for example, be technically true that Islamist terrorists have, in the years since 9/11, cost fewer

Americans their lives than people slipping in their bathtubs. But to emphasize that fact is to ignore the psychological difference between a tragic mishap and a politically motivated crime designed to scare people.

The second step is to commit the necessary resources to fighting terrorism and dismantling extremist networks. Defenders of diverse democracy must not brook any attempt to demonize members of religious minorities. But nor should they be squeamish about discussing the ideological roots of Islamist terror or punishing those who aid and abet violence. Advocates of the great experiment must not hesitate to oppose anybody who justifies violence, whether they be part of the majority or belong to a minority community.

Finally, they should point out that the power of terrorism derives in part from its ability to set people in conflict with one another, to make them return to the safety of their own tribe, and to define others by their ascriptive identities. This is all the more reason to stick to the ideals that unite us in the face of heinous crimes, insisting that the great majority of members of diverse democracies remain committed to living together in peace. Even at the time of greatest difficulty, we must vow not to let terrorists succeed in their mission of destroying democracies that give citizens drawn from a big range of different communities the freedom to live a self-determined life.

WHY OPTIMISM IS IMPORTANT

I know from experience that an insistence on seeing the promising as well as the worrying trends is likely to strike many as tone-deaf. But though the instinct to focus primarily on the bad may feel righteous, it is a poor guide to reality—and might just turn out to be a serious obstacle to improving the world.

A lot of proponents of the great experiment, in particular, assume that a focus on the problems of diverse democracies will motivate their compatriots to act with greater compassion. Once people recognize that the country they love and the institutions they take for granted are deeply racist, the hope goes, they will grow more willing to adopt radical change.

But it is far from clear that this is how things actually play out in the real world. When they are told that injustices that once characterized their countries persist unchanged despite decades of efforts to remedy them, some people are instead likely to conclude that there isn't anything they can do. Others may go one step further. Perhaps, they will tell themselves, things never improve because immigrants and minorities really are to blame for their own lack of progress. (For that reason, it should probably give pessimistic proponents of the great experiment pause that its opponents emphasize some of the same pessimistic themes out of a conviction that it is likely to boost *their* political cause.)

More important, noble intentions alone are, in any case, unlikely to improve the lot of the disadvantaged. As many failed attempts to eradicate poverty or stimulate economic growth have shown, even the most generous programs go wrong if they are based on a faulty assessment of the roots of the problem and the kinds of measures that have—or haven't—worked in the past. Anyone who seeks to remedy the problems that really do persist must first gain a realistic view of their nature.

Imagine your neighbor's house just burned to the ground.

If you merely point out that many houses in the neighborhood still look very pretty, or that most of them are in a much better state today than they were thirty years ago, your neighbors would understandably feel that you are being obtuse. The first order of business should be to help them put out the fire and, if they need accommodation, offer them a place to stay for the night.

But once the fire is out, and your neighbors have somewhere to go, you should insist on figuring out what happened. If you want to stop other houses from burning down in the future, you really do need to get a good idea of why existing safeguards failed.

Let's imagine you find out that there used to be a lot of fires in the neighborhood. To cut down on risks, every house installed new fire alarms. But as it turns out, the number of fires never went down.

This would give you valuable information. Perhaps the fire alarms are faulty. Or perhaps the fire brigade takes too long to get to a burning house. Either way, it seems that the current solution to the problem isn't working. You need a drastic change of course.

Alternatively, let's imagine you find out that there used to be a lot of fires in the neighborhood. To cut down on the risks, most houses replaced outdated electrical systems. And though a few houses have not yet had a chance to install the new system, and continue to catch fire at a high rate, the incidence of fires in the neighborhood as a whole has gone down drastically since these changes were introduced.

This would likely lead you to a very different conclusion. Clearly, the measures taken in the past are making a valuable contribution to fire safety. Perhaps you could make sure they are completed more quickly. Or perhaps you could add additional safety features. But if you want to stop more houses from burning down, you should build on, rather than reverse, the steps the neighborhood has taken so far.

This, it seems to me, comes closer to the situation we now face.

There are very real problems and injustices in our metaphorical neighborhoods. For reasons both moral and prudential, we must seriously investigate them, and commit ourselves to remedying them as best we can. This is an urgent task, and one that will by no means be easy. But as we set out to do so, we can, thankfully, build on the real progress we have made in recent decades.

———

One powerful source of pessimism about diverse democracy is the idea that they are not making any progress toward a more equitable future. Another powerful source of pessimism is the idea that diverse democracies will always be split into two mutually hostile groups: members of the historical majority on the one side, and everybody else on the other.

On this view, the ascriptive identities that are now salient will continue to determine the cultural and political behavior of members of diverse democracies for a long time to come. In the United States, whites will, even thirty or sixty years from now, stand in direct competition with "people of color." And in the Netherlands, politics will for the foreseeable future consist of a competition between those who are "ethnically Dutch" and those who are "descendants of immigrants."

If this outlook proves to be true, it would be politically disastrous. Democracies will be pushed to their breaking point if every election delivers victory to one ethnic block and defeat to another. Even those who are confident that they will be able to cobble together a winning coalition—whether because they manage to retain their majority status by slowing demographic change and disenfranchising minorities or because they belong to groups that are now in the minority but are projected to gain majority status in the coming decades—should be repulsed by a vision of the future in which different ethnic or religious groups are forever locked into existential battle with one another.

But, thankfully, these pessimistic projections are based on a misunderstanding of the present reality and likely future of diverse democracies. Demographically, it is far from clear that any major democracy will soon become "majority minority" in a meaningful sense. Projections that whites will soon be in a minority in the United States, for example, rely on highly questionable assumptions about who should count as white and how people will actually self-identify. Similarly, the common belief that "demography is destiny" fundamentally mischaracterizes the politics of most developed democracies. Despite the confident predictions of demographers and political strategists, it is impossible to predict who will win the next election by counting the number of people who supposedly fall into different demographic categories.

Diverse democracies will always remain at risk of fragmentation. It is impossible to rule out the possibility that the electoral and cultural politics of the future might pit majority against minority, or the traditionally dominant against the historically marginalized. But as I argue in the next chapter, it is wrong to think of that outcome as a foregone conclusion—and anybody who wants the great experiment to succeed should work hard to ensure that it doesn't come to pass.

NINE

Demography Isn't Destiny

t is rare for demographers to make headline news. But when the United States Census Bureau projected that the country would, sometime in the 2040s, become "majority minority," America's newspapers paid plenty of attention. THE U.S. WHITE MAJORITY WILL SOON DISAPPEAR FOREVER, the *Houston Chronicle* headlined. Other newspapers and magazines explored how this shift would alter every aspect of American life, from its elections to its "office dynamics."

Nearly all these articles had one thing in common: they implicitly divided the American population into two distinct blocks. On one side, there were whites, a group portrayed as cohesive despite the vast ethnic and religious differences it subsumes. On the other side, there were members of ethnic minorities—or "people of color"—who were portrayed as having a meaningfully shared identity despite hailing from vastly different parts of the world and comprising individuals from just about every race known to man.

As a result, these seemingly dry demographic projections have come to signify a much broader transformation of the country's culture and politics. For the foreseeable future, the implication goes, America will be characterized by a clash between two mutually hostile blocks—and because of its shrinking size, the group that has traditionally dominated the country will soon lose much of its power.

This framing helps to explain why these projections are capable of inspiring tremendous hope. Many Americans look forward to the 2040s as the decade when their experience will cease to be marginal to the country's narrative. Instead of being the exception, they will finally become the norm.

Political strategists have also set their sights on the moment when the country is supposedly set to become majority minority. Because Hispanics and African Americans tend to support the Democratic Party in greater numbers, many Democrats now hope that the ongoing demographic transformation will help them inflict permanent defeat on the Republican Party—and perhaps even remake the country in keeping with their long-standing social and cultural aspirations.

Among other Americans, that same prospect is capable of provoking enormous fear. Demographic change, in their view, might change the country in which they grew up beyond recognition, or even relegate them to a subordinate position.

In its most extreme form, this fear takes the form of apocalyptic warnings about the "great replacement" that is supposedly taking place in Western societies. Traitorous politicians, far-right activists claim, are plotting to replace the existing population with newcomers whom they hope to control more easily than the native-born.

Because the United States is one of the major developed democracies in which the erstwhile majority group has dwindled most rapidly as a portion of the overall population, this debate is most intense in America. In much of this chapter, I focus on the country as a kind of case study. But in other democracies, whose own demographic transformations will take a few more decades to reach the stage at which America has now arrived, similar assumptions are inspiring the same hopes and fears. To this day, for example, many German disciples of replacement theory cite my television interview about "the great experiment" as supposed proof of their conspiracy theory.

This makes it all the more urgent to examine the premise of the whole conversation. Will America—and, eventually, other diverse democracies from France to Australia—really become majority minority in the sense so many pundits predict? Are the most important political and cultural conflicts within diverse democracies going to pit different demographic groups against one another? And would such changes help the great experiment succeed—or test it to its limits?

My answers to these questions strongly diverge from the received wisdom. Most developed democracies will never become majority minority in any meaningful sense. It is highly premature to assume that the politics of the future will neatly pit "natives" against "immigrants" or "whites" against "people of color." And anybody who wants the great experiment to succeed should celebrate that demography isn't destiny— and do what they can to ensure that the lines of cultural and political conflict in tomorrow's diverse democracies turn out to be a lot more fluid than so many people now predict.

WHEN THE "SCIENCE" ISN'T
ALL THAT SCIENTIFIC

When the United States Census Bureau projected that the country would become majority minority sometime in the 2040s, its demographic model was presented—and treated—as an exercise in science, giving the prediction an air of unassailable fact.

In this view, demographic projections are relatively straightforward exercises in arithmetic. Any American who has ancestors that belong to a relevant minority group, the assumption goes, will become part of the new majority. The future size of that group is a simple function of such factors as how many people belonging to minority groups are currently in the country, how many children they will have, and how many more will move to America over the coming decades.

Because it's impossible to predict these factors with precision, building the necessary models admittedly involves a little guesswork. It is always possible that specific projections will, here and there, turn out to be off by a few percentage points. But so long as the people involved in making the model are highly trained professionals who are doing their best to provide the public with objective information (as, for the most part, they are), the findings they come up with will be directionally correct.

Perhaps America will become majority minority in 2042 or in 2048 rather than in 2045. But sooner or later, whites will be in the minority. That's just science.

But this conceals the extent to which the categories popularized by the Census Bureau to classify Americans as white or nonwhite rely on highly questionable assumptions about how they self-identify now—and even more questionable ones about how they will self-identify in the future. Does the child of a white father and a Chinese mother count as white or Asian? (According to the dominant narrative, the answer is: Asian.) And is someone who has seven white great-grandparents and one black great-grandparent white or black? (Black.)

Seemingly scientific, the projections of the Census Bureau assume that all Americans who have either a drop of nonwhite blood or some distant cultural heritage connecting them to a Spanish-speaking country will be "people of color." This makes them a highly speculative guide to reality.

If we want to get a real sense of what the future of America—or, for that matter, other diverse democracies around the globe—will look like, it is not enough to point to a demographic table that stipulates who is what by employing a simplistic scheme of racial classification; we need to observe real-world behavior. And when you bother to look at how different groups actually see themselves, and are seen by others, it quickly becomes apparent that many of their members don't fit the neat narrative that has been imposed on them.

There are especially big question marks about the role three rapidly growing groups of Americans—who should, according to the prevailing narrative, simply see themselves as "people of color"—will actually play in the country's politics and culture.

THE RISE OF MIXED-RACE AMERICA

Three or four decades ago, a majority of Americans still openly stated that they opposed whites and African Americans dating one another.

Reality reflected these prejudices. In 1980, only 3 percent of newborns in the United States had a mother and a father from different ethnic groups.

In the past three decades, this has changed rapidly and radically. The number of people who oppose interracial marriage is now miniscule. Only one out of every ten Americans say that they would be uncomfortable if a close relative married a member of a different race. And while some of this shift may be down to "social desirability bias"—with respondents changing how they answer survey questions, not how they really feel—there is strong evidence that the actual behavior of young Americans is transforming just as drastically. By the late 2010s, one out of every seven children born in the United States was mixed-race.

The tendency to "marry out" is especially widespread among the fastest growing demographic groups. Nearly one out of every three Hispanic and Asian American newlyweds has a spouse of a different race. All indicators suggest that the number of mixed-race Americans will continue to grow in the coming years.

Because the media usually applies a "one-drop rule" to American identity, every single one of the babies born to these couples is counted as a member of an ethnic minority. But this imposed identity does not square with the findings of sociologists who have actually bothered to study the self-perception of mixed-race children.

Ethnographic accounts of such children usually conclude that most of them are deeply integrated into white America. Children with one white and one Asian American or one white and one Hispanic parent resemble their fully white counterparts in significant respects. As Edward Telles and Vilma Ortiz found in one seminal study, children with one Mexican and one non-Hispanic white parent "were less likely to know Spanish, were more likely to intermarry themselves [and] identified less with their Mexican origin."

Many of these mixed-race Americans even expressly identify as white. As one prominent sociologist summarized in an in-depth report by Pew, "Many Americans with mixed Asian or Hispanic family origins identify with the white majority some of the time."

THE COMPLEX IDENTITY OF LATINOS

In 2014, there were about 55 million people with roots in Spain or Latin America in the United States. At the time, the Census Bureau predicted that, by 2060, there would be 119 million. But while many people of Hispanic origin are black or indigenous, the vast majority, about 103 million, were projected to be white. The big question is whether this group will see itself as distinct or whether it will, like the Italians and Irish of the late nineteenth and early twentieth century, slowly blend into the American mainstream.

The question of how Hispanics will see themselves in thirty years is difficult to answer. American notions of race changed drastically between 1960 and 1990, and again between 1990 and 2020. There is no good reason to think they won't change just as drastically by 2050.

What is clear, though, is that Hispanic identity is already much more fluid than much of the country's political class tends to assume. In the run-up to the 2020 election, for example, two Hispanic progressives conducted a series of focus groups. Ian Haney López and Tory Gavito assumed that Latinos would see themselves as "people of color," and reject concerns about "illegal immigration from places overrun with drugs and criminal gangs" as a racist dog whistle. Instead, López and Gavito found that many of the people they interviewed insisted on being white, and that Latinos were actually *more* likely than non-Hispanic whites to agree with anti-immigrant messages.

Progressives, López and Gavito concluded,

> commonly categorize Latinos as people of color, no doubt partly because progressive Latinos see the group that way and encourage others to do so as well. Certainly, we both once took that perspective for granted. Yet in our survey, only one in four Hispanics saw the group as people of color. In contrast, the majority rejected this designation. They preferred to see Hispanics as a group integrating into the American mainstream, one not overly bound by racial constraints.

THE UNCERTAIN PLACE OF ASIAN AMERICANS

While Hispanics are adding the greatest numbers to the American population, the fastest growing group hails from Asia. Between 2014 and 2060, the number of Asian Americans is projected to increase by more than twofold, from twenty million to forty-six million.

Unlike many Hispanics, Asian Americans will likely continue to see themselves—and to be seen by others—as racially distinct. But that does not mean that they will naturally form a cultural or electoral coalition with other "people of color."

While black Americans continue to earn less than whites, on average, Asian Americans earn significantly more. Korean Americans have a median household income of $72,000; Chinese Americans, of $82,000;

and Indian Americans, of $119,000. The median Asian woman in the United States now earns more than the median white man.

This financial success is rooted in extraordinary educational achievements. While Asian Americans currently make up less than one-tenth of the US population, for example, they make up a quarter of the entering class at Harvard. At schools that are legally prohibited from favoring applicants on the basis of race, their presence is even larger. At Berkeley, for example, nearly half of the domestic students entering the university in 2020 were Asian American.

Neither culture nor politics is ever just about self-interest. Even so, diverging interests may make a lasting coalition between Hispanics, African Americans, and Asian Americans harder to sustain than those who believe in the inevitable rise of a cohesive grouping of ethnic minorities tend to assume.

If the future really does pit whites against "people of color" in the way so many academics and journalists now believe—a prospect that is, in any case, highly doubtful—it is far from clear into which group Asian Americans would belong.

Driven by the media's focus on the country's demographic transformation, most Americans overestimate the nature and the extent of the changes that lie afoot.

Because the country will come to be majority minority according to demographic models that make a host of questionable assumptions, most politically engaged Americans now believe that the white population is rapidly declining. But a close look at the actual facts reveals a future America that drastically differs from these speculative assumptions.

According to the Census Bureau, about 69 percent of the American population of 2060 will, if you include Hispanics who now self-identify as such, be ethnically white. Another 5 percent of Americans will be mixed-race and have some recent white ancestors. Many more will have a spouse or other close relative who is white. It is, in short, far from clear that the most important cleavage in American society will pit whites against people of color.

Should that be a relief or a disappointment to those who seek to make the great experiment succeed? The answer has to do with one of the few big theories about American politics on which large parts of both the left and the right now agree: the idea that the growing share of minority groups as a portion of the overall population will transform the country's politics and make it easy for Democrats to win elections. But as it happens, Democrats' "inevitable demographic majority"—or, as I like to call it, the most dangerous idea in American politics—is just as uncertain.

THE MOST DANGEROUS IDEA
IN AMERICAN POLITICS

In the years after 9/11, the war on terror dominated American politics. The social mood was distinctly conservative, with a series of statewide referenda against same-sex marriage passing by wide margins. And though George W. Bush was derided by many of the country's journalists and intellectuals—who distrusted his evangelical faith and loathed his foreign policies—he was popular among ordinary Americans. So when "Dubya" won a second presidential term in 2004, many concluded that the right enjoys a natural advantage in American politics. The future seemed to belong to Republicans.

Then a couple of contrarians made a startling claim that squarely contradicted the conventional wisdom of the day. Those parts of the American electorate that have traditionally favored Republicans, John Judis and Ruy Teixeira argued in *The Emerging Democratic Majority*, are rapidly shrinking. Those parts of the American electorate that have traditionally supported Democrats are rapidly growing. Soon, this seemingly right-leaning country was likely to become thoroughly progressive.

A part of Judis and Teixeira's thesis touched on social and economic changes. Americans who have college degrees or live in urban centers, they pointed out, have more progressive social values. And because the share of urbanites and college graduates is increasing, the country is likely to move to the left.

But the most influential part of the book was about the shift in relative weight between different ethnic groups. Latinos, African Americans, and Asian Americans, Judis and Teixeira demonstrated, tend to favor Democrats. Because their proportion of the American population was set to grow, they would likely add millions of votes to the Democratic column. Over time, "these groups of voters will continue to support Democrats rather than Republicans, paving the way for a new majority."

These counterintuitive predictions seemed to come true when a man by the name of Barack Hussein Obama began his remarkable ascent. Though Obama was no radical, his policies marked a decisive break with the social conservatism of the Bush years. And when he became the first black politician in the history of the country to move into the White House, his victory rested on the kind of coalition Judis and Teixeira had predicted. Obama won big among the highly educated, made significant gains in urban centers and affluent suburbs, and drew record support from minority groups.

Obama's historic victory seemed to prove that demography was destiny. But while Judis and Teixeira had emphasized the need for Democrats to build a broad coalition—which would have to include a large number of white working-class voters—many of those who embraced their theory now dispensed with such subtleties. In the minds of many progressive journalists and political strategists, an emerging Democratic majority that would have to be carefully cultivated became a demographic majority that was all but inevitable.

Big parts of the American right have, oddly, taken the same empirical assumptions on board. Many Republicans are now just as convinced as Democrats that the transformation of the country's population will push it in a progressive direction. But what fills the hearts of the left with joy has been sowing fear in the ranks of the country's conservatives.

Perhaps the most influential articulation of this panic came in the run-up to the 2016 elections. Writing under a pseudonym, Michael Anton, who later took a senior position in the White House, acknowledged that Donald Trump was an untested candidate who might prove incapable of governing. But that didn't matter. Democrats, Anton warned, are "on the cusp of a permanent victory" because of "the ceaseless importation of Third World foreigners." In Anton's mind, Donald Trump was the last chance for Republicans to rescue the country from the imminent demise brought on by its demographic transformation.

In the lead-up to the election, Trump himself echoed strikingly similar language. "I think this will be the last election that the Republicans have a chance of winning, because you're going to have people flowing across the border," he said at the height of the 2016 campaign. "Once all that happens, you can forget it."

When Trump unexpectedly won the Republican presidential primary in 2016, virtually all pundits and experts were certain that he would lose to Hillary Clinton. Because of the country's demographic transformation, a candidate who primarily sought to appeal to white voters just wouldn't be able to cobble together a winning coalition. "Demography alone appears to give Clinton a clear advantage in this election," an article on NPR's website proclaimed, predicting that she would win 345 votes in the electoral college.

Reality turned out to be very different. When the ballots were counted on the evening of November 8, 2016, the very states that were, according to an analysis by Ruy Teixeira, supposed to cement Democrats' new "progressive dominance" handed Trump his upset victory.

Trump's election started to call the theory of the inevitable demographic majority into serious doubt. Enthralled by the growth of the minority vote, many progressives had seemingly forgotten that a majority of the ballots cast for Obama in both 2008 and 2012 stemmed from white voters without a college degree. Democrats remained far more dependent on the support of the white working class than many of their activists and strategists had come to believe.

Now, even the inventors of the rising demographic majority have come to the conclusion that this will remain the case for the foreseeable future. As Teixeira recently acknowledged, Democrats who seek to be competitive on the national level will have to "retain the votes of a significant portion of the white working class."

In 2020, Democrats managed to unlearn some of the false lessons they had taken on board. After a tense campaign, Joe Biden won a clear victory over Donald Trump. When all the ballots were counted, he beat Trump by nearly seven million ballots and received more than 300 votes in the Electoral College.

But far from resuscitating the theory of the rising demographic majority, the 2020 elections demonstrated just how swiftly groups' electoral behavior can change. Democrats did manage to win important victories in some states with rapidly growing minority populations, such as Nevada and Georgia. But even there, actual vote patterns ran directly counter to the assumptions on which Democrats had relied for the previous decade.

Joe Biden owes his victory to the fact that he did far better among white voters than Hillary Clinton. Donald Trump remained competitive because he made inroads among just about every other demographic group. When he first stood for election, Trump was extremely unpopular with both Muslim Americans and African Americans. Over the following four years, he increased his share of the vote among both groups by about one quarter.

The Latino shift toward Trump was even more striking. The media has made much of the fact that many immigrants from Cuba or Venezuela, which have had bad experiences with leftist leaders, were put off by the rhetorical embrace of socialism among some prominent Democrats. This certainly helps to explain why Trump comfortably carried the state of Florida. But Latinos also swung toward the Republican Party in parts of the country that are overwhelmingly populated by voters who do not have the same historical reasons to be nervous about invocations of socialism. The overwhelmingly Mexican American counties of southwest Texas, for example, recorded some of the biggest swings toward Republican candidates anywhere in the United States.

Counterintuitive as this may be, electoral patterns in the United States have, of late, significantly depolarized by race. As a result, it was harder to predict who a voter was going to support based on their race in 2020 than in 2016.

It's impossible to know whether the remarkable trend of the past four years will continue for the next forty. But the fact that Trump—of all people—unexpectedly picked up millions of votes from "people of color" in his failed bid for reelection should drive home just how naive it is to make confident predictions about the ethnic cleavages of 2032 or 2048.

My political values are left of center. The American politician of the past fifty years I most admire is Barack Obama. Faced with a choice between Joe Biden or Hillary Clinton, on the one hand, and Donald Trump, on the other hand, I'd choose one of the former without a moment's hesitation.

All of this should predispose me to think that the idea of the inevitable demographic majority is a hopeful one. After all, it would supposedly ensure that "my team" will one day dominate American politics. But the more you think about such a supposedly alluring future, the more disturbing it turns out to be.

As should by now be clear, I am deeply skeptical that demography really is destiny in the way so many people believe. But let's assume, for the sake of argument, that predictions of the rising demographic majority come true. The presidential election of 2052 is in full swing. The campaign is bitter and hard-fought. But, deep down, everyone knows that the outcome is foreordained. Counting on the reliable support of the "minority groups" that have, over the past decade, officially come to constitute a majority of the American population, Democrats are cruising for yet another victory.

But this scenario sounds dystopian to me. Ignore that a democratic election in which the outcome is known in advance leaves a sour taste in the mouth. Forget that countries in which one party predominates for many decades tend to suffer from pervasive corruption. What most worries me about this supposed utopia is the way in which politics would still be segregated by race. Walking down the street in New York or San Diego in 2052, I would be able to guess who you're voting for with a high degree of accuracy just by looking at the color of your skin.

Obama once said that we shouldn't slice and dice the electorate into blue states and red states. In the vision that many progressives have mistakenly taken to be comforting, we would, for the foreseeable future, continue to slice and dice the electorate into "blue races" and "red races." That is hardly an attractive vision of the future of diverse democracies.

REASONS TO CELEBRATE THAT DEMOGRAPHY ISN'T DESTINY

Over the course of the past decade, the dominant discourse has started to divide Americans into two neat groups: whites and "people of color." But whites are far less culturally or politically homogeneous, and ethnic minority groups far more culturally and politically heterogeneous, than this clean dichotomy implies.

Thankfully, there is an alternative vision of what America's future might look like. In *The Great Demographic Illusion*, the eminent sociologist Richard Alba argues that what he calls the American mainstream has proved capable of expanding in unexpected ways. Whereas the country's historic ruling elite once feared the changes that Irish and Italian immigrants would bring about, these newcomers were ultimately absorbed into the country's mainstream; today, the distinction between Americans who hail from Sussex and those who hail from Sicily seems quaint.

If Alba is to be believed, the American mainstream will once again prove capable of expanding in ways that now seem difficult to fathom. The first groups to join this new American mainstream would likely include white Hispanics, Asian Americans, and those who are mixed-race. But as the increasingly multiethnic culture of metropoles from Houston to New York City shows, the new mainstream could ultimately grow even more inclusive: in particular, a growing share of black Americans could also be absorbed.

The choice between an America that looks like the projections of the United States Census Bureau and an America that looks like the projections of Richard Alba is straightforward. The country would be a much better place to live, for whites and nonwhites alike, if it managed to integrate an ever-greater array of ethnic and religious groups into an expanding mainstream.

This has important implications for how those of us who are committed to the success of the great experiment should behave.

Electoral politics is important. Whether they are on the left or the right, politicians should resist the temptation to double down on "their" demographic base. Instead, they should seek to appeal to a broader range of voters, helping to depolarize their countries' political systems by race. Thankfully, there is at least one good reason to hope that many of them will, over time, start to make the moral choice: by and large, doing so happens to be in their self-interest.

Democrats in the United States, for example, should neither assume that they are sure to hang on to the vote of Latinos, Asian Americans, and African Americans nor that they are incapable of boosting their standing among whites. Instead of betting the house on the idea that demography is destiny, they must recognize that their future electoral prospects—and the well-being of the country—depends on their ability to appeal to Americans who are drawn from every ethnic group.

The choice faced by Republicans is even more consequential. They can try to double down on an electoral strategy that squarely focuses on white voters. And that strategy might even deliver a few more close-run victories. But at some point, a Republican Party that refuses to broaden its ethnic coalition or cultural appeal would consistently lose elections. It would then face a choice between trying to entrench its power by pursuing ever more extreme strategies for disenfranchising nonwhite voters—or finally doing what it can to make them feel welcome in the Republican Party.

When and if the party starts to reach out to those demographic groups in earnest, it will likely be much more successful than many pundits now assume. For far from being consistently progressive on social or economic policy, many minority voters are much more conservative than their current electoral behavior would suggest. A large number of Latinos, Asian Americans, and even African Americans could be open to the appeal of a racially inclusive conservatism.

Politics is important. But society is much more so. And so the question I am most worried about is what the America of 2052 might look like far away from the political arena.

Will Americans hew closely to the ethnic categories of the Census Bureau, assuming that the interests of white Americans, on the one hand, and those of Hispanics or Asian Americans or African Americans, on the other hand, are implacably opposed? Or will categories of race, while still recognizable, have lost some of their current salience, with the vast majority of Americans integrated into a diverse mainstream?

This is where developments on the ground provide the greatest reason for optimism. Every day, scores of Americans from different demographic groups decide to intertwine their fates as friends, business associates, or romantic partners. At least in their daily lives, most Americans do not seem to buy into the monolithic opposition between whites and "people of color."

But human identities are deeply malleable. They take form—and change nature—in keeping with the narratives imparted by an older generation, the cues given by elites, and the incentives created by institutions. A lot thus depends on whether elementary school teachers and college professors, senators and CEOs help to support the natural processes that are making boundaries between different groups more porous—or whether they, deliberately or inadvertently, reverse that trend.

This is one of the things that most worries me at this moment. For in more and more spheres of American life, well-intentioned people who genuinely believe that they are fighting for righteous causes are doing what they can to make racial identity the all-encompassing dividing line of American life.

An overwhelming focus on the importance of ethnic identity and the irreconcilable conflicts between whites and "people of color" is quickly becoming part of the ruling ideology of the American elite. One of the most pressing questions of the next few decades is whether this elite will succeed in imposing its view of race on the rest of the population—or whether ordinary Americans drawn from every demographic group are able to counter with a more inspiring vision of our collective future.

This chapter has primarily focused on the United States. The reason is simple: the demographic transformation is more advanced in America than it is in most other diverse democracies. And so the debate about the rising demographic majority is further along in America than elsewhere.

And yet the basic terms of debate are increasingly similar in most diverse democracies: progressives dream of a future in which the growing share of ethnic minorities will deliver them secure electoral majorities, while conservatives fear that immigrants and their descendants will fundamentally alter the character of their nations. And there, too, such predictions would represent an acute danger to the success of the great experiment if they came true—but are unlikely to do so.

This is quickly becoming evident in the political sphere. In many European and Anglo-Saxon countries, right-wing parties whose voters had once almost exclusively been concentrated among members of the ethnic and religious majority have broadened their appeal. Many right-of-center leaders owe their victories in part to significant levels of support among minority communities. In Germany, a recent poll showed that a majority of immigrants and their descendants now vote for right-wing parties. And in the United Kingdom, a conservative government has given a majority of the most important cabinet positions to politicians whose parents or grandparents arrived in the country.

Defenders of the great experiment should, irrespective of their personal political leanings, recognize this as a sign of progress. A significant percentage of the citizens of diverse democracies will, whether they be white or brown or black, always hold right-of-center views. Political parties that represent these views without tolerating racism in their midst would help to vanquish the dangerous delusion of demographic determinism now shaping political systems from France to the United States—and thereby make a huge contribution to building democracies that are not only diverse but also tolerant.

—————

Ten years ago, two professors at Northwestern University set out to study how an emphasis on demographic change would alter the racial attitudes of white Americans. Maureen A. Craig and Jennifer A. Richeson recruited participants to their lab and asked each of them to read one of two texts. The first described America's current racial makeup. The second summarized the Census Bureau's projections according to which America was about to become majority minority.

The findings were striking. Participants in the study who were randomly asked to read about the impending end of white America were much more likely to say that it would bother them if their child married someone from a different ethnic background. They also had more negative feelings toward racial minorities. "Rather than ushering in a more tolerant future," Craig and Richeson warned, an emphasis on the (supposed) decline of the white majority "may instead yield intergroup hostility."

Many well-meaning Americans have convinced themselves that emphasizing an empirically dubious theory about the country's demographic future would somehow help them overcome the injustices of the present. But as Craig and Richeson suggest, it is actually likely to make it much harder to create thriving diverse democracies.

The supposedly inevitable demographic majority won't ride to the rescue of diverse democracies. In politics, the lines of battle are ever shifting. Groups that now appear to be cohesive will likely splinter in as yet unpredictable ways. Demography is not destiny. And so the residents of diverse democracies—white and black, Christian and Muslim, majority and minority, left and right, religious and secular—are stuck with one another. For those of us who believe that the great experiment can succeed, a key task for the coming decades consists of fighting for a future in which as many people as possible conceive of themselves, not as members of mutually hostile tribes but rather as proud and optimistic citizens of diverse democracies.

Is there something that the traditional arena of political action—public policy—can do to hurry that outcome along? That is the question I address in the tenth, and final, chapter of this book.

TEN

Policies That Can Help

Books about big ideas often suffer from a serious flaw.

In their first nine chapters, they identify a fascinating problem or challenge. They explain its causes and context. They show why it is worth worrying about and urgently needs to be solved.

But any problem that is big and important enough that someone can write an interesting book about it is unlikely to be solved soon. And so the tenth chapter of these books is nearly always far less satisfying. Either it suggests huge changes of public policy or collective behavior that really would solve the problem—but are highly unrealistic. Or it suggests technical policy fixes or small adjustments in our lives that might actually be achievable—but will at best make a small difference.

It's the chapter 10 problem.

No writer can will the chapter 10 problem out of existence. It is owed to the nature of our limitedly perfectible world. Big problems will always go deeper than their putative solutions. It's far easier to identify what is wrong than to muster the resources to do what is right.

But a recognition of the chapter 10 problem can at least make writers more careful about making promises they cannot keep, and push them to think seriously about how to contribute to building a better future in the absence of a silver bullet. The questions it implies may be less exciting, but they are also far more useful: What real-world trends are already pointing in the right direction (and how can we amplify them)? And what would society need to look like for positive change to be possible (and how can public policy help to put those conditions into place)?

Over the course of the past two chapters, I have started to examine the larger social transformations that are now underway in diverse democracies to see how they can help to attenuate some of today's problems.

One reason to remain optimistic about the prospects for the great experiment, I have argued, is that developments on the ground are much more positive than many observers recognize. In many diverse democracies across the globe, immigrants and other minority groups are making rapid economic progress and reaching new levels of social acceptance.

Another reason to remain optimistic, I have argued, is that demography need not be destiny. Though many pundits and politicians now like to slice and dice diverse democracies into a supposedly monolithic group of insiders and a supposedly monolithic group of outsiders, it is far from clear that they will fragment along such neat ethnic or religious lines. A much more integrated culture and politics is possible.

But this still leaves the question about what diverse democracies would need to look like if they were to succeed, and how public policy might (in however modest a manner) help to bring these conditions about. And the best way to approach that question, it seems to me, is to look at some of the broader obstacles that currently make it hard for diverse democracies to succeed. Four of those seem particularly pertinent.

First, many people have barely experienced any improvements in their living standards in recent years and now worry that they may be even less affluent in the future. As some excellent sociological research shows, this makes them much more likely to look at members of other demographic groups with fear or disdain. It is easier to cheer on the success of members of different groups when you feel that your own future is likely to be bright as well.

Second, some ethnic and religious groups continue to suffer from significantly lower socioeconomic standing. This is especially common among those, like most African Americans, whose ancestors suffered from schemes of "hard domination." This long shadow of past domination therefore raises the danger of turning diverse democracies into hierarchical societies in which the members of some groups will indefinitely enjoy superior standing to those of others.

Third, the institutions of many diverse democracies now struggle to make effective decisions, are insufficiently responsive to public opinion, or exclude key groups from having a full voice in the decision-making process. The resulting sense that citizens don't have any control over their collective fate raises the risk of intergroup tension and makes it easier for extremists who oppose the founding principles of diverse democracies to win power.

And finally, a rise in polarization is making it harder for citizens of diverse democracies to see those with whom they have political disagreements in a charitable light. This lack of mutual respect undermines the ability of these societies to contain conflicts when passions run high.

Fixing any of these problems isn't going to be easy. Fixing all at once is likely to prove impossible. And yet there are meaningful actions that both policy makers and individual citizens can take to improve the background conditions for the great experiment.

Diverse democracies, I argue in this chapter, need to offer citizens "secure prosperity": they should both boost economic growth and ensure that these gains actually end up in the pockets of ordinary citizens. They should double down on "universal solidarity": they need to build a generous welfare state that helps the diadvantaged and avoids pitting members of one ethnic group against those of another ethnic group. They need to build "effective and inclusive institutions": they need to give all citizens the sense that their preferences count. And they need to build a "culture of mutual respect": in diverse democracies, it must be possible for citizens to have robust disagreements without seeing one another as existential enemies.

The diverse democracies of the future should ensure that all of their citizens get to lead a life of affluence and dignity, that children born to any set of parents have genuine opportunities to rise to the top, that citizens feel a sense of collective control over their destiny, and that they cultivate a sense of respect even for those of their compatriots with whom they have serious political disagreements. Nobody can magically make that kind of future appear. But there are plenty of policies and principles that can help to point diverse democracies in that promising direction.

SECURE PROSPERITY

In the late summer of 2018, I stumbled across a large demonstration at the Place de la Republique, in Paris.

Young protesters in fashionable outfits beat drums and chanted environmentalist slogans with joyous abandon. Colorful signs expressed their opposition to consumerism. One still stands out in my memory: HALTE A LA CROISSANCE, it read in big red letters: STOP ECONOMIC GROWTH.

A few months later, a very different kind of mass protest took over the streets of France. When the government proposed to raise its gas tax, millions of citizens all over the country took to the streets in yellow vests.

Sociologists found that the average participant in these protests lived in a rural or exurban community with little economic opportunity and had no more than a thousand euros of monthly after-tax income at their disposal. Though the ideological profile of the yellow vests was diffuse, the demand for a higher standard of living was widely shared.

So, increasingly, was an anger bordering on blind rage. As they wore on, the protests became ever more violent, with a growing share of participants identifying outsiders, from Jews to Arabs, as the true cause of their discontent.

The contrast between these two sets of protests is instructive. When those who are materially comfortable preach an end to economic growth, they are frequently met with the wrath of those who have never had the opportunities they take for granted.

Ever since a watchmaker's son from Geneva unexpectedly won the prestigious prize of the Academy of Dijon with an elegant essay that denounced the morally corrupting impact of affluence and civilization, it has been fashionable to associate economic growth with moral degradation. Most of his contemporaries, Jean-Jacques Rousseau argued in 1755, blamed common vices, such as greed and pride, on the very nature of humanity. But this was to make the mistake of ascribing ills instilled by civilization to the natural condition of mankind.

More than 250 years after its publication, the *Discourse on the Origin and Basis of Inequality Among Mankind* remains highly influential. Building on Rousseau's lament, writers with an anarchist bent like to claim that humans were more peaceable and altruistic before they started to till fields and build settlements. The belief in the corrupting impact of modern civilization has also worked its way into popular culture. When well-heeled westerners return from a trip to some "exotic" locale, for example, they like to show off their photographs of smiling children posing in front of derelict huts, raving about the "simple virtues" of the people they encountered.

But if social scientists are to be believed, poverty and economic stagnation are no guarantors of altruism, much less of tolerance. A host of studies have found that economic crises often provoke a climate of hatred, the rise of far-right political movements, or even sectarian violence. According to a trio of German economists, for example, economic crises from the Great Depression in the 1930s to the Great Recession in the 2000s were followed by a statistically significant increase in extremist political movements. Looking at twenty different countries over a 140-year period, they found that "political parties on the far right appear to be the biggest political beneficiaries of a financial crash," putting a severe "strain on modern democracies."

Rapid economic growth, by contrast, is usually associated with a significant liberalization of social attitudes toward all manners of outsiders, including ethnic, religious, and sexual minorities. According to the World Values Survey, for example, people in rich countries are much more likely than those in poor ones to say that they would welcome somebody from a salient out-group as their neighbor. And as

Benjamin Friedman, an economist at Harvard University, has argued, economic growth "more often than not fosters greater opportunity, tolerance of diversity, social mobility, commitment to fairness, and dedication to democracy."

Fights over the distribution of economic goods or the rightful apportionment of social status are far easier to tolerate when the pie is growing than when it is shrinking. Other things being equal, democracies are more likely to manage the tensions induced by their growing diversity if the bulk of their citizens feel confident about their economic future.

Advocates of diverse democracies should therefore favor policies that boost economic growth. They should oppose monopolies that allow inefficient corporations to quash would-be competitors, and they should favor pouring money into research that has the potential to lead to groundbreaking innovations like the new mRNA vaccines. They should make it easier for ambitious young people to found companies and fight against restrictive building regulations that exclude many underprivileged citizens from opportunity. They should reform educational systems to ensure that all children have a chance to develop their talents and give citizens access to basic welfare benefits like health insurance irrespective of their current employment status.

But economic growth is not enough if it only benefits a small group of highly educated and especially talented people who, by and large, already look toward the future with optimism. To ensure that economic growth makes it easier for people to treat their compatriots with generosity rather than jealousy, it needs to benefit as many people as possible.

Traditionally, modern states have mostly tried to ensure that economic growth would have benefits for all through welfare state programs like unemployment benefits and transfer schemes like the earned income tax credit. To foster the social preconditions for mutual tolerance, diverse democracies should maintain these programs. And in countries with welfare states that still remain woefully incomplete, as in the United States, governments should finally ensure that all citizens gain access to key services like quality health care or core entitlements like paid family leave.

Creating opportunities for all citizens to rise in the social ranks is another key tool for diverse democracies. In many countries, social mobility has stagnated or decreased in recent decades. Societies that hope to ensure that economic growth benefits the many, not the few, should redouble their efforts to give all citizens a fair shot at reaching positions of influence and affluence.

But while entitlement programs like unemployment insurance can help to cushion the fate of the least fortunate, they will still leave many of their beneficiaries feeling that their material means are very modest and the respect they command from society extremely limited. And while it is important for all citizens to have a shot at a better life, it is impossible for everyone to climb the ranks at the same time. What citizens need most urgently, then, is to know that they can earn a dignified living and enjoy real social respect even if they hold down perfectly ordinary jobs.

Countries that succeed in creating an inclusive economy of this kind tend to have a range of different weapons in their arsenal. They usually shape the distribution of material goods through robust schemes of progressive taxation and corporate taxes that don't offer big companies endless loopholes. They create the circumstances that allow employees in many lines of work, including those who do not possess special skills, to bargain for a fair wage. And they invest heavily in professional schools and apprenticeship programs that put people who prefer to work with their hands in a position to earn a decent livelihood.

In the future, more ambitious tools may be necessary to fulfil these same goals. The Biden administration is trying to harmonize international tax systems to make it harder for big corporations to dodge their responsibilities to the societies in which they make their profits; in a promising first step, the nations of the Group of Seven (G7) have recently agreed on a new global minimum tax rate of 15 percent for large multinational corporations. Other ideas whose time may one day come include new forms of industrial policy or even a basic income.

The precise mix of policies that is needed to achieve such inclusive growth will differ from country to country, and from decade to decade. But the goal is likely to remain the same across these different contexts: the more diverse democracies are able to offer their citizens secure prosperity, the better the background conditions for the great experiment to succeed.

UNIVERSAL SOLIDARITY

Most diverse democracies do not just suffer from inequality between the rich and the poor; they are also characterized by significant differences in income and opportunity between members of historically dominant and historically dominated groups. For the great experiment to succeed, this cannot be allowed to turn into a perennial state. If past domination should forever translate into future disadvantage, the promise of treating all citizens as equals would come to ring intolerably hollow.

Thankfully, the past decades suggest that progress on this front is more likely than many people, whether they defend or oppose the great experiment, now believe. In most countries, descendants of immigrants and members of minority groups have rapidly attained greater educational achievements, gained a higher professional status, and started to earn more generous salaries. If past proves to be prologue, we should expect the gap between different demographic groups to keep narrowing.

Public policy can help hurry these changes along. Diverse democracies need robust laws to ensure that employers don't discriminate on the basis of race or religion. They must ensure that the most prestigious institutions of higher learning are genuinely open to high-achieving applicants from all social groups. And they should stop companies and public institutions from offering unpaid internships that make it harder for those without deep-pocketed parents to break into promising careers.

But if diverse democracies are to overcome their historical patterns of domination, they need to focus less on who attends the most famous universities or is hired for the most prestigious jobs, and more on how to ensure that children from disadvantaged backgrounds have a chance to develop their talents in the first place. Even though there is now a strong consensus in pedagogy and developmental psychology that children's early years play a crucial role in determining their future prospects, most countries still invest too little in early childcare, kindergartens, and elementary schools. A significant increase in the resources devoted to maximizing the potential of every child at the moment when it most matters would, among many other benefits, help to speed up the rate at which gaps in socioeconomic outcomes between demographic groups close.

Especially in countries in which the educational system remains deeply segregated and the quality of public schooling varies widely between neighborhoods, giving all children a chance to develop their talents will also require an urgent commitment to providing consistent access to an excellent education. In the United States, for example, the funding available to schools and the salaries paid to teachers depend, in part, on the amount of tax paid by the local community. This makes it all the more important for states and the federal government to offer supplemental funding to schools in poor districts; students who already suffer from significant disadvantages should have access to the same pedagogical resources and enjoy the same quality of education as those who live in wealthier parts of the country.

It is also worth experimenting with more innovative approaches to boost opportunities for all children. So-called baby bonds, for example, would give young adults starting capital to cover the cost of a quality education or take a risk on an entrepreneurial venture. This could help ensure that the children of the poor as well as those of the rich have a chance to chase their dreams.

For many decades, the left emphasized the need for state programs to be as "universal" as possible. When I went to graduate school, progressive political scientists like Theda Skocpol demonstrated that entitlement programs that benefit virtually all citizens, such as social security, enjoy far greater public support than those that are seen as favoring particular ethnic or economic groups, such as food stamps. Those who wanted to build a generous welfare state capable of giving access to opportunity for all, Skocpol concluded, should promote universal programs.

In recent years, many writers and policy makers on the left have embraced the opposite conclusion. As questions of race have come to the forefront of public discourse, they have increasingly insisted on making public policy "race-conscious." In a wide range of areas, from who should get loans at preferential rates to who should first get access to life-saving vaccines, they have advocated measures that would encourage governments to distinguish between citizens on the basis of their race.

Especially in the United States, politicians have actually started to implement such policies. During the presidential transition, for example, Joe Biden vowed that his administration's "priority will be Black, Latino, Asian, and Native American owned small businesses, women-owned businesses." Once in power, his administration attempted to follow through on the promise. Whereas the Small Business Administration had previously awarded emergency grants in keeping with how much of a business's revenue had been lost because of the pandemic, new rules established a racial pecking order, with those owned by African Americans, Latinos, Asians, and women first. Because funds were limited, this effectively ensured that businesses owned by white men would be excluded from accessing emergency aid under this program.

Given the persistence of serious economic and educational disadvantages for some minority groups, including African Americans, it is easy to empathize with the intentions behind such policies. But it is doubtful that defaulting to policies that explicitly distinguish between citizens of diverse democracies by their race will serve such purposes without doing a lot of harm. The program run by the Small Business Administration, for example, would quickly have led to a series of absurdities. It would have barred black entrepreneurs who had built their own businesses from emergency aid if they happened to have a white spouse who legally owned half of the business. It would have prioritized

Asian business owners over white ones even though Asian Americans now outearn whites. And since it was directed at people who own a business, the policy in any case would have done very little to help those who are most in need. (Thankfully, a federal court held that the new rules violated the constitution.)

This suggests that the reasons progressives have long preferred universal policies still hold. Though race-conscious policies might be justified in rare circumstances, they are usually hard to implement and lead to arbitrary distinctions between applicants. A growing body of evidence suggests that they are also inimical to the kind of universal solidarity diverse democracies need to sustain the welfare state.

In a democracy, race-conscious policies don't just need to improve outcomes to be worth pursuing; they must also attract and sustain majority support. That, too, may prove to be difficult.

In a telling study from the United Kingdom, political scientists Robert Ford and Anouk Kootstra set out to understand "how switching the focus of identical equal opportunities and redistribution policies from class or income to ethnicity influences majority group attitudes." When Ford and Kootstra asked a randomly selected sample of white Britons to what extent they felt it was the government's responsibility to reduce inequalities between the rich and the poor, most respondents were enthusiastic. When they asked another randomly selected sample to what extent the government should "reduce inequalities between whites and ethnic minorities," most respondents were markedly less supportive.

Next, Ford and Kootstra tested what happened when they changed the intended beneficiaries of a set of opportunity-enhancing policies like university scholarships. When these policies were meant to help all working-class children and communities, they commanded almost universal approval—only 3 percent opposed them. When they exclusively targeted disadvantaged ethnic groups, opposition to them skyrocketed. Up to 67 percent now opposed them.

Might the situation look different in the United States, where race-conscious policies have a longer history, and members of ethnic minorities—who were not included in Ford and Kootstra's survey—make up a significantly larger share of the overall population? As a number of similar studies suggests, the answer is likely no.

Many proposals to expand the welfare state now find strong support across the political spectrum. A clear majority of Americans favor higher taxes on the rich, a more generous minimum wage, the introduction of universal pre-K, and a public option for health insurance. But most Americans reject race-conscious policies that are explicitly targeted toward a specific demographic group. As a result, policies that disproportionately help minority communities become far less popular if their goal is explicitly cast in terms of racial equity.

A recent paper by two political scientists at Yale University, for example, found that the same policies bled a lot of support when their goals were rendered in terms of race rather than class. American respondents who were presented with race-neutral justifications for policies like a higher minimum wage, the cancellation of student debt, or more permissive zoning laws largely supported these policies. But when respondents were presented with justifications for the same policies that "explicitly use racial justice framing," opposition to them shot up. Strikingly, these race-based justifications not only made the policies less popular among white respondents; they also decreased support for them among Hispanics, Asian Americans, and (to a more moderate extent) African Americans.

Most citizens of diverse democracies, from France to the United States, are outraged when their compatriots experience discrimination on the basis of their religion or ethnicity. They strongly support policies that protect their most vulnerable compatriots against the great misfortunes of life and give kids from a disadvantaged background an opportunity to rise. When cast in universal terms, public policies that help disadvantaged groups close the socioeconomic gap that still separates them from the majority are very popular—even if they disproportionately benefit members of an ethnic or religious minority.

The alternative to this universal solidarity is explicitly race-conscious policies that frequently fail to live up to their lofty promises. They tend to put different groups into direct competition for key material benefits, pitting them against one another in a zero-sum competition. They often fail to attract the majority support that is needed for a welfare state to be sustainable over time. And at times, they even harm the very people they are supposedly designed to help.

There is every reason to fear that, over the long run, all this could exacerbate the kind of fragmentation that has historically made it so difficult for diverse societies to succeed. Rather than encouraging citizens to recognize one another as compatriots who share common interests, race-conscious policies prime them to regard one another as members of competing teams. Given the strong human tendency toward in-group favoritism and out-group hostility, that does not bode well for the future success of diverse democracies.

Everyone who is invested in the success of the great experiment should be concerned about the deep socioeconomic inequalities that still persist between some demographic groups. But, for the most part, a substantive form of universal solidarity, not race-conscious policies explicitly targeted at particular demographic groups, is the best way to remedy them.

EFFECTIVE AND INCLUSIVE INSTITUTIONS

In the fall of 2005, Silvio Berlusconi, the prime minister of Italy, began to fear for his future.

The latest opinion polls were too close to call. A scattering of left-wing parties looked poised to inch past him in upcoming elections. And for Berlusconi, a fall from office could well culminate in a stint in jail.

Ever since a giant corruption scandal imploded the Italian political system in the early 1990s, the billionaire entrepreneur had faced criminal investigations into his shady business dealings. If Berlusconi failed in his bid for reelection, he would also lose the power to impede court proceedings until the statute of limitations on the many accusations against him ran out.

With his back against the wall, Berlusconi decided to manipulate Italy's electoral system. Less than six months before the next election, he pushed two key changes through parliament on a party-line vote. Convinced that he was popular among Italians who live abroad, he created six new members of the upper chamber who would represent territories outside the country. And since he believed that the right was much more capable of uniting under a common banner than the left, he offered a giant seat bonus in the lower chamber to the coalition of parties that got the largest number of votes.

At the time, commentators agreed that these changes would prove to be a boon to Berlusconi. The minister who drafted the bill publicly admitted that it was a "porcata," a "swinish" maneuver to stay in power. The opposition strenuously opposed the reforms. But when Italians finally went to the polls in April 2006, the outcome took the country by surprise.

Because it won most of the overseas senate races, the opposition eked out a paper-thin majority in the upper chamber. And since the new law had given the bickering factions of the left an added incentive to put aside their differences, the newly created Unione beat Berlusconi's Casa delle Libertà by 49.80 percent to 49.73 percent. Under the new electoral rules, those 24,700 extra votes gave Romano Prodi, the new prime minister, a comfortable majority in the lower house.

Politicians, journalists, and academics often convince themselves that they can predict how changes to a country's political institutions will alter the dynamics of the system and the fate of its main political factions. In many countries, this hubris is currently on rich display. Especially in the United States, a number of scholars and activists are now calling for big changes to the political system that, they confidently predict, would solve the crisis of the country's democratic institutions (or at least help their side win).

Some believe that popular anger at the dysfunctional political system would subside if only the country adopted a form of proportional representation. Others argue that Democrats would finally be able to overcome many of the country's injustices if they were willing to pack the Supreme Court. But, most likely, each of these changes would turn out to have a very different impact than their proponents suggest. Like Silvio Berlusconi—and many other politicians and academics who have dabbled in changing institutions to serve some purpose, noble or selfish—those who believe that they can predict the impact of such reforms will likely turn out to be wrong.

This makes me skeptical of the many radical reform proposals that fail to take into account how people with less than noble intentions might be able to abuse their newly changed institutions. But it is also clear that diverse democracies should have something they now lack in many countries: inclusive political institutions that pay due regard to public opinion. And despite the inevitable risk that they, too, may turn out to have unexpected drawbacks, some more modest institutional reforms should be able to make a worthwhile contribution to redressing those shortcomings.

All around the world, many citizens of democracies feel that their political systems are failing to live up to the core promise advertised in their name: to let the people rule. Far from being in control of their collective fate, they lament, they are barely able to influence the direction of their governments.

There are many reasons for this widely shared sentiment. In Europe, for example, it stems from the highly indirect way in which the European Union makes decisions. In the United States, meanwhile, it is partially owed to the many veto powers that make it so difficult to pass legislation.

It will not be easy to solve any of these problems. But a few changes do suggest themselves.

The European project remains an inspiring attempt to overcome the narrow nationalism that shaped the continent, and the world, in the first half of the twentieth century. But European institutions often fail to live up to the noble ideals that motivated their founding. To reduce the EU's democratic deficit, member states should expand the powers of the European Parliament. But even if the powers of the parliament were to be strengthened, Brussels would continue to feel very remote to most Europeans. The block should therefore return decision-making power on some key issues, especially in the social and cultural realm, to the national level.

The United States, meanwhile, suffers from a political system that makes it more difficult for a law to pass than that of just about any other democracy in the world. To take effect, a legislative proposal needs to garner a majority in the House of Representatives, a super-majority in the Senate, the approval of the president, and the (tacit or explicit) assent of the Supreme Court.

In many ways, this intricate system of checks and balances has served the country well. It is, for example, right that the Supreme Court should be able to overrule Congress or the president when they infringe on basic rights guaranteed in the Constitution. But to maintain the bipartisan support it needs to safeguard the rights of the most vulnerable when it really counts, the court should also become much more reluctant to get drawn into big debates about public policy from health insurance to campaign finance.

While the Supreme Court and the presidency have vastly expanded their powers, Congress has become less and less influential, making it more difficult for a minority of senators to block ordinary legislation from passing may help to reverse this trend. But other, less hotly de-bated changes are likely to make as big a difference. In keeping with the informal "Hastert Rule," for example, the Speaker of the House now refuses to bring bills up for debate unless a majority of his or her own members supports it; this effectively ensures the death of many proposals that would be broadly popular in the nation at large. It is time for Congress to make this and other necessary changes to put power back in the hands of elected representatives.

A reform of the electoral system may also help to temper the polarization that makes it so hard for Congress to get anything done. Maine, for example, allows voters to rank candidates by their order of preference, making it possible for them to support their favorite candidate without having to worry about "wasting" their vote if he or she is unlikely to garner strong support. In California, meanwhile, the two candidates who win the largest number of votes in a nonpartisan "jungle primary" now face each other in the general election, irrespective of their party affiliation. Both reforms can give politicians an incentive to appeal beyond their traditional base.

There is also another specifically American problem. Because the country is the oldest democracy in the world, its system for administering elections is now in many ways outdated and continues to bear the mark of past forms of hard domination. This creates many present injustices.

Though the American founders rebelled against the idea of having to pay taxation without enjoying representation, the country continues to exclude some of its citizens from full political participation on the basis of their location. To live up to its core democratic principles, the United States should grant statehood to the residents of the District of Columbia and (if its inhabitants wish) Puerto Rico. Meanwhile, the voice of many citizens throughout the fifty states of the union is diluted because they live in "gerrymandered" constituencies that aim to give one party a partisan advantage or to ensure the existence of majority-minority districts. In keeping with the practice of most other democracies, the

United States should entrust nonpartisan commissions with drawing the boundaries of electoral districts according to neutral criteria, such as geographic contiguity.

Other citizens are targeted on the basis of their race. Democracies have a legitimate interest in enforcing the security of elections. But many Republicans invoke such concerns as an insincere excuse for laws that are designed to suppress voter turnout by minority voters who are more likely to support the Democratic Party. The principled way to put an end to such attacks on voting rights is to bring the administration of American elections closer into line with that of other developed democracies around the world. This would include provisions like automatic voter registration, a greater number of voting locations, free and easy access to secure ID cards, and sensible precautions that curb voter fraud.

But the most urgent threat to a free and fair vote in the United States is rather more novel. After Donald Trump falsely claimed that the outcome of the 2020 election was fraudulent, Republican legislators in a significant number of states have passed laws that give elected politicians a much greater role in certifying the outcome of elections. This raises the risk that they may overrule nonpartisan electoral officials and falsely claim that their preferred presidential candidate has won a key battleground state like Arizona—potentially leading to a terrifying constitutional crisis or an election that really is stolen. To ensure that the outcome of future elections is respected, these laws urgently need to be repealed.

Institutional reforms can help to make diverse democracies more responsive to the preferences of their voters. But it is also incumbent on politicians to be sensitive to the views of their constituents. And there is one area of public policy in which citizens are especially likely to feel that their elected representatives refuse to listen to them: immigration.

Citizens in virtually every democracy have a preference for strong control over their borders. And while five out of every ten respondents in a recent poll of the citizens of developed democracies said that they wanted to reduce the number of immigrants who can move to their countries, only one out of ten preferred to increase that number. (In part because of widespread revulsion at Donald Trump's attacks on immigrants, the United States has in recent years been one of the few exceptions. But even there, the public was less happy with Joe Biden's handling of the southern border than with his performance on any other area of public policy after his first hundred days in office.)

This puts advocates of diverse democracies in a difficult spot. They are deeply committed to the humane treatment of immigrants. Many also believe that high levels of immigration offer more benefits than drawbacks. At the same time, they are—or should be—committed to the democratic ideal of deferring to the persistent and resounding views of the majority. And as the past decade has made painfully clear, moderate or progressive politicians who ignore their voters' preferences over immigration risk feeding a populist backlash liable to undermine their core values in an even more fundamental manner.

So what kind of immigration policies should advocates of diverse democracies favor?

The basic principles of liberal democracy make it impermissible to discriminate between different citizens on the basis of their religion or ethnicity: members of minority groups need to enjoy the same rights and protections as those who belong to the majority. But this does not mean that liberal democracies cannot legitimately determine the number of, or the requirements for, the people they wish to admit in the future. There is nothing inherently illegitimate about limiting access to membership in a country for those who do not already live there.

In practice, each country will have to decide which immigrants to admit on such varied criteria as its historical self-understanding, its geographic location, and its economic needs. The United States of America is, for good reason, likely to adopt immigration policies that differ from those of Sweden, and Sweden is in turn likely to adopt policies that differ from those of Japan. But one broad principle is likely to be helpful to policy makers in all these different contexts.

There appears to be a tight empirical link between border enforcement and public views of immigration. Roughly speaking, countries that have weakened their determination to control their own borders have seen attitudes toward immigration turn more hostile. By contrast, countries that have strengthened their control over their own borders have seen citizens grow more welcoming of immigration. Counterintuitively, those who hope to persuade their compatriots of the benefits of relatively high levels of immigration have good reason to demonstrate that they are capable of exercising real control over who enters the country.

MUTUAL RESPECT

Many democracies around the world have become much more politically polarized in recent years. Rather than seeing other politicians and their supporters as mere adversaries, a growing number of people decry them as enemies or even traitors. The mutual respect that many voters once had for each other is fraying at a dangerous speed.

The rise of populist politicians who denounce their opponents as corrupt or illegitimate is the most important proximate cause for this new era of polarization. But in many countries, its roots lie in a deeper social and cultural divorce between the urban and the rural, the rich and the poor, the highly educated and everybody else.

In postwar America, some of the key identities by which most people defined themselves tended to cut against one another. Lutherans might have been wary of Buddhists, and Democrats of Republicans. But in Lutheran churches and Buddhist temples, there would have been both Democrats and Republicans. Even as any two Americans were divided by some salient social characteristics, they were likely to share others.

Today, the most salient social divides increasingly reinforce one another. Lutherans are now very likely to be Republican and Buddhists to be Democrat. Increasingly, Americans are sorting into two mutually hostile blocks, or "supergroups." If two Americans are divided by one socially salient identity, they are also likely to be divided by a second and a third and a fourth.

The racial polarization of American politics renders this state of affairs even more dangerous. Many voters don't just feel that their political values or partisan loyalties are under threat when the other side wins; they also fear that their compatriots have voted to disrespect their ethnic or racial group.

It is easy to imagine all kinds of reforms and policies that might help to counteract the dangerous polarization of American society. Politicians have an urgent responsibility to appeal to demographic groups that have not traditionally supported their party in great numbers. And reforms to the electoral system might help to give politicians concrete incentives to reach out beyond their base.

Other policies might make a worthwhile contribution as well. Some idealistic reformers, for example, seek to establish a kind of domestic Peace Corps program, allowing young people to get to know very different communities within their own country. Others have called for schools to recommit to a form of civics education that emphasizes the enduring ideals of liberal democracy without airbrushing their countries' serious injustices out of existence. Others still emphasize the importance for elite institutions to be on their guard against turning into an ideological monoculture so as to ensure that the decision makers of the future don't look upon half their compatriots with derision or disdain.

But all these policies and prescriptions are likely to pale in comparison to the scale of the challenge. And so the most important battlefield for how to cultivate some modicum of mutual respect and avoid the formation of two diametrically opposed supergroups is not political; it is social and even personal.

As polarization in many democracies intensifies, and extremists attempt to poison the tone of the public debate, there is a growing temptation to turn politics into a Manichean struggle between "us" and "them." Whether this dangerous development can take hold, shaping what life in diverse democracies will look like, depends on the kind of arguments each citizen makes, cheers, and tolerates. This is why we should all, as best as possible, resolve to hold ourselves—as well as our friends, relatives, and compatriots—to three basic maxims:

1. *Stick to Your Principles*: The more polarized a country gets, the easier it becomes to outsource one's own thinking to one's greatest enemies. Instead of relying on their own commitments to assess a situation, a frightening number of people now seem content to look at the positions of those they most disdain and embrace the opposite point of view. But, shrewd though this may seem, the precept that my enemy's enemy is my friend is strategically stupid because it allows those who have the most reason to harm you to define what you believe and who you embrace. More importantly, it is normatively disastrous because it lures you into a view of the world in which everybody must be either wholly good or wholly bad, forever forcing you to make excuses for the lesser evil. So the only way to make real political progress remains what it has always been: to apply your own standards in a consistent manner.

2. *Be Willing to Criticize Your Own*: One of the difficulties with sticking to your own principles is that it will sometimes require you to criticize people who are on your side. And whenever you dare to point out that some of the people who are usually on your team may have gotten the wrong end of some important stick, you are likely to be accused of committing the sin of looking for equal fault with "both sides." But if those who see themselves as being on the right side of history avoid criticizing members of their own team for fear of being seen to downplay the sins of the other side, it will become impossible for them to hold the worst instincts of their own group in check. In this way, the charge of both-siderism raises

the cost for internal critique, allowing the most immoral and cynical members of each coalition to go unchallenged. That is why you should remain willing to criticize your own even when you believe the sins committed by your side to be far less grave than those committed by your political adversaries.

3. *Don't Ridicule or Vilify; Engage and Persuade*: Far too much of the debate about the future of diverse democracies consists in attempts to ridicule or vilify rather than to engage or persuade. Instead of denouncing each other, we should enter into a real debate about the kind of country we seek to build. For our ultimate ambition should not be to score rhetorical points or win the next election but rather to rally as many of our compatriots to the cause of the great experiment as possible.

As citizens of democratic countries, we do, collectively, hold a lot of political power—and have a corresponding obligation to make our voices heard in moments of crisis. It's incumbent on us to vote for parties that are committed to making the great experiment succeed, to advocate for policies that would realize the promise of diverse democracy, and of course to protest when governments target minorities or deepen discrimination.

And yet to all but the most extreme politics junkies, the explicitly political field of battle will often feel very remote. The question likely to interest them is not how to impact the next election or bring about large changes in public policy but rather how to boost the cause of diverse democracy through concrete steps they can take in their own lives.

A large part of the answer to this question lies in the personal realm.

The project of making diverse democracy thrive is the project of building a meaningfully shared life. It is therefore more likely to succeed if we build deeper connections, empathy, and solidarity between different groups—and that ultimately depends on the millions of small choices we collectively take about where to invest our time and energy.

The best thing you can do to advance the lived reality of a thriving diverse democracy is, quite simply, to get out of your own bubble. Seek out opportunities to build bridges to members of other groups. Look for more diverse groups of friends and acquaintances. Become active in charities or interfaith organizations. Invite your neighbors over for coffee or organize a block party. Spend a little less time arguing about the state of diverse democracy and a lot more time modeling the future you seek.

CONCLUSION

Much of the world is setting out for uncharted territory.

All through human history, some societies have been characterized by ethnic and religious diversity. Virtually all of them subjugated minorities in cruel ways, suffered from structured anarchy, or had to contend with the effects of deep fragmentation. Only a handful were democratic—and even those barely pretended to offer their members true equality.

In some diverse democracies, like the United States, an explicit scheme of domination excluded members of an ethnic underclass from the most basic rights and liberties enjoyed by the majority. In other countries, including much of Europe, an implicit scheme of domination turned immigrants and their descendants into second-class citizens or permanent "guests." The stability of these democracies was, to a significant degree, purchased by the exclusion of millions of people.

Only one kind of polity has, in the long annals of human history, been conspicuous by its absence: a democracy that grants true equality to a highly diverse set of citizens. And yet dozens of countries around the world are now attempting to construct such a society.

That is *The Great Experiment*. Can it possibly succeed?

The last decade has made it tempting to answer this question in the negative.

When I arrived in the United States, the first black presidential candidate with a realistic chance of moving into the White House was running on a message of hope and change. When Barack Obama was duly elected the forty-fourth president of the United States, many commentators declared that the country was about to enter a "post-racial future."

In the following years, it quickly became obvious that such predictions had been hopelessly naive. The Great Recession took an especially heavy toll on the economic standing of minority groups. Opposition to the country's first black president increasingly focused on a conspiracy theory about his place of birth. The spread of cell phones with video cameras made visible the extent of police brutality against African Americans.

Inspired to take a closer look at their own practices, many people and institutions that prided themselves on their own tolerance started to recognize how frequently they, too, had failed to live up to their ideals. When I lived in New York as an exchange student at Columbia, I was impressed by how diverse both the city and the university were. The longer I stayed in America, the more I recognized that even self-consciously inclusive institutions like Ivy League universities remained structured along racial lines. Black students were much more likely to sit next to other black students, and white students to be friends with other white students.

Then the bad news turned worse. Donald Trump became the forty-fifth president of the United States by belittling members of minority groups and questioning the legitimacy of his predecessor. Authoritarian populists in some of the most powerful and populous democracies of the world, from Brazil to India, pulled off similar upsets. Their success makes painfully clear how high the stakes of the great experiment are. If diverse democracies should fail, their most vulnerable members will be subjected to unspeakable cruelty—and even those who escape the worst injustices because they are part of the dominant group will be in danger of losing their democratic rights.

The setbacks of the past decade have inspired two responses that now vie for dominance in much of the mainstream debate about the future of diverse democracies.

The first consists of unadulterated pessimism. Countries like the United Kingdom or the United States, many of their most self-critical citizens believe, have always been characterized by enormous injustices and are unlikely to experience significant improvements in the future. Socially dominant groups will always find a way to cling to power and avoid the indignity of being treated, merely, as an equal. The future of diverse democracy looks bleak.

The second response is rooted in the premise that diverse democracies are characterized by a fundamental battle between different identity groups. In North America and Western Europe, this has, historically, allowed members of the white majority to subjugate everyone else. But since the balance of demographic forces is now shifting, the future is likely to look very different. One day soon, the formerly subjugated shall supposedly inherit the earth.

From the perspective of overcoming historical injustices, the second prediction seems to look more promising. But the closer you look, the more dystopian it turns out to be. For it, too, assumes that different members of diverse democracies will forever look at one another as something more akin to enemies than fellow citizens.

That's why it's time to recommit to a more ambitious vision for the future of diverse democracies. If the great experiment is to be truly successful, it must offer a realistic account of human nature and be honest about the injustices of the past. But it must also be unapologetically sanguine about the possibility that members of different groups can pull together to build fair and thriving democracies whose members share a sense of common purpose.

———

Humans are groupish.

We are wired to distinguish between those who count as "one of us" and those who are "one of them." How we treat others strongly depends on the category into which they fall. Even people who are no more moral than average often treat members of their in-group with real consideration and generosity. And even people who are no more immoral than average can, under the wrong circumstances, treat members of an out-group with stunning disregard or cruelty.

Humanity's groupish nature has plenty of advantages. It is the reason the world does not resemble the war of all against all that so terrified Thomas Hobbes. It facilitates humans' distinctive ability to cooperate with each other on a massive scale. It is implicated in all the biggest wonders of civilization, from beautiful religious temples to moving symphony concerts.

But our groupish nature is also responsible for many of history's most bitter tragedies and injustices. It explains how god-fearing people can slaughter infidels in good conscience and why highly civilized human beings might wish to kill members of another race by the use of bombers or bayonets.

Faced with history's rich parade of horrors, many people understandably despair for their country, their culture, their race. "How could *we* have done such terrible things?" they ask. Often, the answers they identify have to do with the specific attributes of their group. They point to the darkest chapters of their history, to the most noxious prejudices that pervade their culture, or to the dangerous tendency of some of their own compatriots to see themselves as members of a superior race.

These laments are usually right insofar as they go. Most countries really do have shameful chapters in their histories. And for the most part, those chapters really do have roots in long-standing features of the societies in which they took place. Occasions for shame are rich, the need for commemoration real.

But precisely because the human capacity for evil is so universal, these answers leave out something just as important. In history, war and slaughter, oppression and subordination are closer to the norm than the exception. Societies that have never inflicted injustices usually owe their superior moral status to a lack of opportunity rather than a surfeit of moral virtue. If you want to corrupt a group, history suggests, you have but to bestow great power upon it.

Any attempt to understand one instance of horror in abstraction from all the others will, then, lead to conclusions that are at best partial. The great historical puzzle is not why some societies have been capable of doing terrible things; virtually all of them have. It is why

other societies have at times done a little better—and how they might
be able to keep improving.

Compared with the long sweep of human history, what is striking
about the current state of France or Japan, Australia or the United
States is not so much the things these societies continue to get wrong,
real and maddening though they are; it is what they get right.

Most diverse democracies around the world are vastly more just and
inclusive today than they were fifty or a hundred years ago. The United
States has abolished slavery, granted African Americans civil rights, and
adopted far more inclusive views and practices in areas ranging from
cultural representation to interracial marriage. European countries like
Germany and Spain have rejected fascism, broadened their conception
of who truly belongs in their societies, and started to embrace an everyday culture that is deeply diverse. Even comparatively homogeneous
democracies like Japan have in recent decades become a little more willing to see members of other cultures as equals and accept immigrants
as compatriots.

A fair assessment of these countries' current condition needs to feature the good alongside the bad. Today's America is characterized both
by a serious problem of police violence and by the millions of people
who protested it in the midst of a deadly pandemic. Today's Germany
is marked both by the resurgence of a scary far-right movement and by
the millions of people who have seriously grappled with the country's
Nazi past. Today's Japan is characterized both by prime ministers who
honor the graves of war criminals and by attitudes toward immigrants
and minorities that are gradually becoming more welcoming. And in
all these countries, members of minority groups and descendants of

immigrants are rapidly climbing the economic and educational ranks, occupying positions of higher prestige than their parents or grandparents thought possible.

It is common for writers to deemphasize the positive side of the ledger. Going on about progress when so many things remain far from perfect, they worry, will be seen as a form of quietism; perhaps they might even be accused of seeking to preserve persistent injustices by downplaying their severity. But this is to misunderstand why progress matters. The point of being as forthright about the good as the bad is not to soothe anybody's conscience; it is to give us the courage we need to fight for a better future—and show us how to do so successfully.

Advocates of diverse democracies need the courage and confidence to take the fight to their detractors.

From Europe to America, and from Asia to Australia, there are still a lot of people who believe that we must abandon the great experiment before it is too late. Immigration and ethnic diversity, they claim, bring few benefits and a lot of problems. The best course of action is to limit or end the arrival of newcomers—and make it clear to those outsiders who are already in the country that the historically dominant group will always call the shots. If somebody doesn't like that, they can leave.

To win the fight against these detractors, those of us who are committed to diverse democracies need to embrace a confident vision of a better future. The various horror scenarios beloved by enemies of diverse democracies are unlikely to come true. Contrary to what they say, our countries are capable of integrating newcomers, of building a common bond with people who do not share the same race or religion, and of embracing new national narratives. The future need not consist of a pitched battle between different demographic groups.

But to make that case convincingly, the advocates of diverse democracy will also have to keep in check the pessimists in their own midst. For some of the loudest voices in the debate now claim that race and religion will forever separate the citizens of diverse democracies to such an extent that they are barely able to understand one another. Society, in their vision, will forever be characterized by a clash between the historically dominant and the historically oppressed, or between whites and "people of color." Even thirty or sixty years from now, race will remain the defining attribute of residents of diverse democracies.

Such a vision of the future is unlikely to sustain the political solidarity we need to overcome historical injustices. Instead of growing the resolve of those who care about the fate of the great experiment, it inadvertently validates the fears of its most devoted detractors. It would be both a moral and a strategic mistake to settle for such a cynical vision of the future.

Thankfully, there is a better alternative. Defenders of diverse democracies should aim for a society in which as many citizens as possible feel that they are embarking on a meaningfully shared life. While they should never be naive about the difficulty of understanding those who come from different ethnic or religious groups, they should trust their ability to build a future in which most citizens come to regard one another as compatriots to whom they owe empathy and consideration. Most importantly, they must aim to construct diverse democracies in which racial markers become less important over time—not because their citizens blind themselves to the extent to which these now shape societies around the world but rather because they have managed to overcome the injustices they still inspire.

Of late, I've spent a lot of time listening to the songs of Manu Chao.

There is something compellingly joyous about his music. His is the sort of beat that helps get you out of bed in the morning, the sort of sound you want to have playing on a road trip. During the isolated months of the global pandemic—months during which the compelled loneliness of the shutdowns was, in my case, deepened by the self-imposed discipline required to write a book—I found myself comforted by its promise of adventure to come in the near future.

But there is, I now realize, also a deeper reason why I have found myself drawn to albums like *Próxima Estación: Esperanza* (Next Station: Hope). They remind me of a faith in the existence of a common humanity and the compassion required to recognize it that have recently become all too rare.

Manu Chao was born in France, in 1961, the son of Spanish parents who had fled the fascist dictatorship of Francisco Franco. He grew up in the highly diverse suburbs of Paris, soaking up cultural influences from across Europe, Africa, the Caribbean, and the Middle East. His politics are not at all mine (though my fifteen-year-old self would, probably, have agreed with him on just about everything). While I believe in the virtues of liberal democracy, he has a long history of supporting insurrectionist movements.

And yet there is something in his style and his songs that I savor. Chao's music is a kind of patchwork. It bears the influence of a wide variety of genres, from punk to salsa, from French folklore to Jamaican ska. He and his collaborators sing in a bewildering array of different languages, from Spanish to English to Arabic to Wolof. His is the sound of encounter, of mutual cultural influence, of people from different countries clashing and, together, creating the world anew.

This does not mean that Manu Chao's songs are silent about the difficulties and injustices that many members of diverse democracies face. Much of *Clandestino*, his first album, is told in the voice of illegal immigrants who have to contend with the indifference of the people they encounter. On the album's second song, "Desaparecido," he vividly describes the predicament of a street vendor who has to flee whenever he spots the police, making a touching plea to see him as, simply, human:

> They call me the one who's disappearing
> A phantasma that never stays
> They call me the one who's profiteering
> But that doesn't express the truth
> In my body, I carry a pain
> That doesn't let me breathe
> In my body, I carry a sentence
> That always makes me leave.

These lines encapsulate much of the cultural message of Manu Chao's albums, and of a whole humanistic thought world that can now feel disturbingly anachronistic. For all the flaws it had then, and for all the ways in which the past decades make additional amendments to it inescapable, I believe that it would be a grave mistake to abandon it altogether.

Appeals to our common humanity, even when accompanied by a catchy tune, will only do so much good. "Desaparecido" can no more show us a realistic recipe for how to build diverse democracies than "Kumbaya" or "We Are the World."

Even so, I believe that there is something in the spirit of Manu Chao's songs that is worth recovering. It expresses a faith in a shared humanity and its ability to inspire empathy that was once dominant in much of the mainstream. And that is an optimistic vision for our ability to build better societies, and relate to each other as equals, that is far more attractive than the various dystopias peddled by the pessimists who now dominate the discourse.

Constructing diverse democracies that command the enthusiastic consent of the great majority of their citizens is going to be hard. We really have embarked on an unprecedented experiment. It really might fail. But if those of us who are committed to its values want to maximize its chances of success, we need to have the courage to paint the vision of a shared future that most people would actually want to live in—one in which as many people as possible conceive of themselves as proud and optimistic citizens of diverse democracies, choosing to emphasize what we have in common rather than what divides us.

Let's get to it.

ACKNOWLEDGMENTS

If it takes a village to raise a child, it takes an international republic of letters to write a book. That is probably why I have always found sitting down to write acknowledgments to be both a humbling and an anxiety-inducing experience: humbling because you realize just how much gratitude you owe to how many, some of it impossible to put in words or fully repay, and anxiety-inducing because it is impossible not to feel that you are leaving someone important out (and usually do).

My first and my deepest thanks go to Penguin Press, one of the world's great publishing houses, and the home of so many authors I admire. I am very grateful to Ann Godoff and Scott Moyers for taking on this project, to Natalie Coleman for excellent and patient editorial support throughout the process, to Mia Council and Elizabeth Furlong for generous comments on an early draft, and to Elisabeth Calamari, Shina Patel, and so many others on the team for doing an amazing job in making sure that the book reaches the attention of readers like you.

Many writer friends complain about the long weeks—or sometimes the long months—between when they send a book manuscript to their editor and when they get any kind of response. With Scott, I may, once or twice, have complained about the opposite. After finishing a full draft and sending it off to him, I looked forward to forgetting about the book for a few weeks, only to find detailed and insightful comments in my inbox within a few days. This book is both a lot stronger and a lot more subtle thanks to

Scott's guidance, and I am extremely grateful to have him on board as my intellectual companion for future projects.

I am also incredibly grateful to my international publishers for helping to make sure that this book finds an international audience. Special thanks goes to Alexis Kirschbaum, Mari Yamazaki, Jasmine Horsey, and Anna Massardi at Bloomsbury; to Muriel Beyer, Adèle van Reeth, Severine Courtaud, and Jeanne de Saint-Hilaire at Editions L'Observatoire; to Margit Ketterle, Thomas Blanck, Esther von Bruchhausen, and Johannes Schermaul at Droemer, as well as to the teams at *Feltrinelli*, *Paidos*, *Companhia*, *Het Spectrum* and *Prostor*, among others.

When I was trying to figure out what to write as a follow-up to *People vs Democracy*, Molly Atlas patiently pushed me toward more ambition and higher conceptual ground. I will forever remain grateful for her guidance, wisdom, and calm. Thanks are also due to Claire Nozières and Karolina Sutton for helping to place this manuscript with wonderful publishers outside the United States.

Since January 2019, my academic home has been at Johns Hopkins University. I am deeply grateful to Ron Daniels for bringing me to Homewood and for his principled leadership of the university. It is very exciting to be part of the SNF Agora Institute, a new institute devoted to renewing democracy at home and abroad, and I am especially grateful to its inaugural director, Hahrie Han, as well as to Stephen Ruckman, Elizabeth Smyth, Catherine Pierre, and Kristine Wait. I am also grateful to Eliot Cohen, Jim Steinberg, Vali Nasr, Kent Calder, Andrew Mertha, Miji Bell, and Julie Micek at the School of Advanced International Studies, and to countless wonderful and inspiring faculty colleagues on both campuses, for making me feel so at home at the university.

I am also incredibly lucky to have joined a wonderful community of thinkers and scholars at the Council on Foreign Relations. I am especially indebted to Richard Haass, James Lindsay, and Shannon O'Neil, as well as two anonymous peer reviewers, for their perceptive and thorough comments on an earlier version of this manuscript; both their suggestions and their criticisms were immensely useful during the revision process. I am also very grateful for everybody who made me feel so welcome in the Fellows Program, or helped shepherd *The Great Experiment* through the CFR Books process, including Amy Baker, Patricia Lee Dorff, Lisa Shields, Shira Schwartz, Anya Schmemann, Aliya Medetbekova, David Gevarter, and Gideon Weiss. Gideon Rose and Daniel Kurtz-Phelan, both excellent leaders of *Foreign Affairs*, have helped sharpen my ideas about public policy and international politics, to the great benefit of this book. Finally, this book is part of the Diamonstein-Spielvogel Project on the Future of Democracy; I am tremendously grateful to Dr. Barbaralee Diamonstein-Spielvogel and the late Ambassador Carl Spielvogel for their generous support.

For the last years, I have been lucky to be able to develop my ideas about this topic—and so much else besides—in the pages of *The Atlantic*, the most vibrant and intellectually diverse magazine in America today. My thanks go to Jeff Goldberg and Yoni Appelbaum for putting their trust in me, to Juliet Lapidos for being an excellent and exacting editor, and to so many other wonderful colleagues and editors who have sharpened my thinking about the world over the course of the last years.

For the past two years, I have had the great pleasure to lead and edit *Persuasion*, a magazine and community fighting for the liberal ideals to whose defense this book, too, is devoted. I am especially grateful to David Hamburger, without whose counsel, reliability, and skilled leadership I would never have found the time to complete this book; to Seth Moskowitz and Luke Hallam, two excellent young editors who will go far; to Rob Stein, Mike Berkowitz, and Rachel Pritzker, the best advisors any philanthropic organization could wish for; to Sahil Handa, who was part of the project from the very first hour; to Moisés Naím and Emily Yoffe, whose editorial guidance has been invaluable; as well as to Eleni Arzoglou, Anne Bagamery, Thomas Chatterton Williams, Martin Eiermann, Bea Frum, Samantha Holmes, Nat Rachman, Tom Rachman, Rebecca Rashid, Brendan

Ruberry, John Taylor Williams, and the members of *Persuasion*'s Board of Advisors.

I have been extremely lucky to have the assistance of a number of excellent research assistants while preparing this manuscript. Megan Rutkai was of immense help in assembling secondary literature and summarizing scholarly debates in the early stages of research. David Gevarter was very helpful with research on far-flung places and bibliographical assistance. Brittin Alfred, to whom I owe the biggest thanks, was incredibly resourceful in everything from intellectually demanding research to more mundane tasks like fact-checking the book and putting the footnotes in order.

An extraordinary number of friends and collaborators have taken the time to read this manuscript or the book proposal in an early version, or to help shape my thoughts about this topic during in-depth conversations. They include Anne Applebaum, Ian Bassin, A. B., Sheri Berman, Larry Diamond, Martin Eiermann, Roberto Foa, David Frum, Francis Fukuyama, Jonathan Haidt, David Hamburger, Samantha Hill, C. M., Henry Midgley, David Miliband, Russ Muirhead, Michael Lind, George Packer, David Plunkett, Nancy Rosenblum, Bernardo Zacka, and Dan Ziblatt.

But my biggest debt goes to those who went far beyond the call of duty to give me advice, again and again, on everything from how to phrase a particular point to how to conceive of this project. Shira Telushkin was indefatigable in offering me concrete suggestions for how to improve the manuscript during the final revision process. Sam Koppelman has read innumerable drafts of every iteration of this project. And Andrew Wylie has been a fierce advocate and wonderful advisor on all matters literary, big and small.

Finally, my most personal thanks goes to the friends and family members who have kept me sane through these strange past few years, including Thierry Artzner, Eleni Arzoglou, Matteo Borselli, Thomas Chatterton Williams, Guillermo del Pinal, Alex Drukier, N. G., Helena Hessel, Samantha Holmes, Tom Meaney, Alicja Mounk, Carl Schoonover, and William Seward.

NOTES

Introduction

1 **sat down for a live interview:** *Tagesthemen*, February 20, 2018. Aired at 22:15. Link to interview: https://www.tagesschau.de/multimedia/sendung/tt-5821.html. Time stamp: 24:45.

2 **"Who agreed to this experiment?":** "Das hatte die Redaktion der Tagesthemen nicht geplant," *Tichys Einblick*, February 22, 2018, https://www.tichyseinblick.de/daili-es-sentials/das-hatte-die -redaktion-der-tagesthemen-nicht-geplant.

3 **Finally, the word reached *The Daily Stormer*:** "Daily Stormer: Cloudflare Drops Neo-Nazi Site," BBC, August 17, 2017, https://www.bbc.com/news/technology-40960053.

3 **Putting my name in triple brackets:** Andrew Anglin, "(((Yascha Mounk)))'s 'Unique Historical Experiment': Transforming a Mono-Ethnic Country into a Multi-Ethnic One," *The Daily Stormer*, February 23, 2018, https://dailystormer.su/yascha-mounks-unique-historical-experiment -transforming-a-mono-ethnic-mono-cultural-democracy-into-a-multi-ethnic-one.

3 **Invoking Arbeit Macht Frei:** Anglin, "Yascha Mounk's 'Unique Historical Experiment.'"

3 **In one sense, an experiment:** "Experiment," Lexico, accessed June 6, 2021, https://www.lexico .com/en/definition/experiment.

4 **affiliation with elite institutions:** At the time of the interview, I was a lecturer in Harvard University's Department of Government.

4 **"a course of action tentatively adopted":** "Experiment," Lexico.

4 **a "long train of abuses":** "Creating the United States," Library of Congress, accessed June 6, 2021, https://www.loc.gov/exhibits/creating-the-united-states/interactives/declaration-of-independence /abuses/index.html.

7 **At the end of World War II:** Keith Lowe, "Five Times Immigration Changed the UK," BBC, January 20, 2020, https://www.bbc.com/news/uk-politics-51134644.

7 **Today, it is one in seven:** See "Migrants in the UK: An Overview," The Migration Observatory, University of Oxford, November 6, 2020, https://migrationobservatory.ox.ac.uk/resources/brief ings/migrants-in-the-uk-an-overview; and Lowe, "Five Times Immigration Changed the UK."

7 **Now one in five Swedish residents:** "Foreign-Born Population," OECD Data, 2016–2019, accessed September 24, 2021, https://data.oecd.org/migration/foreign-born-population.htm.

8 **In Germany and Switzerland:** Bill Wirtz, "The German Economic Miracle Depended on Immigrants," Foundation for Economic Education, March 28, 2018, https://fee.org/articles/the -german-economic-miracle-depended-on-immigrants; and Switzerland: Thomas Liebig et al.,

"The Labour Market Integration of Immigrants and Their Children in Switzerland," OECD Social, Employment and Migration Working Paper No. 128: Directorate for Employment, Labour and Social Affairs, OECD Publishing, 2012, https://www.oecd.org/migration/49654710.pdf.

8 **In France and the United Kingdom:** Erik Bleich, "Colonization and Immigrant Integration in Britain and France," *Theory and Society* 34, no. 2 (April 2005): 171–95, https://www.jstor.org/stable/4501720?seq=1.

8 **In Denmark and Sweden, generous asylum laws:** On Denmark, see Ulf Hedetoft, "Denmark: Integrating Immigrants into a Homogenous Welfare State," *Migration Policy Institute.* November 1, 2006. https://www.migrationpolicy.org/article/denmark-integrating-immigrants-homogeneous -welfare-state, and Arno Tanner, "Overwhelmed by Refugee Flows, Scandinavia Tempers Its Warm Welcome." *Migration Policy Institute,* February 10, 2016. On Sweden, see Bernd Parusel, "Sweden's U-Turn on Asylum." *Forced Migration Review,* no. 52 (2016): 89–90, *ProQuest,* https://www .proquest.com/scholarly-journals/swedens-u-turn-on-asylum/docview/1790567102/se-2?accoun tid=11752, and James Traub, "The Death of the Most Generous Nation on Earth." *Foreign Policy,* February 10, 2016, https://foreignpolicy.com/2016/02/10/the-death-of-the-most-generous-nation -on-earth-sweden-syria-refugee-europe.

9 **When the peculiarly cruel institution:** The Emancipation Proclamation effectively ended slavery in much of the United States two years earlier, in 1863. But it was not until the ratification of the Thirteenth Amendment, in 1865, that the process of abolishing it was finally complete in the whole of the country.

9 **But as the backlash to Reconstruction:** For a classic history of the promise and ultimate failure of reconstruction, see Eric Foner, *Reconstruction: America's Unfinished Revolution 1863–1877,* rev. ed. (New York: HarperPerennial, 2014).

9 **When Chinese laborers:** Kevin Allen Leonard, "'Is That What We Fought For?' Japanese Americans and Racism in California, the Impact of World War II," *The Western Historical Quarterly* 21, no. 4 (November 1990): 463–82, https://doi.org/10.2307/969251.

9 **Starting in 1875:** As Congressman Horace F. Page, the sponsor of one key bill, made clear, its primary purpose was to "end the danger of cheap Chinese labor and immoral Chinese women." George Anthony Peffer, "Forbidden Families: Emigration Experiences of Chinese Women Under the Page Law, 1875–1882," *Journal of American Ethnic History* 6, no. 1 (1986): 28, https://www .jstor.org/stable/27500484. Less than a decade later, the Chinese Exclusion Act extended this partial ban to all Chinese immigrants. See "Immigration and Relocation in U.S. History: Legislative Harassment," Library of Congress, accessed September 24, 2021, https://www.loc.gov/classroom -materials/immigration/chinese/legislative-harassment, and "Chinese Exclusion Act," *Encyclopaedia Britannica,* accessed September 24, 2021, https://www.britannica.com/topic/Chinese-Exclusion -Act.

9 **Laws passed in the 1920s:** See "Modern Immigration Wave Brings 59 Million to U.S., Driving Population Growth and Change through 2065—Chapter 1: The Nation's Immigration Laws, 1920 to Today," Pew Research Center, September 28, 2015, https://www.pewresearch.org/his panic/2015/09/28/chapter-1-the-nations-immigration-laws-1920-to-today, and "The Immigration Act of 1924 (The Johnson-Reed Act)," US State Department: Office of the Historian, accessed September 24, 2021, https://history.state.gov/milestones/1921-1936/immigration-act.

9 **Only in 1965:** "Modern Immigration Wave Brings 59 Million to U.S.," Pew Research Center.

9 **"It will not reshape the structure":** Lyndon B. Johnson, "Remarks at the Signing of the Immigration Bill, Liberty Island, New York, October 3, 1965," The American Presidency Project, accessed September 24, 2021, https://www.presidency.ucsb.edu/documents/remarks-the-signing-the-immi gration-bill-liberty-island-new-york.

10 **During the 2010s:** "Modern Immigration Wave Brings 59 Million to U.S.," Pew Research Center.

14 **In some places, they have even succeeded:** When Donald Trump sought to impose what he himself called a "Muslim ban," lower courts initially held that his proposal violated the

Constitution's prohibition on favoring one religion over another. But when his administration issued a lightly revised executive order, which emphasized that it would bar citizens from a number of Muslim-majority countries, the Supreme Court gave it the benefit of barely credible doubt. In effect, Trump banned millions of people from traveling to America on the grounds that they follow a religion that differs from that of the majority. (Joe Biden has since reversed the policy.)

Narendra Modi, the prime minister of India, has been even more successful in his aspiration of changing his country's character. Under proposals put forward by his government, a National Register of Citizens will soon track who is in the country legally and who should be subject to deportation. Since birth certificates were uncommon until a few decades ago, this plan endangers the rights of millions of Muslims who lack the necessary documentation to prove that they are citizens. Though they have every right to be in the country, they must now fear deportation. (Technically, the National Register of Citizens could also ensnare Hindu immigrants who fled to India after being expelled from neighboring countries. To assuage their fears, Modi is giving unauthorized immigrants from Muslim-majority countries an express path to naturalization if they face religious persecution in their place of origin. Asked for similar assurances by India's two hundred million Muslims, he has steadfastly refused to provide them with the same comfort.) See Jeffrey Gettleman and Suhasini Raj, "India Steps toward Making Naturalization Harder for Muslims," *New York Times*, December 9, 2019, https://www.nytimes.com/2019/12/09/world/asia/india-muslims -citizenship-narendra-modi.html.

14 **Growing up in Wenatchee:** David Kamp, "Heidi Schreck Is Giving New Meaning to Political Theater," *Vogue*, October 16, 2020, https://www.vogue.com/article/heidi-schreck-political-theater -vogue-august-2019-issue.

15 **Is the Constitution failing to deliver:** Ramtin Arablouei and Rund Abdelfatah, "The Shadows of the Constitution," *Throughline*, podcast, November 12, 2020, 46:38, https://www.npr.org/tran scripts/933825483.

15 **"I actually don't think our Constitution is failing":** Andrew Ferguson, "Who Is the Constitution For?," *The Atlantic*, August 28, 2019, https://www.theatlantic.com/ideas/archive/2019/08/who-con stitution/596341.

15 **At the end of her smash hit:** Jesse Green, "Review: Can a Play Make the Constitution Great Again?," *New York Times*, March 31, 2019, https://www.nytimes.com/2019/03/31/theater/what -the-constitution-means-to-me-review.html.

15 **She leaves viewers in little doubt:** Naureen Khan, "The Tony-Nominated Play That Savages the U.S. Constitution," *The Atlantic*, June 8, 2019, https://www.theatlantic.com/entertainment/archive /2019/06/what-constitution-means-me-takes-easy-out/591040.

15 **"Notwithstanding the dark picture":** Frederick Douglass, "What to the Slave Is the Fourth of July?," in *The Speeches of Frederick Douglass*, eds. John R. McKivigan and Julie Husband (New Haven, CT: Yale University Press, 2018), 52–92.

16 **And yet he too remained determined:** Martin Luther King Jr. and James Melvin Washington. "I Have a Dream." *A Testament of Hope: The Essential Writings and Speeches of Martin Luther King, Jr.* (San Francisco, CA: HarperSanFrancisco, 1991), 217–21.

18 **And though the racial gap in income:** I make the case for optimism about the socioeconomic progress made by immigrant and minority groups in most developed democracies in much greater detail in chapter 8.

18 **But they also worry:** It might seem as though I am implicitly taking the perspective of members of the majority in this passage. But polling suggests that many descendants of immigrants and members of minority groups are just as torn on these issues. For example, a substantial portion of them favors harsh policies to crack down on illegal immigration. For a longer treatment of the political and cultural views of minority groups, especially in the United States, see chapter 9.

Part One: When Diverse Societies Go Wrong

27 **According to most scientists:** Yvonne Rekers, Daniel B. M. Haun, and Michael Tomasello, "Children, but Not Chimpanzees, Prefer to Collaborate," *Current Biology* 21 (October 2011): 1756–58, https://doi.org/10.1016/j.cub.2011.08.066.

27 **As Michael Tomasello:** Cited in Jonathan Haidt, *The Righteous Mind: Why Good People Are Divided by Politics and Religion* (New York: Vintage Books, 2013), 237.

27 **By the age of three or four:** See, for example, Michael Tomasello et al., "Two Key Steps in the Evolution of Human Cooperation: The Interdependence Hypothesis," *Current Anthropology* 53, no. 6 (December 2012): 673–92, https://www.journals.uchicago.edu/doi/10.1086/668207#sc2.

Chapter One: Why Everyone Can't Just Get Along

32 **Upon his liberation:** For an overview of his life, see, for example, Gustav Jahoda, "Tajfel, Henri [*formerly* Hersz Mordche]," Oxford Dictionary of National Biography, September 23, 2004, https://www.oxforddnb.com/view/10.1093/ref:odnb/9780198614128.001.0001/odnb-978019 8614128-e-58393.

32 **If you are like most Americans:** On Australia, see Wesley Kilham and Leon Mann, "Level of Destructive Obedience as a Function of Transmitter and Executant Roles in the Milgram Obedience Paradigm," *Journal of Personality and Social Psychology* 29, no. 5 (May 1974): 696–702, https://doi.org/10.1037/h0036636. On Germany, see David Mark Mantell, "The Potential for Violence in Germany," *Journal of Social Issues* 27, no. 4 (April 2010): 101–12, https://doi.org /10.1111/j.1540-4560.1971.tb00680.x. On Jordan, see M. E. Shanab and Khawla A. Yahya, "A Cross-Cultural Study of Obedience," *Bulletin of the Psychonomic Society* 11 (1978): 267–69, https://doi.org/10.3758/BF03336827.

32 **Over the course of a few days:** See Muzafer Sherif, B. Jack White, and O. J. Harvey, "Status in Experimentally Produced Groups," *American Journal of Sociology* 60 (1955): 370–79, https://www .journals.uchicago.edu/doi/abs/10.1086/221569. For a critical reappraisal, see Maria Konnikova, "Revisiting Robbers Cave: The Easy Spontaneity of Intergroup Conflict," *Scientific American*, September 5, 2012, https://blogs.scientificamerican.com/literally-psyched/revisiting-the-robbers-cave -the-easy-spontaneity-of-intergroup-conflict.

33 **This is the intellectual puzzle:** Henri Tajfel, "Experiments in Intergroup Discrimination," *Scientific American* 223, no. 5 (1970): 96–103, https://www.jstor.org/stable/10.2307/24927662.

33 **In the second stage of the experiment:** In reality, the boys were assigned to two different groups on an entirely random basis to rule out the remote possibility that the tendency to underestimate or overestimate the number of dots in some arbitrary exercise might somehow be related to the tasks they were asked to perform next.

34 **researchers have replicated Tajfel's findings:** Dave Hauser (@DavidJHauser), "In case you are teaching social psych soon, know that it is easy to replicate the minimal groups paradigm effect in class if you replace 'which art do you prefer' with 'is a hotdog a sandwich?,'" Twitter, December 5, 2019, 10:26 a.m., https://twitter.com/DavidJHauser/status/1202610237934592000.

34 **"Outgroup discrimination," Tajfel concluded:** Tajfel, "Experiments in Intergroup Discrimination," 102.

36 **French pupils learn:** "'Your Ancestors Were Gauls,' France's Sarkozy Tells Migrants," Reuters, September 20, 2016, https://www.reuters.com/article/us-france-election-sarkozy/your-ancestors -were-gauls-frances-sarkozy-tells-migrants-idUSKCN11Q22Y.

36 **The Chinese call:** Luke S. K. Kwong, "What's in a Name: Zhongguo (or Middle Kingdom) Reconsidered," *Historical Journal* 58, no. 3 (September 2015): 781–804, https://www.jstor.org/stable /24532047.

36 **The Mauri claim:** Jennifer Garlick, Basil Keane, and Tracey Borgfeldt, *Te taiao = Māori and the Natural World* (Auckland: New Zealand Ministry for Culture and Heritage 2010), https://manu kau.primo.exlibrisgroup.com/discovery/fulldisplay?context=L&vid=64MANUKAU_INST:64 MANUKAU&search_scope=MyInst_and_CI&tab=Everything&docid=alma99427685340 5101.

36 **Jews and Zoroastrians really are descended:** On Zoroastrians, see Saioa Lopez et al., "The Genetic Legacy of Zoroastrianism in Iran and India: Insights into Population Structure, Gene Flow and Selection," *American Journal of Human Genetics* 101 (September 2017): 353–68, https://doi .org/10.1016/j.ajhg.2017.07.013. On Jews, see Michael Balter, "Tracing the Roots of Jewishness," *Science*, June 3, 2010, https://www.sciencemag.org/news/2010/06/tracing-roots-jewishness, and Gil Atzmon et al., "Abraham's Children in the Genome Era: Major Jewish Diaspora Populations Comprise Distinct Genetic Clusters with Shared Middle Eastern Ancestry," *American Journal of Human Genetics* 86, no. 6 (June 2010): 850–59, https://dx.doi.org/10.1016%2Fj.ajhg .2010.04.015.

37 **Over the decades, doctors have realized:** Hui Li et al., "Refined Geographic Distribution of the Oriental ALDH2*504Lys (née 487Lys) Variant," *Annals of Human Genetics* 73, no. 3 (2009): 335–45, https://www.ncbi.nlm.nih.gov/pmc/articles/PMC2846302.

37 **African Americans have a higher propensity:** See, for example, Centers for Disease Control and Prevention, "Data & Statistics on Sickle Cell Disease," accessed March 24, 2020, https://www.cdc .gov/ncbddd/sicklecell/data.html, and Nadia Solovieff et al., "Ancestry of African Americans with Sickle Cell Disease," *Blood Cells, Molecules, and Diseases* 47 (June 2011): 41–45, https://www.ncbi .nlm.nih.gov/pmc/articles/PMC3116635.

37 **Ashkenazi women are in greater danger:** Centers for Disease Control and Prevention, "Jewish Women and BRCA Gene Mutations," accessed March 24, 2020, https://www.cdc.gov/cancer /breast/young_women/bringyourbrave/hereditary_breast_cancer/jewish_women_brca.htm, and Ellen Warner et al., "Prevalence and Penetrance of BRCA1 and BRCA2 Gene Mutations in Unselected Ashkenazi Jewish Women with Breast Cancer," *Journal of the National Cancer Institute* 91, no. 14 (July 1999): 1241–47, https://doi.org/10.1093/jnci/91.14.1241.

37 **Like millions of Brazilians:** My account of the story of Maíra Mutti Araújo is based on Cleuci De Oliveira, "One Woman's Fight to Claim Her 'Blackness' in Brazil," *Foreign Policy,* July 24, 2017, https://foreignpolicy.com/2017/07/24/one-womans-fight-to-claim-her-blackness-in-brazil.

39 **Compared with many other settler colonies:** See Edward Telles, *Race in Another America: The Significance of Skin Color in Brazil* (Princeton, NJ: Princeton University Press, 2006), as well as "Race Relations: Slavery's Legacies," *The Economist,* September 10, 2016, https://www.economist .com/international/2016/09/08/slaverys-legacies.

39 **Rather than counting as fully black:** I do not mean to suggest that all of these sexual encounters were voluntary. Like in other settler colonies, there were of course many cases of rape. But the existence of legally sanctioned unions between members of different groups had important consequences for the overall scheme of racial classification. Unlike in the United States, which adopted the "one-drop rule" in part because children of white fathers and black mothers did not count as "legitimate," the children from these marriages enjoyed a different social and legal status.

39 **Increasingly, people's membership:** Edward Telles, "Racial Discrimination and Miscegenation: The Experience in Brazil," *UN Chronicle*, accessed September 24, 2021, https://www.un.org/en /chronicle/article/racial-discrimination-and-miscegenation-experience-brazil.

40 **In the United States, by contrast:** For an extensive treatment of the origin and development of the "one-drop rule" in racial categorization schemes and in the US census, see, for example, Christine B. Hickman, "The Devil and the One Drop Rule: Racial Categories, African Americans, and the U.S. Census," *Michigan Law Review* 95, no. 5 (March 1997): 1161–265, https://repository.law .umich.edu/mlr/vol95/iss5/2.

40 *Octoroon,* **one of the most:** The audience could root for love to win out in part because Zoe, the octoroon, was "white" in manners and appearance; despite her legal classification, she was not, the play implied, "really black." *The Octoroon by* Dion Boucicault, The Winter Garden Theatre, New York, NY, 1859.

40 **But whereas, in Brazil, Araújo:** The point of comparing Brazil to the United States is not to say that one scheme of racial categorization is somehow less unjust or more enlightened than the other.

The history of slavery in Brazil is no less cruel than that in the United States. The owners of the country's plantations forcibly brought an even larger number of people to the country, the most of any in the world. As in North America, a significant portion of them died of disease, exhaustion, malnutrition, or violent punishment for supposed infractions. Both countries are products of deep historical injustices.

For a long time, Brazilians celebrated the relative fluidity of their racial categories. One famous historian of the country called it a "racial democracy." The weaker social taboos about contact between members of different races really have helped the country avoid *some* of the most pernicious injustices with which the United States still has to deal today, like residential segregation.

And yet it is also clear that the relative fluidity of racial categories in Brazil cannot compensate for the history of injustice that many of its residents suffer. Even today, Brazilians with lighter skin are commonly viewed positively, while those with darker skin face prejudice and discrimination. The country's elite is predominantly white, while its sprawling slums—though not nearly as segregated as some neighborhoods in America's inner cities—are home to a disproportionate share of dark-skinned residents.

41 **Should Americans who are descended:** See "About Hispanic Origin," United States Census Bureau, last revised on October 16, 2020, https://www.census.gov/topics/population/hispanic-origin/about.html, and Lucia Benadiaz, "Why Labeling Antonio Banderas a 'Person of Color' Triggers Such a Backlash," NPR, February 9, 2020, https://www.npr.org/2020/02/09/803809670/why-labeling-antonio-banderas-a-person-of-color-triggers-such-a-backlash.

41 **Many Native Americans protested:** Ginger Gibson, "Democratic Hopeful Warren Apologizes for Native American Ancestry Claims," Reuters, August 19, 2019, https://www.reuters.com/article/us-usa-election-warren/democratic-hopeful-warren-apologizes-for-native-american-ancestry-claims-idUSKCN1V91QY.

41 **A new activist group:** See for example "The Road Map to Reparations," ADOS: American Descendants of Slavery, https://adoschicago.org/roadmap-to-reparations/.

41 **As Karen and Barbara Fields have pointed out:** Karen E. Fields and Barbara Fields, *Racecraft: The Soul of Inequality in American Life* (London: Verso Books, 2014), 262.

43 **Drawn up as the result:** Collins Mtika, "Malawi and Zambia Struggle to Mark Their Border," DW, September 7, 2009, https://www.dw.com/en/malawi-and-zambia-struggle-to-mark-their-border/a-4459275.

44 **The reason, Posner demonstrated:** One obvious explanation for the difference between Zambia and Malawi, for example, might be that villagers on one side of the border are less aware of their cultural differences than those on the other side of it. But Posner was able to rule that possibility out. Though respondents in Zambia were much less hostile toward one another, they were just as capable of enumerating the cultural differences that divide them.

Another obvious explanation would be that one of these countries might be more "modern" or developed than another, making ethnic identity and different cultural practices less salient to its inhabitants. But Posner was able to rule that possibility out too. The villages on both sides of the border had similar levels of education and economic development. Daniel N. Posner, "The Political Salience of Cultural Difference: Why Chewas and Tumbukas Are Allies in Zambia and Adversaries in Malawi," *American Political Science Review* 98, no. 4 (November 2004): 529–45, https://www.jstor.org/stable/4145323.

45 **Chinese immigrants in Jamaica:** Orlando Patterson, "Context and Choice in Ethnic Allegiance: A Theoretical Framework and Caribbean Case Study," in *Ethnicity: Theory and Experience*, eds. Nathan Glazer and Daniel P. Moynihan (Cambridge, MA: Harvard University Press, 1975), 305–49.

45 **Political entrepreneurs in countries:** See, for example, Robert H. Bates, "Ethnic Competition and Modernization in Contemporary Africa," *Comparative Political Studies* 6, no. 4 (January 1974): 457–84, https://journals.sagepub.com/doi/pdf/10.1177/001041407400600403. See also Bates, *Markets and States in Tropical Africa: The Political Basis of Agricultural Policies* (Berkeley: University of California Press, 2014).

45 **And the deterioration of relationships:** Barry R. Posen, "The Security Dilemma and Ethnic Conflict," *Survival* 35, no. 1 (Spring 1993): 27–47, http://www.rochelleterman.com/ir/sites/default /files/posen-1993.pdf.

46 **Anti-Semitism was widespread:** Daniel Schatz, "Poland Reckons with Its 1968 Campaign Against Jews," CNN, March 15, 2018, https://www.cnn.com/2018/03/15/opinions/expulsion -polish-jews-50th-anniversary-schatz.

46 **Unlike the lab experiments:** Political scientists who study topics like tribalism, ethnicity, and civil war tend to have starkly divergent views about the roots of conflict between different groups.

One set of scholars believes that groups that fight with each other tend to have a long history of in-group identification and out-group hostility. They insist that there is an important truth to "primordial" explanations of conflict.

Another set of scholars emphasizes the strategic or "instrumental" aspect of intergroup conflict. They tend to concentrate on the ways in which ethnic or religious coalitions allow their members to win power and distribute concrete benefits to its members. Whether these authors focus on unscrupulous leaders who build ethnic coalitions to gain power, or on the agency of ordinary citizens who hope to gain concrete benefits by organizing along ethnic lines, their theories show how political incentives help to shape who is in and who is out.

A final set of scholars emphasizes the power of rhetoric. They focus on the way in which identities are "constructed" through the actions of colonial administrators, the choices of governments, or the influence of mass media.

But these three theories are not nearly as mutually exclusive as its main proponents seem to believe. All three capture an important aspect of reality. It is only by seeing how the features of the world to which they call our attention interrelate that we can understand the stakes facing diverse democracies around the globe.

Chapter Two: Three Ways Diverse Societies Fail

52 **"Nature," Hobbes argued:** Thomas Hobbes and W. G. Pogson Smith, *Hobbes's Leviathan* (Oxford, UK: Clarendon Press, 1943), chapter 13.

52 **But "when all is reckoned":** Hobbes and Smith, *Hobbes's Leviathan*, chapter 13.

52 **there is no place for industry:** Hobbes and Smith, *Hobbes's Leviathan*, chapter 13.

53 **The conflict is over when:** William Lomas, "Conflict, Violence and Conflict Resolution in Hunter-Gatherer Societies," Brewminate, November 3, 2018, https://brewminate.com/conflict -violence-and-conflict-resolution-in-hunting-and-gathering-societies. Based on Jean L. Briggs, "Conflict Management in a Modern Inuit Community," in *Hunters and Gatherers in the Modern World: Conflict, Resistance, and Self-Determination*, eds. Megan Biesele, Robert K. Hitchcock, and Peter P. Schweitzer (New York: Berghahn Books, 2006), 110–24.

54 **According to careful studies:** Debra L. Martin and Ryan P. Harrod, "Bioarchaeological Contributions to the Study of Violence," *American Journal of Physical Anthropology* 156 (February 2015): 116–45, https://doi.org/10.1002/ajpa.22662.

54 **"Between the late Middle Ages":** Steven Pinker, *The Better Angels of Our Nature: Why Violence Has Declined* (New York: Viking, 2011), xxiv.

54 **In El Salvador, where:** Based on data from 2017. On the United States, Singapore, and El Salvador, see UNODC, *Global Study on Homicide 2019* (United Nations: Vienna, Austria, 2019), 17, https://www.unodc.org/documents/data-and-analysis/gsh/Booklet2.pdf.

54 **Some of the most dangerous places:** Institute for Economics and Peace, *Global Peace Index 2020: Measuring Peace in a Complex World* (IEP: Sydney, Australia, June 2020), 9, https://reliefweb.int/sites/reliefweb.int/files/resources/GPI_2020_web.pdf. On Venezuela, see William Finnegan, "Venezuela, a Failing State," *New Yorker*, November 6, 2016, https://www.newyorker.com/magazine/2016/11/14/venezuela-a-failing-state. On the Central African Republic, see Hans de Marie Heumgoup, "In Search of the State in the Central African Republic," International Crisis Group, March 13, 2020, https://www.crisisgroup.org/africa/central-africa/central-african-republic/search-state-central-african-republic.

57 **"They came to kill":** Flora Drury, "Afghan Maternity Ward Attackers 'Came to Kill the Mothers,'" BBC, May 15, 2020, https://www.bbc.com/news/world-asia-52673563. On details of the attack, see further contemporaneous news accounts, including "Babies among 24 Killed as Gunmen Attack Maternity Ward in Kabul," Al Jazeera, May 13, 2020, https://www.aljazeera.com/news/2020/5/13/babies-among-24-killed-as-gunmen-attack-maternity-ward-in-kabul, and Orooj Hakimi, Abdul Qadir Sediqi, and Hamid Shalizi, "Maternity Ward Massacre Shakes Afghanistan and Its Peace Process," Reuters, May 13, 2020, https://www.reuters.com/article/us-afghanistan-attacks-hospital-insight/maternity-ward-massacre-shakes-afghanistan-and-its-peace-process-idUSKBN22P2F5.

57 **Both groups denied responsibility:** Kathy Gannon and Tameen Akhgar, "US Blames Brutal Attack on Afghan Maternity Hospital on IS," AP News, May 15, 2020, https://apnews.com/article/eebcd4af6c821e5530f3795352542f9f.

57 **Far from being engaged in a chaotic war:** For a good journalistic account, see Ruhullah Khapalwak, David Rohde, and Bill Marsh, "Tribal Custom and Power in Daily Life," *New York Times*, January 31, 2010, https://archive.nytimes.com/www.nytimes.com/imagepages/2010/01/31/weekinreview/13rohde-grfk-2.html?action=click&module=RelatedCoverage&pgtype=Article&region=Footer.

57 **"state of nature":** Nor are the heads of different groups complete strangers to one another. Rather, each tribal chief or local warlord has a strong sense of the political, material, and military resources he has at his disposal, and the kind of price this allows him to demand for entering into an—often brittle—political alliance with either the country's nominal government or the rebel forces that have, for most of the past five decades, sought to overthrow it.

　　　See the interesting recent research on the idea of a "political marketplace" in countries from Somalia to parts of Africa, for example, Alex De Waal, *The Real Politics of the Horn of Africa: Money, War and the Business of Power* (New York: John Wiley & Sons, 2015), and Alex De Waal, "Introduction to the Political Marketplace for Policymakers," *JSRP Policy Brief* 1 (London: JSRP, 2016).

57 **The country as a whole:** Thomas J. Barfield, *Afghanistan: A Cultural and Political History* (Princeton, NJ: Princeton University Press, 2010), 18.

58 **His access to arable land:** Khapalwak, Rohde, and Marsh, "Tribal Custom and Power in Daily Life."

58 **Women, who are subject:** See, for example, Special Inspector General for Afghanistan Reconstruction, *Support for Gender Equality: Lessons from the US Experience in Afghanistan* (Arlington, VA: Government Printing Office, 2021).

58 **Most of its citizens have at best:** Hamid Shalizi, "Who Is an Afghan? Row over ID Cards Fuels Ethnic Tension," Reuters, February 8, 2018, https://www.reuters.com/article/uk-afghanistan-politics-idUKKBN1FS1WH.

58 **The quality of schools in Afghanistan:** "Afghanistan—Education," UNICEF, accessed September 25, 2021, https://www.unicef.org/afghanistan/education.

58 **Welfare benefits are minimal:** Abdul Majeed Labib, "The Islamic Republic of Afghanistan: Updating and Improving the Social Protection Index," Asian Development Bank, August 2012, https://www.adb.org/sites/default/files/project-document/76049/44152-012-reg-tacr-01.pdf.

58 **Even before COVID-19 hit:** "Coronavirus Pushing Millions into Poverty: SIGAR," Al Jazeera, July 31, 2020. https://www.aljazeera.com/economy/2020/7/31/coronavirus-pushing-millions-of-afghans-into-poverty-sigar.

58 **There are whole stretches:** "Afghanistan," CIA World Factbook, April 21, 2021, https://www.cia.gov/the-world-factbook/countries/afghanistan.

58–59 **Only 43 percent of Afghanistan's population:** "Interview: 'Literacy Rate in Afghanistan Increased to 43 percent,'" UNESCO Institute for Lifelong Learning, March 17, 2020, https://uil.unesco.org/interview-literacy-rate-afghanistan-increased-43-cent#:~:text=Currently%2C%20over%2010%20million%20youth,increased%20to%2043%20per%20cent.

59 **Out of every one thousand:** "Country Profile: Afghanistan," UNICEF, accessed September 25, 2021, https://data.unicef.org/country/afg.

59 **In 2018, the average life expectancy:** "Life Expectancy at Birth—Afghanistan," The World Bank, accessed September 25, 2021, https://data.worldbank.org/indicator/SP.DYN.LE00.MA.IN?locations=AF.

60 **Anthony Burns was born:** Joshua D. Rothman, "Anthony Burns and the Resistance to the Fugitive Slave Act," We're History, July 27, 2018, http://werehistory.org/anthony-burns-and-the-resistance-to-the-fugitive-slave-act.

60 **Determined to win his liberty:** Charles Emery Stevens, *Anthony Burns, a History* (Boston: J. P. Jewett and Co., 1856, 154–55, https://docsouth.unc.edu/neh/stevens/stevens.html.

60 **set up a secret school:** Stevens, *Anthony Burns*, 172.

60 **In his late teens, Burns:** Stevens, *Anthony Burns*, 172–73.

60 **On a cold morning in February 1854:** Stevens, *Anthony Burns*, 177.

61 **On the basis of the Fugitive Slave Act:** Rothman, "Anthony Burns and the Resistance to the Fugitive Slave Act."

61 **Within weeks, a notorious slave hunter:** Stevens, *Anthony Burns*, 16.

61 **Richard Henry Dana Jr., the scion:** Jeffrey L. Amestoy, "Richard Henry Dana's Second Act," *Los Angeles Times*, July 31, 2015, https://www.latimes.com/opinion/op-ed/la-oe-amnestoy-richard-dana-birthday-20150831-story.html.

61 **Guards beat them back:** Rothman, "Anthony Burns and the Resistance to the Fugitive Slave Act."

61 **President Franklin Pierce ordered a company:** "Anthony Burns Captured, 1854," PBS, accessed September 25, 2021, https://www.pbs.org/wgbh/aia/part4/4p2915.html.

62 **"They had hoisted American flags":** Rothman, "Anthony Burns and the Resistance to the Fugitive Slave Act."

62 **Burns was put on a ship:** Rothman, "Anthony Burns and the Resistance to the Fugitive Slave Act."

63 **Southern states imported about three hundred thousand:** "Trans-Atlantic Slave Trade: Estimates: 1501–1866," Slave Voyages, accessed September 25, 2021, https://www.slavevoyages.org/assessment/estimates.

64 **As a result, black people in the United States:** "On Views of Race and Inequality, Blacks and Whites Are Worlds Apart," Pew Research Center, June 27, 2016, 18–26, https://www.pewresearch.org/social-trends/2016/06/27/1-demographic-trends-and-economic-well-being.

64 **the indigenous in Australia:** On education, see "Australia's Welfare: Indigenous Education and Skills," Australian Government: Australian Institute of Health and Welfare, September 11, 2019, https://www.aihw.gov.au/reports/australias-welfare/indigenous-education-and-skills. On income, see "Australia's Welfare: Indigenous Income and Finance," Australian Government: Australian Institute of Health and Welfare, September 11, 2019, https://www.aihw.gov.au/reports/australias-welfare/indigenous-income-and-finance.

64 **members of lower castes in India:** Maitreyi Bordia Das and Soumya Kapoor Mehta, "Poverty and Social Exclusion in India: Dalits," World Bank, 2012, https://openknowledge.worldbank.org/han dle/10986/26336, License: CC BY 3.0 IGO.

66 **When Christians took control:** "Reconquista," *Encyclopaedia Britannica*, accessed September 25, 2021, https://www.britannica.com/event/Reconquista.

66 **As late as the seventeenth century:** See "History of Europe: Wars of Religion," *Encyclopaedia Britannica*, accessed September 25, 2021, https://www.britannica.com/topic/history-of-Europe /The-Wars-of-Religion, and "Peace of Augsburg," *Encyclopaedia Britannica*, accessed September 25, 2021, https://www.britannica.com/event/Peace-of-Augsburg.

66 **important scientific advantages:** Even those times were hardly models of justice or harmony, of course. In the Baghdad of the ninth century, for example, religious minorities suffered from a host of important disadvantages. They were excluded from key offices of the state, had to pay a punitive tax, and were prohibited from certain forms of dress. Minorities in Istanbul and Vienna faced similar disabilities. But by the standards of their time, these multiethnic empires were astoundingly tolerant. For the millennium and a half between the sacking of Rome and the rise of modern nation-states,, they represented some of the brightest examples of the promise of diverse societies.

68 **But in countries from Iraq to Rwanda:** See, for example, Andrew Cockburn, "Iraq's Oppressed Majority," *Smithsonian*, December 2003, https://www.smithsonianmag.com/history/iraqs-oppressed -majority-95250996; "Rwanda Genocide: 100 Days of Slaughter," BBC, April 4, 2019, https:// www.bbc.com/news/world-africa-26875506; Oded Haklai, "A Minority Rule over a Hostile Majority: The Case of Syria," *Nationalism and Ethnic Conflict* 6, no. 3 (September 2000): 19–50, https://doi.org/10.1080/13537110008428602; and "Guatemala's State Corruption and the Heirs of Colonial Privilege," Al Jazeera, July 18, 2019, https://www.aljazeera.com/opinions/2019/7/18 /guatemalas-state-corruption-and-the-heirs-of-colonial-privilege.

68 **the ruling elite has traditionally:** The roots of minority dominance are many. In some colonies, foreign powers promoted minority groups to powerful positions because they thought that these would be less able to challenge them; when they were finally forced to grant independence to their former colonies, these minority groups were in a strong position to commandeer the machinery of the state.

In other countries, the origins of minority rule lie in religious or cultural traditions. In India, for example, the upper castes that have long dominated the ranks of government and the economy are far less numerous than the lower castes that have been relegated to menial work.

But because both shared a set of beliefs that provided a religious justification for this hierarchy, challenges to it have long remained much more muted than the extreme inequality in the country might otherwise suggest.

Different rates of demographic growth are yet another reason why minorities can sometimes come to rule over majorities. The ruling families of the United Arab Emirates, for example, have traditionally shared an ethnic and religious identity with their subjects. But because the country has attracted an enormous number of immigrants during the decades of its rapid growth, Emirati citizens are now vastly outnumbered by noncitizens who hail from a much greater diversity of cultures and ethnicities. In the UAE, the minority rules simply because it was once the majority and has never let go of its power.

69 **has termed "herrenvolk democracy":** Pierre Louis Van den Berghe, *Race and Racism: A Comparative Perspective* (New York: John Wiley & Sons, 1978).

69 **The great majority lacked the vote:** "South Africa—The National Party and Apartheid," *Encyclopaedia Britannica*, accessed September 25, 2021, https://www.britannica.com/place/South-Africa /The-National-Party-and-apartheid.

70 **Within a few months, even Sunnis:** Sabrina Tavernise, "For Sunnis, Dictator's Degrading End Signals Ominous Dawn for the New Iraq," *New York Times*, https://www.nytimes.com/2007/01

/01/world/middleeast/01sunnis.html. See also George Packer, *The Assassins' Gate: America in Iraq* (London: Faber and Faber, 2007).

70 **Between Shia attempts to monopolize:** Rwanda is yet another tragic illustration of this depressingly common pattern. In 1959, Hutus managed to challenge the long-standing rule of the Tutsi minority by forcing the king to flee the country. Exiled Tutsis formed a rebel group that invaded Rwanda in 1990. A power-sharing agreement, struck in 1993, proved insufficient to hold the peace. After a plane carrying the president of Rwanda, a Hutu, was shot down the following year, extremist leaders incited their followers to take their revenge on hundreds of thousands of innocent Tutsis. Within three months, Hutu soldiers and villagers across Rwanda murdered at least 500,000 Tutsis.

72 **Even institutions like hospitals:** Staf Hellemans, "Pillarization ('Verzuiling'): On Organized 'Self-Contained Worlds' in the Modern World," *The American Sociologist* 51, no. 2 (June 2020): 124–47, https://doi.org/10.1007/s12108-020-09449-x.

73 **as Lijphart said in a recent interview:** Nivek Thompson and Arend Lijphart, "Patterns of Democracy with Professor Lijphart," September 24, 2017, in *Real Democracy Now*, podcast, season 3, episode 2, 34:20 (discussed at 2:30 minutes), https://realdemocracynow.com.au/podcast/podcasts/season-3-elections.

73 **And might some of the new nations:** Lijphart sets out to answer this question in his book *The Politics of Accommodation: Pluralism and Democracy in the Netherlands*. On page 70 he asks: "What can this case [Holland] tell us about the conditions of stable and effective democracy?" Arend Lijphart, *The Politics of Accommodation: Pluralism and Democracy in the Netherlands* (Berkeley: University of California Press, 1976).

73 **If "the majority and minority are fixed":** Donald L. Horowitz, "Democracies in Divided Societies," *Journal of Democracy* 4, no. 4 (October 1993): 18–38 (quote on page 29). See also his classic account of the problems facing democracy in divided societies in Donald L. Horowitz, *Ethnic Groups in Conflict* (Berkeley: University of California Press, 2001).

74 **"the textbook case of democratic":** Horowitz, "Democracies in Divided Societies," 29. In other countries, the problem is slightly different. There, the balance of power between different ethnic groups may be more even. But if they are sufficiently hostile toward one another each of these groups is likely to fear that the other will rig the system as soon as it gets the chance. The stakes of every election will then come to feel existential.

74 **The Netherlands, Lijphart argued:** Lijphart, *The Politics of Accommodation*, 112–13. The Netherlands' Social and Economic Council consisted of forty-five members, each carefully selected through different appointment processes by the various socialist, Catholic, and Protestant unions, employer blocs, or cabinet members. The council's membership was thus intentionally representative to the proportions of socialists, Catholics, and Protestants among the broader population. While its formal decision-making powers were limited, Lijphart writes that the council's advice was "often tantamount to future national policy."

74 **Instead of giving the victor:** Lijphart, *The Politics of Accommodation*, 112, subheading "The Institutionalization of Accommodation." See also Arend Lijphart, "Typologies of Democratic Systems," *Comparative Political Studies* 1, no. 1 (April 1968): 7–44, https://doi.org/10.2307/421322.

75 **The president of the republic would always:** For an overview, see Imad Harb, "Lebanon's Confessionalism: Problems and Prospects," United States Institute of Peace, March 30, 2006, https://www.usip.org/publications/2006/03/lebanons-confessionalism-problems-and-prospects.

75 **"A multiple balance of power":** Lijphart, "Typologies of Democratic Systems."

75 **When Lijphart first presented his theory:** Lijphart, "Typologies of Democratic Systems." The canonical statement of the theory came a year later, in a 1969 *World Politics* article titled "Consociational Democracy." Arend Lijphart, "Consociational Democracy," *World Politics* 21, no. 2 (January 1969): 207–25, https://www.jstor.org/stable/i308670.

76 **Lijphart was serving as the president:** "APSA Presidents and Presidential Addresses: 1903 to Present," American Political Science Association, accessed September 25, 2021, https://www.apsanet.org/about/governance/apsa-presidents-1903-to-present.

76 **Lijphart was putting the finishing touches:** Arend Lijphart, *Democracy in Plural Societies: A Comparative Exploration* (New Haven, CT: Yale University Press, 1977).

76 **Lebanon fell into a bloody:** "Lebanon: History: Lebanon after Independence: Civil War," *Encyclopaedia Britannica*, accessed September 24, 2021, https://www.britannica.com/place/Lebanon/Lebanon-after-independence.

76 **In the country that long served:** It had, probably, always been a little preposterous to think that institutions that worked well in a country like the Netherlands would bring about similarly positive results in a country like Lebanon.

The Netherlands have a long history of religious toleration going back to the Dutch Republic of the seventeenth century. The main "pillars" of its society consisted of different denominations of the same religion. In one form or another, it had been a sovereign nation for many centuries. In the 1960s, when Lijphart was developing his theory, the country was rapidly growing more secular. It had come to be embedded in the European Community (as it was then called), a powerful supernational organization that helped to protect the rights of religious and ethnic minorities. On all sides, it was surrounded by peaceful and affluent countries.

Lebanon, by contrast, had often experienced bouts of ethnic conflict. The country's population was split between different religions with a long history of mutual hostility. Its borders were largely artificial. Some of its major groups had strong ties to allies in neighboring countries. Lebanon is located in a highly volatile region. Since its founding, it has been involved in periodic warfare with one of the two countries with which it shares a physical border.

Many of the other countries to which political scientists tried to apply the supposed lessons of consociationalism faced similar obstacles. Compared with the Netherlands, they were poorer, more deeply divided, and located in far less forgiving environments. With the benefit of hindsight, it was hubris to think that any set of clever institutional mechanisms—whether the more consensual ones prevalent in Belgium or Switzerland, or the more majoritarian ones prevalent in Australia and the United Kingdom—could have fixed the problems faced by countries like Lebanon.

77 **I remembered those weeks fondly:** For details on the wedding, as well as the broader context of nondenominational weddings in Lebanon, see Martin Chulov, "Society Couple Said 'I Do'—but Lebanon Won't Accept That They Are Married," *Guardian*, August 25, 2019, https://www.theguardian.com/world/2019/aug/25/lebandon-high-society-wedding-tests-civil-freedom.

77 **Even today, marriages across:** "Interfaith Marriages Still a Rarity in the Muslim World," DW, September 11, 2019, https://www.dw.com/en/interfaith-marriages-still-a-rarity-in-the-muslim-world/a-50391076.

77 **"the state has completely subjugated":** Chulov, "Society Couple Said 'I Do'—but Lebanon Won't Accept That They Are Married."

77 **"We want Lebanon to be a country for all":** Chulov, "Society Couple Said 'I Do'—but Lebanon Won't Accept That They Are Married."

78 **If you are a Sunni who wishes:** Nayla Geagea and Lama Fakih, "Unequal and Unprotected: Women's Rights under Lebanese Personal Status Laws," Human Rights Watch, January 19, 2015, https://www.hrw.org/report/2015/01/19/unequal-and-unprotected/womens-rights-under-lebanese-personal-status-laws.

78 **But the decision is ultimately:** Alice Fordham, "A Wedding and a Challenge: Lebanese Couples Fight for Civil Marriage," NPR, May 22, 2015, https://www.npr.org/sections/parallels/2015/05/22/407769876/a-wedding-and-a-challenge-lebanese-couples-fight-for-civil-marriage.

Like Lebanon, India has separate laws for a number of key religious groups, including Hindus, Muslims, Christians, and Parsis. To avoid giving religious authorities quite as much power, India has opted to enact these kinds of laws by the same route as other legislation: a majority vote in the Lok Sabha, the country's parliament. But this creates a problem of legitimacy all its own, for it means that representatives elected by hundreds of millions of Hindus and Muslims get to amend "The Parsi Marriage and Divorce Act," which governs the personal lives of the 60,000 Zoroastrians who now remain in the country.

78 **Any set of institutions that actually:** One approach to doing so is to introduce so-called centripetal institutions. While their exact nature depends on the local context, they try to force politicians and political actors to cooperate across the boundaries of traditional social cleavages. In deeply divided countries with a strong geographic split, for example, they may make representation in the national parliament dependent on a party's ability to garner a significant share of the vote in all parts of the country. For both an explanation and a critique of centripetalism, see, for example, Donald L. Horowitz, "Ethnic Power Sharing: Three Big Problems," *Journal of Democracy* 25, no. 2 (April 2014): 5–20, https://muse.jhu.edu/article/542442.

79 **"internal political cohesion":** Lijphart, "Typologies of Democratic Systems," 25–26.

80 **Over the past decades, both sets:** On Germany, see Edith Palmer, "Citizenship Pathways and Border Protection: Germany," Library of Congress, updated December 30, 2020, https://www.loc.gov/law/help/citizenship-pathways/germany.php. On Uruguay and other Latin American countries, see Deisy Del Real, "Migrant Legalization and Rights: Ideas and Strategies from South America," University of Southern California: Equity Research Institute, April 6, 2021, https://dornsife.usc.edu/eri/blog-migrant-legalization-rights-ideas-strategies, and Diego Acosta, "Free Movement in South America: The Emergence of an Alternative Model?," Migration Policy Institute, August 23, 2016, https://www.migrationpolicy.org/article/free-movement-south-america-emergence-alternative-model. On Japan, see Deborah J. Milly, "Japan's Labor Migration Reforms: Breaking with the Past?," Migration Policy Institute, February 20, 2020, https://www.migrationpolicy.org/article/japan-labor-migration-reforms-breaking-past.

80 **The United States finally granted minority:** "Civil Rights Act; July 2, 1964," Yale Law School, accessed September 24, 2021, https://avalon.law.yale.edu/20th_century/civil_rights_1964.asp.

82 **Across North America and Western Europe:** On North America, see, for example, Rachel Wetts and Rob Willer, "Privilege on the Precipice: Perceived Racial Status Threats Lead White Americans to Oppose Welfare Programs," *Social Forces* 97, no. 2 (December 2018): 793–822, https://doi.org/10.1093/sf/soy046. On Europe, see Christian Albrekt Larsen, "Ethnic Heterogeneity and Public Support for Welfare: Is the American Experience Replicated in Britain, Sweden and Denmark?," *Scandinavian Political Studies* 34, no. 4 (October 2011): 332–53, http://dx.doi.org/10.1111/j.1467-9477.2011.00276.x; Dennis C. Spies and Alexander W. Schmidt-Catran, "Immigration and Welfare Support in Germany: Methodological Reevaluations and Substantive Conclusions," *American Sociological Review* 84, no. 4 (July 2019): 764–68, http://dx.doi.org/10.1177/0003122419858729; and Maureen A. Eger, "Even in Sweden: The Effect of Immigration on Support for Welfare State Spending," *European Sociological Review* 26, no. 2 (April 2010): 203–17, http://dx.doi.org/10.1093/esr/jcp017.

Parts of the left have loudly rejected these findings, perhaps in part because they fear that they serve as a justification for anti-immigrant policies. But interestingly, a structurally similar thesis is highly popular on the left in a more specifically American context: the idea that white American voters have turned against the provision of generous public goods once they had to share them with African Americans. See, for example, Heather McGhee, *The Sum of Us: What Racism Costs Everyone and How We Can Prosper Together* (New York: One World, 2021), and Jeff Wiltse, *Contested Waters: A Social History of Swimming Pools in America* (Chapel Hill: University of North Carolina Press, 2007).

82 **Detailed rules ensure that every group:** See, for example, Rebecca Collard, "How Sectarianism Helped Destroy Lebanon's Economy," *Foreign Policy*, December 13, 2019, https://foreignpolicy.com/2019/12/13/sectarianism-helped-destroy-lebanon-economy.

83 **ordinary Lebanese people find it:** Ellen Francis and Alaa Kanaan, "Protests Sweep Lebanon as Fury at Ruling Elite Grows over Economic Corruption," Reuters, October 18, 2019, https://www .reuters.com/article/us-lebanon-economy-protests/protests-sweep-lebanon-as-fury-at-ruling -elite-grows-over-economic-corruption-idUSKBN1WX0Q8.

83 **historically dominant groups:** See, for example, Robin DiAngelo, *White Fragility: Why It's So Hard for White People to Talk about Racism* (Boston, MA: Beacon Press, 2018).

Chapter Three: How to Keep the Peace

85 **On December 6, 1992:** Mark Tully, "Tearing Down the Babri Masjid," BBC, December 5, 2002, http://news.bbc.co.uk/2/hi/south_asia/2528025.stm.

85 **a famous mosque in the city:** Lauren Frayer, "Nearly 27 Years after Hindu Mob Destroyed a Mosque, the Scars in India Remain Deep," NPR, April 25, 2019, https://www.npr.org/2019/04/25 /711412924/nearly-27-years-after-hindu-mob-destroyed-a-mosque-the-scars-in-india-remain-dee.

85 **Waving religious flags and chanting:** Akash Bisht, "Babri Mosque Demolition Case: India's BJP Leaders Acquitted," Al Jazeera, September 30, 2020, https://www.aljazeera.com/news/2020/9/30 /indian-court-acquits-all-accused-in-babri-mosque-demolition-case.

85 **politicians allied with the Bharatiya:** See Praveen Jain, "Babri Mosque: The Build-Up to a De-molition That Shook India," BBC, December 5, 2017, https://www.bbc.com/news/world-asia -india-42106056, and Bisht, "Babri Mosque Demolition Case: India's BJP Leaders Acquitted." (There was also a heavy presence of politicians from another allied Hinduist party, the Vishwa Hindu Parishad Pary, or VHP.)

85 **Around noon, a young religious devotee:** Jain, "Babri Mosque: The Build-Up to a Demolition That Shook India."

85 **It only took them a few hours to raze:** See Tully, "Tearing Down the Babri Masjid," and Jain, "Babri Mosque: The Build-Up to a Demolition That Shook India."

86 **More than two thousand people died:** "Timeline: Ayodhya Holy Site Crisis," BBC, December 6, 2012, https://www.bbc.com/news/world-south-asia-11436552.

86 **When the killing finally subsided:** For details on this gruesome episode, see Ashutosh Varshney, "Ethnic Conflict and Civil Society: India and Beyond," *World Politics* 53 (April 2001): 381, http:// dx.doi.org/10.1353/wp.2001.0012, and Barbara Crosette, "Aligarh Journal; Campus Under Fire: Not Just a Crisis of Identity," *New York Times*, January 10, 1991, https://www.nytimes.com/1991 /01/10/world/aligarh-journal-campus-under-fire-not-just-a-crisis-of-identity.html.

86 **Many cities all across the country:** Sanjoy Hazarika, "Muslim-Hindu Riots in India Leave 93 Dead in 3 Days," *New York Times*, December 10, 1990, https://www.nytimes.com/1990/12/10 /world/muslim-hindu-riots-in-india-leave-93-dead-in-3-days.html.

86 **understated name of "communal violence":** For an example of the uses of the term, see, for ex-ample, Sruthisagar Yamunan and Ipsita Chakravarty, "Divided City: How Violence Occurred on Frontiers between Hindu and Muslim Neighbourhoods in Delhi," Scroll.In, February 28, 2020, https://scroll.in/article/954560/divided-city-how-delhi-violence-occurred-on-frontiers -between-hindu-and-muslim-neighbourhoods.

86 **But, strangely, other cities:** Varshney, "Ethnic Conflict and Civil Society: India and Beyond," 362–98.

86 **Both are midsized cities:** Varshney, "Ethnic Conflict and Civil Society: India and Beyond," 373.

86 **false rumors about supposed massacres:** Varshney, "Ethnic Conflict and Civil Society: India and Beyond," 380.

86 **And yet Kozhikode has so far:** Varshney, "Ethnic Conflict and Civil Society: India and Beyond," 381–82.

86 **"Aligarh figures in the list":** Varshney, "Ethnic Conflict and Civil Society: India and Beyond," 380.

86 **Kozhikode "has not had a single riot":** Varshney, "Ethnic Conflict and Civil Society: India and Beyond," 380.

87 **Gordon W. Allport was born:** "Gordon Allport," *Encyclopaedia Britannica*, accessed September 25, 2021, https://www.britannica.com/biography/gordon-w-allport.

87 **a bestselling exposé of infamous:** Samuel Hopkins Adams, *The Great American Fraud: Articles on the Nostrum Evil and Quackery* (Chicago: American Medical Association, 1912), 118, text available at https://archive.org/details/greatamericanfra00adamuoft/page/118/mode/2up.

87 **After attending Harvard University:** "Gordon Allport of Harvard Dies: 'Maverick' Psychologist, 69, Outspoken on Prejudice," *New York Times*, October 10, 1967, 47, https://timesmachine.ny times.com/timesmachine/1967/10/10/83635986.pdf?pdf_redirect=true&ip=0.

87 **"Each corner of the earth":** G. W. Allport, *The Nature of Prejudice* (Boston: Addison-Wesley, 1954), xiii.

88 **psychologists found evidence of the salutary:** Thomas F. Pettigrew, "Intergroup Contact Theory," *Annual Review of Psychology* 49, no. 1 (February 1998): 65–85, http://dx.doi.org/10.1146 /annurev.psych.49.1.65.

88 **American soldiers who had frequent contact:** Allport, *The Nature of Prejudice*, 267.

88 **White soldiers in mixed platoons:** Allport, *The Nature of Prejudice*, 277.

88 **Among civilians, whites living in integrated:** Allport, *The Nature of Prejudice*, 271.

89 **Through painstaking work, researchers:** For a recent overview, see, for example, Loris Vezzali and Sofia Stathi, eds., *Intergroup Contact Theory: Recent Developments and Future Directions* (London: Routledge, 2016).

89 **But among whites who had exclusively:** Allport, *The Nature of Prejudice*, 274.

89 **Allport formulated four broad conditions:** As Thomas F. Pettigrew, a professor at the University of California at Santa Cruz, wrote in an influential meta-analysis of hundreds of studies in 1998, Allport's conditions "continue to receive support across a great variety of situations, groups, and societies." Pettigrew, "Intergroup Contact Theory," 68. The summary of the conditions on intergroup contact in the following paragraphs is based on the formulation by Pettigrew.

90 **they need to work together to solve:** This is the basis for the important idea of "jigsaw pedagogy" described by Elliot Aronson. See Elliot Aronson, *The Jigsaw Classroom* (Beverley Hills, CA: Sage, 1978).

90 **Subsequent work has mostly vindicated:** Pettigrew, "Intergroup Contact Theory," 65–85.

90 **But these benefits will only accrue:** Allport, *The Nature of Prejudice*, 281.

90 **The more voluntary associations:** The classic work on social capital is Robert D. Putnam, *Making Democracy Work: Civic Traditions in Modern Italy* (Princeton, NJ: Princeton University Press, 2006). See also the later Robert D. Putnam, *Bowling Alone: The Collapse and Revival of American Community* (New York: Simon & Schuster, 2000).

91 **"bridging" social capital:** On the distinction between "bonding" and "bridging" social capital, see Robert D. Putnam, "E Pluribus Unum: Diversity and Community in the Twenty-First Century: The 2006 Johan Skytte Prize Lecture," *Scandinavian Political Studies* 30, no. 2 (June 2007): 137–74, https://doi.org/10.1111/j.1467-9477.2007.00176.x. Compare also Putnam, *Bowling Alone*, 22.

91 **These are the core insights:** Varshney, "Ethnic Conflict and Civil Society: India and Beyond."

91 **About 90 percent of Hindu and Muslim:** Ashutosh Varshney, *Ethnic Conflict and Civic Life: Hindus and Muslims in India* (New Haven, CT: Yale University Press, 2002), 383.

91 **Both the residents of Aligarh:** Varshney, *Ethnic Conflict and Civic Life*, 381.

92 **But most of these cater:** Varshney, *Ethnic Conflict and Civic Life*, 384–85.

92 **There are integrated trade groups:** Varshney, *Ethnic Conflict and Civic Life*, 384.

92 **"Much like Tocqueville's America":** Varshney, *Ethnic Conflict and Civic Life*, 384.

92 **they helped to dispel unfounded rumors:** Varshney, *Ethnic Conflict and Civic Life*, 388.

94 **Human nature is another important:** As Elizabeth Anderson has put it in her explanation for why it makes sense to focus on what philosophers call "non-ideal theory" in discussing topics like

integration and segregation, "we need to tailor our principles to the motivational and cognitive capacities of human beings. . . . Just institutions must be designed to block, work around, or cancel out our motivational and cognitive deficiencies, to harness our nonmoral motives to moral ends, to make up for each other's limitations by pooling our knowledge and wills. To craft such designs, we must analyze our motivational and cognitive biases, diagnose how they lead people to mistreat others, and how institutions may redirect them to better conduct." Elizabeth Anderson, *The Imperative of Integration* (Princeton, NJ: Princeton University Press, 2010), 3–4.

Chapter Four: What Role Should the State Play?

106 **"To know oneself as such a social":** Alasdair MacIntyre, *After Virtue: A Study in Moral Theory*, 2nd ed. (Notre Dame, IN: University of Notre Dame Press, 1984), 33–34. Patrick Deneen condemns liberalism in even more extreme terms. In *Why Liberalism Failed*, he argues that some of the central problems of the modern world flow directly from the failings of this ideology. Because liberalism puts individual autonomy on a pedestal, it grants citizens rights and liberties that harm the interests of the collective. Rotten to its roots, Deneen concludes, liberalism should be abandoned. Patrick J. Deneen, *Why Liberalism Failed* (New Haven, CT: Yale University Press, 2018).

106 **the ideal of an "illiberal democracy":** Of late, more sophisticated thinkers have made a more "refined" case for the majority to assert itself. Oddly, this includes writers who come from communities that themselves are unlikely to constitute the majority in the countries in which they are writing. For example, according to Adrian Vermeule, a professor at Harvard Law School, "nonliberal actors [should] strategically locate themselves within liberal institutions and work to undo the liberalism of the state from within." Adrian Vermeule, "Integration from Within," *American Affairs* 2, no. 1 (Spring 2018), https://americanaffairsjournal.org/2018/02/integration-from-within. Sohrab Ahmari, the opinion editor of the *New York Post*, even argues that conservatives should aim to build "a public square re-ordered to the common good and ultimately the Highest Good." Sohrab Ahmari, "Against David French-ism," *First Things*, May 29, 2019, https://www.firstthings.com/web-exclusives/2019/05/against-david-french-ism.

107 **The state itself, he argues, is:** Chandra Kukathas, "Cultural Toleration," *Nomos* 39 (1997): 94.

108 **On August 20, 2020, at 8:06 a.m.:** André Orban, "An S7 Flight with Alexey Navalny Onboard Diverted after Suspected Poisoning of Russian Opposition Leader," Aviation24.be, August 20, 2020, https://www.aviation24.be/airlines/s7-airlines/an-s7-flight-with-alexey-navalny-onboard-diverted-after-suspected-poisoning-of-russian-opposition-leader.

108 **Disoriented, he made his way:** BBC Russian, "Alexei Navalny: Two Hours That Saved Russian Opposition Leader's Life," BBC, September 4, 2020, https://www.bbc.com/news/world-europe-54012278.

108 **Medical workers carried the sick:** BBC Russian, "Alexei Navalny."

108 **By the time Alexei Navalny:** Anton Zverev and Gleb Stolyarov, "Exclusive: Russian Paramedics' Accounts Challenge Moscow's Explanation for Navalny's Coma—Sources," Reuters, September 14, 2020, https://www.reuters.com/article/us-russia-politics-navalny-health-exclus/exclusive-russian-paramedics-accounts-challenge-moscows-explanation-for-navalnys-coma-sources-idUSKBN265298.

109 **Alexander Murakhovsky, the chief:** "Doctor Who Treated Navalny and Denied Novichok Poisoning Promoted to Regional Health Minister," *Moscow Times*, November 7, 2020, https://www.themoscowtimes.com/2020/11/07/omsk-doctor-who-treated-navalny-and-denied-novichok-poisoning-promoted-to-regional-health-minister-a71980.

109 **When Navalny's wife, Yulia:** Luke Harding and Andrew Roth, "A Cup of Tea, Then Screams of Agony: How Alexei Navalny Was Left Fighting for His Life," *Guardian*, August 20, 2020, https://www.theguardian.com/world/2020/aug/20/a-cup-of-tea-then-screams-of-agony-how-alexei-navalny-was-left-fighting-for-his-life.

109 **But thanks to immense:** "Alexei Navalny: Russian Doctors Agree to Let Putin Critic Go to Germany," BBC, August 21, 2020, https://www.bbc.com/news/world-europe-53865811.

109 **Navalny's new doctors quickly:** "Statement by Charité: Clinical Findings Indicate Alexei Navalny Was Poisoned," Charité: Universitätsmedizin Berlin, press release, August 24, 2020, https://www.charite.de/en/service/press_reports/artikel/detail/statement_by_charite_clinical_findings_indicate_alexei_navalny_was_poisoned.

109 **Less than a month after his collapse:** Anton Troianovski, "Aleksei Navalny Says He'll Return to Russia on Sunday," *New York Times*, January 13, 2021, https://www.nytimes.com/2021/01/13/world/europe/aleksei-navalny-russia-return.html.

109 **When Navalny was finally ready:** Associated Press, "Poisoned Kremlin Critic Alexei Navalny Detained after Landing in Moscow," *Los Angeles Times*, January 17, 2021, https://www.latimes.com/world-nation/story/2021-01-17/navalny-plans-to-return-to-russia-after-recovery-in-germany.

109 **"Bring us some vodka":** Anton Troianovski and Ivan Nechepurenko, "Navalny Arrested on Return to Moscow in Battle of Wills with Putin," *New York Times*, January 17, 2021, https://www.nytimes.com/2021/01/17/world/europe/navalny-russia-return.html.

109 **As soon as he stepped:** Troianovski and Nechepurenko, "Navalny Arrested on Return to Moscow in Battle of Wills with Putin."

109 **a court in Moscow sentenced:** Anton Troianovski, "Russian Activist Navalny Sentenced to More Than 2 Years in Prison," *New York Times*, February 2, 2021, https://www.nytimes.com/2021/02/02/world/europe/russia-navalny-putin.html.

109 **By leaving Russia to be treated:** Troianovski, "Russian Activist Navalny Sentenced to More Than 2 Years in Prison."

110 **"They're imprisoning one person":** *Washington Post* Editorial Board, "Opinion: Navalny's Fiery Indictment of the 'Small Man in a Bunker' Could Rattle Putin's Autocracy," *Washington Post*, February 2, 2021, https://www.washingtonpost.com/opinions/global-opinions/navalnys-fiery-indictment-of-the-small-man-in-a-bunker-could-rattle-putins-autocracy/2021/02/02/2a79140e-657e-11eb-8468-21bc48f07fe5_story.html.

110 **Though the naked power of the Kremlin:** *New York Times* Editorial Board, "Opinion: Vladimir the Poisoner of Underpants," *New York Times*, February 4, 2021, https://www.nytimes.com/2021/02/03/opinion/navalny-putin-speech.html.

110 **Even today, oppressive regimes:** "North Korea: Systematic Repression," Human Rights Watch, January 14, 2020, https://www.hrw.org/news/2020/01/14/north-korea-systematic-repression.

110 **Even failing to express your loyalty:** "Report of the Commission of Inquiry on Human Rights in the Democratic People's Republic of Korea," United Nations Human Rights Council, UN Document Number A/HRC/25/CRP.1, 62, https://www.ohchr.org/en/hrbodies/hrc/coidprk/pages/reportofthecommissionofinquirydprk.aspx.

110 **Some unfortunate souls:** For some striking examples of death sentences or other severe punishments imposed for trivial transgressions, see Faine Greenwood, "North Korean Military Officer Executed—by Mortar Round—for Drinking during Mourning Period for Kim Jong Il," *The World*, October 25, 2012, https://www.pri.org/stories/2012-10-25/north-korean-military-officer-executed-mortar-round-drinking-during-mourning, and Maya Salam and Matthew Haag, "Atrocities Under Kim Jong-un: Indoctrination, Prison Gulags, Executions," *New York Times*, June 11, 2018, https://www.nytimes.com/2018/06/11/world/asia/north-korea-human-rights.html.

110 **Unlike North Koreans, the citizens:** On Nicaragua, see, for example, Ned Price, "Nicaragua's Foreign Agents Law Drives Nicaragua toward Dictatorship, Silencing Independent Voices," United States Department of State, press release, February 8, 2021, https://www.state.gov/nicaraguas-foreign-agents-law-drives-nicaragua-toward-dictatorship-silencing-independent-voices. On Turkey, see, for example, Simon Tisdall, "Recep Tayyip Erdoğan: A Dictator in All but Name Seeks Complete Control," *Guardian*, April 19, 2018, https://www.theguardian.com/world/2018

/apr/19/recep-tayyip-erdogan-turkey-president-election-dictator-seeks-total-control. On Zimbabwe, see, for example, Farai Mutsaka, "Zimbabwe Continues Arrests of Critics, Says Opposition Party," *Washington Post*, August 3, 2020, https://www.washingtonpost.com/world/africa/zimbabwe-continues-arrests-of-critics-says-opposition-party/2020/08/03/1434e6ba-d586-11ea-a788-2ce86ce81129_story.html.

111 **Even countries whose citizens have:** In the Philippines, for example, President Rodrigo Duterte claims the right to kill drug dealers on sight. Unsurprisingly, his henchmen often wind up killing the innocent. See Howard Johnson and Christopher Giles, "Philippines Drug War: Do We Know How Many Have Died?," BBC, November 12, 2019. https://www.bbc.com/news/world-asia-50236481.

111 **As Larry Diamond has chronicled:** Larry Diamond, "Facing Up to the Democratic Recession," *Journal of Democracy* 26, no. 1 (January 2015): 141–55, https://www.journalofdemocracy.org/articles/facing-up-to-the-democratic-recession.

111 **During each of the past fifteen years:** "These withering blows marked the 15th consecutive year of decline in global freedom. The countries experiencing deterioration outnumbered those with improvements by the largest margin recorded since the negative trend began in 2006. The long democratic recession is deepening." Sarah Repucci and Amy Slipowitz, "Freedom in the World 2021: Democracy under Siege," Freedom House, accessed September 26, 2021, https://freedomhouse.org/report/freedom-world/2021/democracy-under-siege.

111 **Fewer than one in five people:** "New Report: The Global Decline in Democracy Has Accelerated," Freedom House, press release, March 3, 2021, https://freedomhouse.org/article/new-report-global-decline-democracy-has-accelerated.

112 **Even in supposedly consolidated democracies:** On the shortcomings of the "consolidation paradigm" and the possibility of democratic deconsolidation in developed countries, see Roberto Stefan Foa and Yascha Mounk, "The Signs of Deconsolidation," *Journal of Democracy* 28, no. 1 (January 2017): 5–15, https://www.journalofdemocracy.org/articles/the-signs-of-deconsolidation.

112 **A state can facilitate:** In some cases, this form of state-tolerated persecution can even be perpetrated by an ideologically committed minority group that enjoys the sanction of public officials.

114 **By the time the sun next rose:** For details on the episode, see Shruti Jain, "Bikaner: Hindu Woman's Family Kill Muslim Man ahead of Her 'Arranged' Marriage," *Wire*, May 3, 2018, https://thewire.in/communalism/in-rajasthans-bikaner-man-killed-over-inter-faith-relationship, and Harsha Kumari Singh, "Bikaner Man, Killed by Girlfriend's Family, Was Also Run Over," NDTV, May 5, 2018, https://www.ndtv.com/india-news/bikaner-man-killed-by-girlfriends-family-was-also-run-over-by-car-1847509. On the long tradition of opposition to interfaith marriages, see also Vikram Seth's seminal novel, *A Suitable Boy* (London: Phoenix, 1995).

The story of a local community punishing a young man for falling in love with somebody who doesn't belong to the same group is, sadly, no aberration. They are depressingly common in India and many other countries around the world. Just a few months earlier, for example, Ankit Saxena, a twenty-three-year-old Hindu man, had fallen in love with Shehzadi, a young Muslim woman. When Shehzadi's family found out that she had agreed to marry Ankit without their permission, they staged an elaborate traffic accident to take revenge. In the early evening of February 1, 2018, Shehzadi's mother deliberately crashed a scooter into Ankit's vehicle. When he got out to help, the whole family set upon him, and his fiancé's father slit his throat. See Shiv Sunny, "Eyewitnesses Recount Delhi Street Horror, Say Girl's Family Feigned Road Rage to Stab Ankit to Death," *Hindustan Times: New Delhi News*, February 5, 2018, https://www.hindustantimes.com/delhi-news/girl-s-mother-feigned-road-rage-to-draw-ankit-out-of-car-eyewitnesses/story-Fj1W2VBCvc3V4nTe4SGNhM.html, and Hemani Bhandari, "Over a Year after Ankit Saxena's Death, Shehzadi Talks about Her Transformation to a Woman in Charge of Her Life," *Hindu*, June 9, 2019, https://www.thehindu.com/news/cities/Delhi/ankit-saxena-murder-shehzadi-opens-up/article27700098.ece.

114 **As Daron Acemoglu:** Daron Acemoglu and James A. Robinson, *The Narrow Corridor: States, Societies, and the Fate of Liberty* (New York: Penguin Press, 2019).

114 **the absence of a state:** Thomas Hobbes and W. G. Pogson Smith, *Hobbes's Leviathan* (Oxford: Clarendon Press, 1943), chapter 13.

114 **"dominance on people":** Acemoglu and Robinson, *The Narrow Corridor*, 19.

114 **From fundamentalist Christians in Topeka:** Topeka, Kansas, is the headquarters of the Westboro Baptist Church. See also Larissa MacFarquhar, "When One Parent Leaves a Hasidic Community, What Happens to the Kids?," *New Yorker*, November 30, 2020, https://www.newyorker.com/maga zine/2020/12/07/when-one-parent-leaves-a-hasidic-community-what-happens-to-the-kids; Richard Orange and Alexandra Topping, "FGM Specialist Calls for Gynecological Checks for All Girls in Sweden," *Guardian*, June 27, 2014, https://www.theguardian.com/society/2014/jun/27/fe male-genital-mutilation-fgm-specialist-sweden-gynaecological-checks-children; and Yassin Musharbash, "Man lebte in Kreuzberg, aber wohl nicht in Deutschland," *Der Spiegel*, April 4, 2006, https://www.spiegel.de/panorama/justiz/ehrenmord-prozess-man-lebte-in-kreuzberg-aber-wohl -nicht-in-deutschland-a-411283.html.

115 **As Lord Acton put it:** Sydney Ahistrom, "Lord Acton's Famous Remark," *New York Times*, March 13, 1974, https://www.nytimes.com/1974/03/13/archives/lord-actons-famous-remark.html.

116 **in the words of John Locke:** John Locke, *Locke: Two Treatises on Government* (Cambridge, UK: Cambridge University Press, 1967).

117 **the individuals who occupy key roles:** The one obvious exception in the United States is the Supreme Court, which is composed of judges with lifetime appointments and now exerts tremendous influence over the country's political life.

117 **Though Mugabe, Chávez, and dozens:** Mugabe ultimately resigned from the presidency in November 2017, at the age of ninety-three, some thirty-seven years after he had first begun to rule the country as prime minister. See, for example, Alan Cowell, "Robert Mugabe, Zimbabwe's 'Founding Father' and Tyrant, Dies," *New York Times*, September 7, 2019, https://www.nytimes.com /2019/09/06/obituaries/robert-mugabe-dead.html, and Norimitsu Onishi and Jeffrey Moyo, "Robert Mugabe Resigns as Zimbabwe's President, Ending 37-Year Rule." *New York Times*, November 21, 2017, https://www.nytimes.com/2017/11/21/world/africa/zimbabwe-mugabe-mnan gagwa.html.

119 **But as long as the state adopts:** Some philosophers refer to this as the state's obligation to "maintain viewpoint neutrality"—for a discussion (and limited critique) of this theory, see, for example, Corey Brettschneider, "Value Democracy as the Basis for Viewpoint Neutrality: A Theory of Free Speech and Its Implications for the State Speech and Limited Public Forum Doctrines," *Northwestern University Law Review* 107, no. 2 (2013): 603–45, https://scholarlycommons.law.northwest ern.edu/nulr/vol107/iss2/7—or "respect the moral autonomy of citizens." See, for example, Joseph Raz, *The Morality of Freedom* (Oxford, UK: Oxford University Press, 2000), and Chris Mills, "How Should Liberal Perfectionists Justify the State?," *Moral Philosophy and Politics* 4, no. 1 (January 2017): 43–65, http://dx.doi.org/10.1515/mopp-2016-0035. Others speak about "the priority of the right over the good." See, for example, John Rawls, *A Theory of Justice* (Oxford, UK : Clarendon Press, 1971) as well as the later reformulations in John Rawls, *Political Liberalism* (New York: Columbia University Press, 1993), and John Rawls, "The Priority of Right and Ideas of the Good," *Philosophy and Public Affairs* 17, no. 4 (Fall 1988): 251–76, https://www.jstor.org/stable /i31376. But though these formulations point to important differences in emphasis, the underlying ambition remains the same: diverse democracies should recognize that there are important aspects of life—questions of faith and morality, of conscience and conviction—in which the state must leave citizens free to make their own choices.

121 **How should a diverse democracy go:** As the British Ghanaian philosopher Anthony Kwame Appiah has pointed out, communitarian societies may do rather less well at recognizing the associational rights of comparatively new organizations. Whether to treat a group with great respect, or to allow other groups to continue to exercise some form of quasi-sovereignty over its members, may ultimately come to depend on whether some agent of the state judges it to have the necessary

group-like characteristics. As Appiah puts the point in a discussion of what kind of social practices communitarians should allow if that question turns on it being sanctioned by a recognized group: "How, in short, are we to establish the boundaries of the group deserving deference? One imagines a vast brigade of state-employed ethnographers, tasked with certifying this or that practice as legitimized by this or that social group." Kwame Anthony Appiah, *The Ethics of Identity* (Princeton, NJ: Princeton University Press, 2010), 76.

121 **If you are a gay man born:** To make things worse, democracies that conceive of themselves as an "association of associations" would also limit the ability of their citizens to intermingle. In a state founded upon ethnic or religious groups that jealously guard the right to rule over the lives of "their own" members, any person who does not fit into a preexisting category becomes a challenge to the entire system. If you have roots in more than one group, you may find that a clash of jurisdictions makes it impossibly difficult to gain a birth certificate or accept an inheritance. And if you wish to marry out of your own tribe, you may, like my friend Abdallah, face a government that simply refuses to register your partnership.

122 **They should be committed to protecting:** This is not to deny that liberals, like adherents of any other viewpoint, will have to make difficult judgment calls in this arena. There will be cases when diverse democracies have to balance the need to free individuals from the cage of norms against the weighty reasons why the state should be highly cautious in telling cultural or religious communities how to constitute themselves. No philosophical standard can wish those kinds of hard cases out of existence. But the way to assess a theoretical framework is whether it adequately captures the competing considerations and liberalism, unlike communitarianism, does.

Chapter Five: Can Patriotism Be a Force for Good?

127 **he had joined an international band of idealists:** George Orwell, *A Homage to Catalonia* (Boston: Mariner Books, 1980).

127 **"The energy that actually shapes the world":** George Orwell, "Wells, Hitler and the World State," *Horizon* 4, no. 20 (August 1941): 133, text available at https://gutenberg.net.au/ebooks03/0300011h.html.

127 **But it is precisely because Orwell:** Orwell's best-known essays on patriotism are "Notes on Nationalism" and "The Lion and the Unicorn: Socialism and the English Genius." But it is in "Wells, Hitler and the World State" that he formulates the problems posed by a lack of healthy patriotism most clearly. See George Orwell, "Notes on Nationalism," The Orwell Foundation: Essays and Other Works, https://www.orwellfoundation.com/the-orwell-foundation/orwell/essays-and-other-works/notes-on-nationalism, George Orwell, "The Lion and the Unicorn: Socialism and the English Genius," The Orwell Foundation: Essays and Other Works, https://www.orwellfoundation.com/the-orwell-foundation/orwell/essays-and-other-works/the-lion-and-the-unicorn-socialism-and-the-english-genius, and Orwell, "Wells, Hitler and the World State."

128 **"we might be watching the SS men":** Orwell, "Wells, Hitler and the World State," 133.

128 **Many activists and intellectuals had managed:** Orwell, "Wells, Hitler and the World State," 133.

129 **Perhaps the rise of noxious nationalists:** For the best defense of cosmopolitanism, see Kwame Anthony Appiah, *Cosmopolitanism: Ethics in a World of Strangers* (New York: W. W. Norton, 2007). Compare also Martha Nussbaum, "Patriotism and Cosmopolitanism," in *The Cosmopolitanism Reader*, eds. Garrett W. Brown and David Held (Cambridge, UK: Polity, 2010), 155–62.

129 **After all, philosophers have a point:** The classic formulation of this point, which also applies to other local attachments beyond the nation, was made in Peter Singer, "Famine, Affluence, and Morality," *Philosophy and Public Affairs* 1, no. 3 (Spring 1972): 229–43, https://www.jstor.org/stable/2265052.

129 **If more people took these obligations:** I say likely since many altruistic efforts to help the poor in distant countries have historically failed to have a positive impact. See William Easterley, *The*

White Man's Burden: Why the West's Efforts to Aid the Rest Have Done So Much Ill and So Little Good (New York: Penguin Press, 2006).

130 **But when decent people succeed:** The last paragraphs build on my argument in Yascha Mounk, *The People Versus Democracy: Why Our Freedom Is in Danger and How to Save It* (Cambridge, MA: Harvard University Press, 2018), chapter 7.

131 **Founded on the basis of ideals:** On India, see, for example, "Republic Day, January 26: History, Significance & Celebration," *Times of India*, January 25, 2020, https://timesofindia.indiatimes .com/home/education/news/republic-day-january-26-history-significance-celebration/articleshow /73604790.cms, and Christophe Jaffrelot, "The Fate of Secularism in India," Carnegie Endowment for International Peace, April 4, 2019, https://carnegieendowment.org/2019/04/04/fate-of -secularism-in-india-pub-78689.

131 **Even countries like Germany:** See Dolf Sternberger, *Verfassungspatriotismus* (Frankfurt: Insel Verlag, 1990), and Jürgen Habermas, "Eine Art Schadensabwicklung," *Die Zeit* 29 (July 11, 1986): 40, https://www.zeit.de/1986/29/eine-art-schadensabwicklung.

132 **His beloved city, Pericles:** See "Pericles," *Encyclopaedia Britannica*, accessed September 26, 2021, https://www.britannica.com/biography/Pericles-Athenian-statesman, and Thomas R. Martin, *Pericles: A Biography in Context* (Cambridge, UK: Cambridge University Press, 2016), 155.

132 **In order to speak in the assembly:** On the privileges of citizenship, see John K. Davies, "Athenian Citizenship: The Descent Group and the Alternatives," *The Classical Journal* 73, no. 2 (December 1977–January 1978): 105, https://www.jstor.org/stable/i366015. On ancestry, see K. R. Walters, "Perikles' Citizenship Law," *Classical Antiquity* 2, no. 2 (October 1983): 316–17, https://doi.org /10.2307/25010801.

133 **The inhabitants of more distant territories:** See, for example, "Civitas," *Encyclopaedia Britannica*, accessed September 26, 2021, https://www.britannica.com/topic/civitas, "Roman Citizenship," Oxford Reference, accessed September 26, 2021, https://www.oxfordreference.com/view /10.1093/oi/authority.20110803095613737, and "Africa," *Encyclopaedia Britannica*, accessed September 26, 2021, https://www.britannica.com/place/Africa.

134 **From Hindus in today's:** Idi Amin expelled all South Asians, the majority of whom were Muslims. On Uganda, see, for example, Reem Shaddad, "Uganda's Asian Exodus: Rose-Tinted Memories and Current Realities," Al Jazeera, June 19, 2018, https://www.aljazeera.com/features/2018/6 /19/ugandas-asian-exodus-rose-tinted-memories-and-current-realities, and "1972: Asians Given 90 Days to Leave Uganda," BBC, August 7, 1972, http://news.bbc.co.uk/onthisday/hi/dates/stories /august/7/newsid_2492000/2492333.stm. On Bangladesh, see Ajaz Ashraf, "Interview: Hindus in Bangladesh Have Faced Ethnic Cleansing Since 1947," Scroll.in, September 17, 2017, https:// scroll.in/article/847725/interview-hindus-in-bangladesh-have-faced-ethnic-cleansing-since -1947.

134 **the birth of postcolonial states:** The most important exceptions to the rule are nations, like India or the United States, that were founded on a form of civic patriotism. I will discuss these in greater detail later in this chapter.

134 **Just as ancient Athens condemned:** See, for example, David Whitehead, "Aristotle the Metic," *Proceedings of the Cambridge Philological Society* 21, no. 201 (January 1975): 94–99, https://doi.org /10.1017%2FS0068673500003734.

136 **To be proud to be an American:** For one influential defense of the civic republican model of patriotism and its contrast to an ethnic form of nationalism, see Maurizio Viroli, *For Love of Country: An Essay on Patriotism and Nationalism* (Oxford, UK: Clarendon Press, 2003).

137 **"The basis of citizenship":** Ramachandra Guha, "The Indian Tragedy," *Liberties* 1, no. 1 (2021): 65, https://libertiesjournal.com/articles/issue/volume-01-number-01.

137 **The Grundgesetz should become:** See Habermas, "Eine Art Schadensabwicklung," and Jürgen Habermas, *The Crisis of the European Union: A Response* (Cambridge, UK: Polity, 2012). See also Jan-Werner Müller, *Constitutional Patriotism* (Princeton, NJ: Princeton University Press, 2007).

138 **For Narendra Modi:** Azeem Ibrahim, "Modi's Slide towards Autocracy," *Foreign Policy*, July 13, 2020, https://foreignpolicy-com.proxy1.library.jhu.edu/2020/07/13/modi-india-hindutva-hindu -nationalism-autocracy.

139 **A lot of Americans have a strong:** "Partisan Antipathy: More Intense, More Personal," Pew Research Center, October 10, 2019, https://www.pewresearch.org/politics/2019/10/10/how -partisans-view-each-other.

139 **But few Americans can explain:** Chris Cillizza, "Americans Know Literally Nothing about the Constitution," CNN, September 13, 2017, https://www.cnn.com/2017/09/13/politics/poll-con stitution/index.html.

140 **Britain would "still be the country":** John Major, "Mr. Major's Speech to Conservative Group for Europe—22 April 1993," The Rt. Hon. Sir John Major KG CH, April 22, 1993, https://johnma jorarchive.org.uk/1993/04/22/mr-majors-speech-to-conservative-group-for-europe-22-april -1993. For context, see also Frances Perraudin, "How Politicians Have Struggled to Define British-ness," *The Guardian*, June 10, 2014, https://www.theguardian.com/uk-news/2014/jun/10/how -politicians-have-struggled-to-define-britishness.

140 **an editorial in *The Independent*:** *Independent* Editorial Board, "Leading Article: What a Lot of Tosh," *Independent*, April 24, 1993, https://www.independent.co.uk/voices/leading-article-what -a-lot-of-tosh-1457335.html.

140 **The idea that warm beer:** When I asked my old friend and sherpa to all things English, William Seward, about the meaning of "pool fillers," he told me: "I assume that pools fillers are people who play the football pools. . . . Ironically it was Major himself who did for the football pools when he introduced the National Lottery in 1994."

140–41 **"National characteristics," Orwell wrote:** Orwell, "The Lion and the Unicorn."

141 **One has historical links:** Hamburg was a key member of the Hanseatic League, which also in-cluded free cities like Stettin in today's Poland, Stockholm in today's Sweden, and Kaliningrad in today's Russia. See, for example, Donald Harreld, *A Companion to the Hanseatic League* (Leiden: Brill, 2015).

141 **The other has long been influenced:** Offenburg was part of the French zone of occupation after World War II; see "Strasbourg History," French Moments, accessed September 26, 2021, https:// frenchmoments.eu/strasbourg-history.

142 **help to determine the "cultural scripts":** Cliff Goddard and Anna Wierzbicka, "Cultural Scripts: What Are They and What Are They Good For?," *Intercultural Pragmatics* 1, no. 2 (January 2004): 157, http://dx.doi.org/10.1515/iprg.2004.1.2.153.

142 **But as Goddard and Wierzbicka:** Goddard and Wierzbicka, "Cultural Scripts," 157.

143 **When asked about their favorite:** See, for example, "Umfrage: Das essen die Deutschen am lieb-sten," *Volksstimme*, July 22, 2013, https://www.volksstimme.de/leben/gesundheit/umfrage-das -essen-die-deutschen-am-liebsten-549578#:~:text=Damit%20liegt%20der%20SPD% 2DKanzlerkandidat,auf%20fast%20acht%20Kilo%20Nudeln, and Shireen Khalil, "Germany's Favourite Fast Food," BBC, February 9, 2017, http://www.bbc.com/travel/story/20170203 -germanys-favourite-fast-food.

144 **And when Americans think about dishes:** Claire Nowak, "This Is Officially America's Favorite Food—It's Not Burgers," *Reader's Digest*, November 16, 2020, https://www.rd.com/article /america-favorite-food.

144 **Scots of Indian extraction:** See, for example, Frankie Allan, "In Pictures: South Asian Culture in Scotland over 30 Years," BBC, December 9, 2018, https://www.bbc.com/news/uk-scotland -46291009, and Sonal Nerukar, "Kilt Meets Kirpan," *Times of India*, September 21, 2014, https:// timesofindia.indiatimes.com/home/Sunday-times/deep-focus/kilt-meets-kirpan/articleshow /43047014.cms.

145 **"When you come back to England":** Orwell, "The Lion and the Unicorn."

Chapter Six: Must the Many Become One?

151 **David Quixano, the fictional protagonist:** Neil Larry Shumsky, "Zangwill's 'The Melting Pot': Ethnic Tensions on Stage," *American Quarterly* 27, no. 1 (March 1975): 29, https://www.jstor.org/stable/i327424.

151 **he would be seized by terrifying:** Israel Zangwill, *The Melting-Pot: Drama in Four Acts* (New York: Macmillan, 1909), 40.

151 **David was determined to use:** Zangwill, *The Melting-Pot*, 47.

151 **His ambition was nothing less:** Zangwill, *The Melting-Pot*, 150.

151 **When immigrants arrived at Ellis Island:** Zangwill, *The Melting-Pot*, 37.

151 **But, he hoped, they "won't be":** Zangwill, *The Melting-Pot*, 37.

151 **The crucible of America would prove:** Zangwill, *The Melting-Pot*, 37.

151 **David's symphony was to express:** Zangwill, *The Melting-Pot*, 38.

151 **Vera Revendal devoted herself:** Zangwill, *The Melting-Pot*, 18.

151 **Inspired by David's vision:** Zangwill, *The Melting-Pot*, 143–45.

152 **"Nothing can separate us":** Zangwill, *The Melting-Pot*, 98.

152 **But as soon as David took:** Zangwill, *The Melting-Pot*, 160–65.

152 **"There is a river of blood":** Zangwill, *The Melting-Pot*, 166.

152 **Four months passed:** Zangwill, *The Melting-Pot*, 173.

152 **Unable to bear the well-wishers:** Zangwill, *The Melting-Pot*, 173–74.

152 **"Failure?" she asked:** Zangwill, *The Melting-Pot*, 192.

152 **"God tried me with his supreme test":** Zangwill, *The Melting-Pot*, 193.

153 **"Shall the shadow of Kishineff":** Zangwill, *The Melting-Pot*, 197.

153 **"Yes," David responded:** Zangwill, *The Melting-Pot*, 197.

153 **As the curtain fell, David:** Zangwill, *The Melting-Pot*, 197.

153 **The vision of America it expressed:** Shumsky, "Zangwill's 'The Melting Pot': Ethnic Tensions on Stage," 29–41.

154 **they haven't actually read Zangwill's:** See, for example, Mike Wallace, "Against the 'Melting Pot' Metaphor," *Lit Hub*, October 30, 2017, https://lithub.com/against-the-melting-pot-metaphor/, William Booth, "The Myth of the Melting Pot: One Nation, Indivisible: Is It History?," *Washington Post*, February 22, 1998, https://www.washingtonpost.com/wp-srv/national/longterm/meltingpot/melt0222.htm, and Timothy Egan, "A Narrative Shattered by Our National Crack-up," *New York Times*, October 27, 2017, https://www.nytimes.com/2017/10/27/opinion/the-national-crackup.html.

155 **Because of the restrictive immigration:** See Elizabeth M. Grievo et al., "The Size, Place of Birth, and Geographic Distribution of the Foreign-Born Population in the United States: 1960 to 2010," US Census Bureau, Population Division Working Paper No. 96, October 2012, https://www.census.gov/content/dam/Census/library/working-papers/2012/demo/POP-twps0096.pdf, and Campbell Gibson and Kay Jung, "Historical Census Statistics on the Foreign-Born Population of the United States: 1850 to 2000," US Census Bureau. Population Division Working Paper No. 81, February 2006, https://www.census.gov/content/dam/Census/library/working-papers/2006/demo/POP-twps0081.pdf, table 1, page 37 of PDF ("Nativity of the Population and Place of Birth of the Native Population: 1850-2000").

156 **Instead, they now embraced a vision:** Sidney Ratner, "Horace M. Kallen and Cultural Pluralism," *Modern Judaism* 4, no. 2 (May 1984): 185–200, https://www.jstor.org/stable/i260692.

156 **guiding ideal as a salad bowl:** On both mosaic and salad bowl, see, for example, Julia Higgins, "The Rise and Fall of the American 'Melting Pot,'" *The Wilson Quarterly*, December 2015, https://www.wilsonquarterly.com/stories/the-rise-and-fall-of-the-american-melting-pot.

157 **The aspiration to build a "multicultural":** For the standard philosophical defenses of multiculturalism, see Will Kymlicka, *Multicultural Citizenship: A Liberal Theory of Minority Rights* (Oxford,

UK: Clarendon Press, 1995), and Charles Taylor and Amy Gutmann, *Multiculturalism: Examining the Politics of Recognition* (Princeton, NJ: Princeton University Press, 1994).

157 **Especially in Europe, most countries:** On Germany, see Yascha Mounk, *A Stranger in My Own Country: A Jewish Family in Modern Germany* (New York: Farrar, Straus and Giroux, 2014), 200. On Italy, see Demetrios G. Papademetriou and Kimberly A. Hamilton, *Converging Paths to Restriction: French, Italian, and British Responses to Immigration* (Washington, DC: Carnegie Endowment for International Peace, 1996), chapter 3.

157 **Even once that self-serving myth:** On opposition to the cultural changes caused by immigration at the highest level of European politics, see, for example, Carl Altaner, "The Weight of Public Opinion: Tracing the Social and Political Genealogy of the British Nationality Act 1981," University of Oxford: Centre on Migration, Policy and Society, Working Paper No. 152, 2020, 17–18, and Claus Hecking, "Kohl Wanted Half of Turks Out of Germany," *Der Spiegel*, August 1, 2013, https://www.spiegel.de/international/germany/secret-minutes-chancellor-kohl-wanted -half-of-turks-out-of-germany-a-914376.html.

157 **Town councils all over Europe:** This was also reflected in cultural policy at both the national and the European level. See, for example, Oriane Calligaro, "From 'European Cultural Heritage' to 'Cultural Diversity'? The Changing Core Values of European Cultural Policy," *Politique Européenne* 45, no. 3 (2014): 60–85, https://www.cairn.info/revue-politique-europeenne-2014-3-page-60 .htm.

157 **In Germany, the Green Party:** "The Integration Debate in Germany: Is Multi-Kulti Dead?," *Economist*, October 22, 2010, https://www.economist.com/newsbook/2010/10/22/is-multi-kulti -dead. See also the sections on Claudia Roth in Yascha Mounk, "How a Teen's Death Became a Political Weapon," *New Yorker*, January 21, 2019, https://www.newyorker.com/magazine/2019/01 /28/how-a-teens-death-has-become-a-political-weapon.

157 **imperial nostalgia of "Rule Britannia":** "Cool Britannia," *Economist*, March 12, 1998, https:// www.economist.com/leaders/1998/03/12/cool-britannia.

158 **an "association of associations":** See, for example, Arend Lijphart, "Typologies of Democratic Systems," *Comparative Political Studies Journal* 1, no. 1 (April 1968): 7–44, https://doi.org /10.2307/421322, and Chandran Kukathas, "Cultural Toleration," *Nomos* 39 (1997): 94, https:// www.jstor.org/stable/24219972.

158 **Muslim children would be educated:** See, for example, "Facts about Faith Schools," *Guardian*, November 14, 2001, https://www.theguardian.com/education/2001/nov/14/schools.uk2, and Emily Dugan, "Inside Britain's First Hindu State-Funded Faith Schools," *Independent*, February 10, 2014, https://www.independent.co.uk/news/education/education-news/inside-britain-s-first -hindu-state-funded-faith-school-1711566.html.

158 **David Bell, then the chief inspector:** See Tony Halpin, "Islamic Schools Are Threat to National Identity," *Sunday Times*, January 18, 2005, https://www.thetimes.co.uk/article/islamic-schools -are-threat-to-national-identity-says-ofsted-tmhw6w2sgtb, and Rebecca Smithers, "Anger at Muslim Schools Attack," *Guardian*, January 18, 2005, https://www.theguardian.com/uk/2005/jan/18 /schools.faithschools.

158 **"Why should state-funded schools":** Anthea Lipsett, "MPs to Voice Concerns over Faith Schools," *Guardian*, January 2, 2008, https://www.theguardian.com/education/2008/jan/02 /schools.faithschools.

158 **majority of the population has long:** Toby Helm and Mark Townsend, "Taxpayers' Cash Should Not Be Used to Fund Faith Schools, Say Voters," *Guardian*, June 14, 2014, https://www.theguard ian.com/education/2014/jun/14/taxpayers-should-not-fund-faith-schools.

158 **found guilty of rigging the vote:** Dave Hill, "Labour's Tower Hamlets Win Is Deserved, but John Biggs Cannot Be Complacent," *Guardian*, June 12, 2015, https://www.theguardian.com/com mentisfree/2015/jun/12/labour-tower-hamlets-lutfur-rahman-john-biggs.

158 **Local critics who dared to speak:** Oscar Rickett, "London's Most Controversial Mayor Got Kicked Out of Office for Corruption," *Vice*, April 24, 2015, https://www.vice.com/en/article /yvxz95/lutfur-rahman-kicked-out-corruption-399.

160 **Playing to that reluctance, Rahman:** Hill, "Labour's Tower Hamlets Win Is Deserved, but John Biggs Cannot Be Complacent." For further details on Rahman, see also Ed Davey, "Tower Hamlets Election Case Witnesses 'Intimidated,'" BBC, October 31, 2014, https://www.bbc.com/news /uk-england-london-29850569.

160 **Out of a misguided reluctance:** Renée Kool and Sohail Wahedi, "Criminal Enforcement in the Area of Female Genital Mutilation in France, England and the Netherlands: A Comparative Law Perspective," *International Law Research* 3, no. 1 (April 2014): 1–15, https://dx.doi.org/10.2139 /ssrn.2433554, and Richard Orange and Alexandra Topping, "FGM Specialist Calls for Gynecological Checks for All Girls in Sweden," *Guardian*, June 27, 2014, https://www.theguardian .com/society/2014/jun/27/female-genital-mutilation-fgm-specialist-sweden-gynaeco logical-checks-children.

160 **In 2014, for example, Anissa:** Orange and Topping, "FGM Specialist Calls for Gynecological Checks for All Girls in Sweden."

160 **multiculturalism requires respect:** Ellen Gruenbaum, *The Female Circumcision Controversy: An Anthropological Perspective* (Philadelphia: University of Pennsylvania Press, 2001).

160 **Sara Johnsdotter, told *The Guardian*:** Orange and Topping, "FGM Specialist Calls for Gynecological Checks for All Girls in Sweden."

161 **the new multicultural dish:** The more you think about it, the less welcoming the metaphor of the salad bowl appears. Nobody would want to eat a salad that is completely dry—or mostly consists of croutons. So the ingredients of a salad may retain some of their original character. But for the salad to be edible, somebody needs to make a tasty dressing and select the ingredients—and the ratio between them—with great care.

Taken seriously, the salad bowl thus suggests a strangely paranoid vision of how diverse democracies might work. Do politicians carefully need to monitor what kind of immigrant groups are added to the existing mix, lest one of them should come to predominate, clash with existing groups, or make the bowl overflow? And do we all need to impose some kind of shared culture to tie the dish together? (Similar objections apply to mosaics, which may consist of many different elements but have to be arranged with the utmost care if they are to make up a coherent whole.)

To be sure, few metaphors work if you insist on taking them *that* literally. But the real-world difficulties that result when democracies think of themselves as being composed of different elements which barely need to be in communication with one another are much harder to wave away.

Chapter Seven: Can We Build a Meaningfully Shared Life?

170 **three different approaches to the informal rules:** There are many different ways to answer each of the questions that are now widely debated, and more ways still to combine each of these different answers into an overall vision. The number of possible futures is large, and any attempt to condense them into a few basic models—as I do here—necessarily incomplete. And yet I do believe that much of the public debate is now taken up by three broad sets of perspectives that have a certain amount of internal coherence. Even though they will not capture the position of each and every participant in these debates, they amount to useful "ideal types" that can help to elucidate the basic set of options facing the future of diverse democracies.

171 **"When someone gets beaten up":** The description of Benjamin Jahn Zschocke and the far-right protests in Chemnitz is drawn from an article I originally published in *The New Yorker*: Yascha Mounk, "How a Teen's Death Became a Political Weapon," *New Yorker*, January 21, 2019, https:// www.newyorker.com/magazine/2019/01/28/how-a-teens-death-has-become-a-political-weapon.

172 **Matteo Salvini, the leader of Italy's:** Rachel Donadio, "The New Populist Playbook," *Atlantic*, September 5, 2019, https://www.theatlantic.com/international/archive/2019/09/matteo-salvini-italy -populist-playbook/597298.

172 **Donald Trump's campaign slogan:** Brooke Seipel, "Trump: 'Make America Great Again' Slogan 'Was Made Up by Me,'" *The Hill*, April 2, 2019, https://thehill.com/homenews/administration /437070-trump-make-america-great-again-slogan-was-made-up-by-me.

173 **By opposing most forms of immigration:** On Central Europe, see, for example, "Multicultural-ism Doesn't Work in Hungary, Says Orban," Reuters, June 3, 2015, https://www.reuters.com /article/us-hungary-orban/multiculturalism-doesnt-work-in-hungary-says-orban-idUSKB N0OJ0T920150603, and Kata Karath, "Viktor Orbán's Bigoted Vision Leaves Me Ashamed to Be Hungarian," *Guardian,* March 7, 2021, https://www.theguardian.com/commentisfree/2018/mar/07 /hungary-young-national-pride-viktor-orban-europe. On East Asia, see, for example, Alanna Schu-bach, "The Case for a More Multicultural Japan," Al Jazeera, November 12, 2014, http://america .aljazeera.com/opinions/2014/11/multiculturalismjapanantikoreanprotests.html.

173 **In Switzerland, for example:** Nick Cumming-Bruce and Steven Erlanger, "Swiss Ban Building of Minarets on Mosques," *New York Times*, November 29, 2009, https://www.nytimes.com/2009/11 /30/world/europe/30swiss.html.

173 **A number of other democracies ban:** See "Legal Restrictions on Religious Slaughter in Europe," The Law Library of Congress, March 2018, https://www.loc.gov/law/help/religious-slaughter/reli gious-slaughter-europe.pdf, and "EU Court Backs Ban on Animal Slaughter without Stunning," BBC, December 17, 2020, https://www.bbc.com/news/world-europe-55344971.

174 **the United States grew more diverse:** See William H. Frey, "The Nation Is Diversifying Even Faster Than Predicted, According to New Census Data," Brookings, July 1, 2020, https://www .brookings.edu/research/new-census-data-shows-the-nation-is-diversifying-even-faster-than -predicted, and "Polling Update: Americans Continue to Resist Negative Messages about Immi-grants, but Partisan Differences Continue to Grow," National Immigration Forum, September 18, 2020, https://immigrationforum.org/article/polling-update-americans-continue-to-resist-negative -messages-about-immigrants-but-partisan-differences-continue-to-grow.

178 **Variously identified as "woke":** This term was coined by Wesley Yang. See, for example, my inter-view with Wesley Yang, "The Woke Future," Persuasion, January 6, 2021, https://www.persuasion .community/p/the-woke-future.

180 **A true emancipation from racism:** Karen Elise Fields and Barbara J. Fields, *Racecraft: The Soul of Inequality in American Life* (New York: Verso, 2012).

180 **Many people suffer severe disadvantage:** Gayatri Chakravorty Spivak, *The Spivak Reader: Se-lected Works of Gayatri Chakravorty Spivak,* eds. Donna Landry and Gerald MacLean (London: Taylor & Francis Group, 1995), especially pages 204–5.

181 **"If you prick us, do we not bleed":** William Shakespeare, *The Merchant of Venice* (Oxford: Claren-don Press, 1993), quote from act 3, scene1.

181 **stories posted by Humans of New York:** Humans of New York, accessed June 1, 2021, https:// www.humansofnewyork.com.

181 **As Salman Rushdie once put it:** Quoted in Robert Andrews, *The Columbia Dictionary of Quota-tions* (New York: Columbia University Press, 1993), 531.

181 **prove the benefits of literature:** David Comer Kidd and Emanuele Castano, "Reading Literary Fiction Improves Theory of Mind," *Science* 342, no. 6156 (October 2013): 377–80, https://sci ence.sciencemag.org/content/342/6156/377.abstract?sid=f192d0cc-1443-4bf1-a043 -61410da39519.

182 **Those who have a comparatively privileged:** For an academic discussion of "standpoint episte-mology," see, for example, Sandra Harding, "Rethinking Standpoint Epistemology: What's 'Strong Objectivity?,'" *Centennial Review* 36, no. 3 (Fall 1992): 437–70, https://www.jstor.org/stable /23739232. For an instance of standpoint epistemology in public discourse, see, for example,

Lorraine Devon Wilke, "No, White People Will Never Understand the Black Experience," *Huff-Post*, December 6, 2017, https://www.huffpost.com/entry/no-white-people-will-neve_b_7875608.

183 **"full of carvings, curios":** Ross Coggins, "The Development Set," January 27, 2012, https://more newsfromafar.wordpress.com/2012/01/27/the-development-set-by-ross-coggins-2. The poem goes on: "Eye-level photographs subtly assure / That your host is at home with the rich and the poor."

183 **Understandably worried about the history:** Wesley Morris, "For Centuries, Black Music, Forged in Bondage, Has Been the Sound of Complete Artistic Freedom. No Wonder Everybody Is Always Stealing It," *New York Times*, August 14, 2019, https://www.nytimes.com/interactive/2019/08/14 /magazine/music-black-culture-appropriation.html.

183 **donned the clothing of minority cultures:** Terry Tang, "Debate Erupts over Halloween Costumes Crossing Racial Lines," PBS, October 28, 2018, https://www.pbs.org/newshour/nation/debate -erupts-over-halloween-costumes-crossing-racial-lines.

183 **advocates of the challenger ideology:** For philosophical discussions of cultural appropriation, see, for example, Richard A. Rogers, "From Cultural Exchange to Transculturation: A Review and Reconceptualization of Cultural Appropriation," *Communication Theory* 16, no. 4 (November 2006): 474–503, https://doi.org/10.1111/j.1468-2885.2006.00277.x; James O. Young, "Profound Offense and Cultural Appropriation" *Journal of Aesthetics and Art Criticism* 63, no. 2 (Spring 2005): 135–46, https://www.jstor.org/stable/3700467; Erich Hatala Matthes, "Cultural Appropriation without Cultural Essentialism?," *Social Theory and Practice* 42, no. 2 (April 2016): 343–66, https://www.jstor.org/stable/24871347; and C. Thi Nguyen and Matthew Strohl, "Cultural Appropriation and the Intimacy of Groups," *Philosophical Studies* 176, no. 4 (April 2019): 981–1002, https://link.springer.com/article/10.1007/s11098-018-1223-3. For a journalistic exploration, see Rivka Galchen and Anna Holmes, "What Distinguishes Cultural Exchange from Cultural Appropriation?," *New York Times*, June 8, 2017, https://www.nytimes.com/2017/06/08 /books/review/bookends-cultural-appropriation.html.

183 **And while it remains acceptable to cook:** Carolina Moreno, "Portland Burrito Cart Closes after Owners Are Accused of Cultural Appropriation," *HuffPost*, May 25, 2017, https://www.huffpost .com/entry/portland-burrito-cart-closes-after-owners-are-accused-of-cultural-appropriation_n _5926ef7ee4b062f96a348181.

184 **have gotten into serious trouble:** Mira Miller, "New Toronto Clothing Store Ditches Broth Bar after Cultural Appropriation Complaints," *blogTo*, November 2020, https://www.blogto.com/eat _drink/2020/11/toronto-clothing-store-ditches-broth-bar-cultural-appropriation-complaints.

185 **Because Latinos and African Americans:** Raul A. Reyes, "Hispanic Republicans? Yep, and They're Here to Stay, Says Author Geraldo Cadava," NBC, June 2, 2020, https://www.nbcnews .com/news/latino/hispanic-republicans-yep-they-re-here-stay-says-author-geraldo-n1215556; Jessica Fulton and Ryan Pougiales, "A Nuanced Picture of What Black Americans Want in 2020," Third Way, December 30, 2019, http://thirdway.imgix.net/pdfs/a-nuanced-picture-of-what -black-americans-want-in-2020.pdf.

189 **politicians like India's Narendra Modi:** Shekhar Gupta, "India Has a New Political Divide—Majority Kanwarias vs Elite Halloweeners," *Print*, November 10, 2018, https://theprint.in/na tional-interest/kanwarias-vs-halloweeners-indias-new-political-faultline/147733.

189 **to Valentine's Day, as dangerous attacks:** Aditya Sharma, "India's Modi Gets Invitation for Valentine's Day from Citizenship Law Protesters," DW, February 14, 2020, https://www.dw.com/en /indias-modi-gets-invitation-for-valentines-day-from-citizenship-law-protesters/a-52376124.

189 **must be preserved with chloral hydrate:** M. E. Schauff, "Collecting and Preserving Insects and Mites: Techniques and Tools," *U.S. Department of Agriculture: Agricultural Research Service*, Publication No. 84791 Systematic Entomology Laboratory, USDA and National Museum of Natural History, NHB, Washington, DC, 1998, https://www.ars.usda.gov/ARSUserFiles/80420580 /CollectingandPreservingInsectsandMites/collpres.pdf.

191 **Tex-Mex restaurant while "Old Town Road":** Elias Leight, "Lil Nas X's 'Old Town Road' Was a Country Hit. Then Country Changed Its Mind," *Rolling Stone*, March 26, 2019, https://www.rollingstone.com/music/music-features/lil-nas-x-old-town-road-810844.

192 **groups that have long been discriminated:** For a subtle philosophical defense of the need for such groups, especially in the context of African Americans, see Tommie Shelby, *We Who Are Dark: The Philosophical Foundations of Black Solidarity* (Cambridge, MA: Harvard University Press, 2009).

Chapter Eight: Reasons for Optimism

201 **surprise bestsellers have argued:** On France, see Eric Zemmour, *Le Suicide Francais* (Paris: Albin Michel, 2015), and Eleanor Beardsley, "A French Best-Seller's Radical Argument: Vichy Regime Wasn't All Bad," NPR, November 5, 2014, https://www.npr.org/2014/11/05/361790018/a-french-best-sellers-radical-argument-vichy-regime-wasnt-all-bad. On Japan, see Sharin Yamano, *Manga Kenkanryu* (Tokyo: Shin'yūsha, 2011); Leo Lewis, "Neighbor Fails to See Funny Side of Comic," *Times*, November 1, 2005, https://www.thetimes.co.uk/article/neighbour-fails-to-see-funny-side-of-comic-tcjqpjwdmg7; and the books of Ko Bunyu. On Germany, see Thilo Sarrazin, *Deutschland Schafft Sich Ab: Wie wir unser Land aufs Spiel setzen* (Munich: DVA, 2010). On America, see Ann Coulter, *Adios America: The Left's Plan to Turn Our Country into a Third World Hellhole* (New York: Regnery, 2015).

203 **Europe's largest sewage treatment plant:** "Europe's Largest Wastewater Project Gets Boost by KSB Pumps," Waterworld, April 7, 2017, https://www.waterworld.com/international/wastewater/article/16203176/europes-largest-wastewater-project-gets-boost-by-ksb-pumps.

203 **Her sixth graders asked for advice:** The description of Lamya Kaddor is drawn from an article I originally published in *Harper's Magazine*. Yascha Mounk, "Echt Deutsch," *Harper's Magazine*, April 2017, https://harpers.org/archive/2017/04/echt-deutsch.

205 **"a background of migration":** See "German Population of Migrant Background Rises to 21 Million." DW, July 28, 2020, https://www.dw.com/en/german-population-of-migrant-background-rises-to-21-million/a-54356773, and "Germany: In 20 years, 1 in 3 People Will Have Migrant Roots," DW, April 11, 2019, https://www.dw.com/en/germany-in-20-years-1-in-3-people-will-have-migrant-roots/a-51101172.

205 **From Italy to Switzerland:** See Catherine Edwards, "What Does It Mean to Be a 'New Italian'? The Question Facing a Divided Italy," *The Local*, July 21, 2017, https://www.thelocal.it/20170721/who-are-the-new-italians-second-generation-children-migrants-ius-soli-citizenship, and AFP, "'We're Italian Too': Second-Generation Migrants Renew Calls for Citizenship," *Local*, August 25, 2020, https://www.thelocal.it/20200825/were-italian-too-second-generaton-immigrants-renew-calls-for-citizenship; Philip Olterman, "Switzerland Puzzles over Citizenship Test after Lifelong Resident Fails," *Guardian*, July 18, 2017, https://www.theguardian.com/world/2017/jul/18/switzerland-puzzles-over-citizenship-test-after-lifelong-resident-fails.

206 **A significant minority of Europeans:** Bruce Stokes, "What It Takes to Be Truly 'One of Us': 3. Birthright Nationality," Pew Research Center, February 1, 2017, https://www.pewresearch.org/global/2017/02/01/birthright-nationality.

206 **But for some Americans:** Marta Maria Maldonado, "'It Is Their Nature to Do Menial Labour': The Racialization of 'Latino/a Workers' by Agricultural Employers," *Ethnic and Racial Studies* 32, no. 6 (July 2009): 1017–36, http://dx.doi.org/10.1080/01419870902802254.

206 **Something similar holds true for Poles:** Ros Taylor, "'I Want to Try and Tell Them the Facts': Adolescents Challenging the Negative Stereotypes of Polish Migration," *LSE Blog*, June 24, 2019, https://blogs.lse.ac.uk/brexit/2019/06/24/i-want-to-try-and-tell-them-the-facts-adolescents-challenging-the-negative-stereotypes-of-polish-migration.

A similar phenomenon even helps to limit the prospects of one of the most successful minority groups in the United States. Thanks to their remarkable educational achievement and economic success, Asian Americans are often celebrated as a "model minority." But as Wesley Yang has chronicled, they often hit a "bamboo ceiling." Perceived as lacking the intangible characteristics needed for leadership, college admissions counselors dismiss them as having a "bad personality," and big corporations deny them promotion to leadership roles. In corporate America, Yang wrote in a viral 2011 essay in *New York*, there are "lots of Asians at junior levels, quite a few in middle management, and virtually none in the higher reaches of leadership." Wesley Yang, "Paper Tigers," *New York*, May 6, 2011, https://nymag.com/news/features/asian-americans-2011-5.

207 **In one fictional scenario he develops:** Sarrazin, *Deutschland Schafft Sich Ab: Wie wir unser Land aufs Spiel*.

208 **only one in five schoolchildren:** "Die Auswertung der Einschulungsstatistik ergab, dass 2045 noch 48 Prozent, 2075 lediglich 30 Prozent und 2105 gar nur noch 20 Prozent der Einschüler für den muttersprachlichen Unterricht das Fach Deutsch wählten," excerpted in Thilo Sarrazin, "Deutschland in 100 Jahren—Traum oder Albtraum," *Bild*, August 28, 2010, https://www.bild.de/politik/2010/deutschland-in-100-jahren-traum-oder-albtraum-13775464.bild.html.

208 **"Unlike past immigrant groups, Mexicans":** Samuel P. Huntington, "The Hispanic Challenge," *Foreign Policy*, March 2004, https://foreignpolicy.com/2009/10/28/the-hispanic-challenge.

209 **But, especially in Western Europe:** Stokes, "What It Takes to Be Truly 'One of Us.'"

209 **The number of people who believe:** Compared to Latinos and Asians, African Americans have long been much more likely to be seen as "truly American." Most white Americans trace their arrival in the New World to the nineteenth or twentieth centuries. A majority of African Americans have at least some ancestors who were forcibly brought to the country by the time the American Republic was founded in the late eighteenth century. So while most other minority groups are always liable to be told to "go back where you came from," even bigots and racists usually pay African Americans the courtesy of recognizing that, second only to Native Americans, they have one of the most indefeasible claims to belonging in this country. Obviously enough, however, this does not protect African Americans from other forms of discrimination, which are in many ways even more pernicious. For a discussion of the particular challenge they pose to an optimistic account of the current state of diverse democracies, see the end of the next section, on "The Gap in Jobs and Education."

209 **more than two out of every three new citizens:** See Alex Nowrasteh and Andrew C. Forrester, "Immigrants Recognize American Greatness: Immigrants and Their Descendants Are Patriotic and Trust America's Governing Institutions," February 4, 2019, CATO Institute, https://www.cato.org/publications/immigration-research-policy-brief/immigrants-recognize-american-greatness-immigrants, and Zaid Jilani, "Immigrants Are Far More Patriotic Than the Right Fears or the Left Hopes," Persuasion, July 29, 2020, https://www.persuasion.community/p/immigrants-are-far-more-patriotic.

210 **A great many households:** See, for example, Richard Alba, "Bilingualism Persists, but English Still Dominates," Migration Policy Institute, February 1, 2005, https://www.migrationpolicy.org/article/bilingualism-persists-english-still-dominates; Michael Skapinker, "Immigrants' Descendants Lose the Language—Sadly," *Financial Times*, May 14, 2019, https://www.ft.com/content/d16f54b6-730f-11e9-bbfb-5c68069fbd15; and David Cho, "Separated by a Wall of Words," *Washington Post*, April 11, 2001, https://www.washingtonpost.com/archive/politics/2001/04/11/separated-by-a-wall-of-words/ed1cb1d3-18ed-4c0b-ac2a-da629399f68f.

210 **While a clear majority of first-generation:** Mark Hugo Lopez, Jens Manuel Krogstad, and Antonio Flores, "Most Hispanic Parents Speak Spanish to Their Children but This Is Less the Case in Later Immigrant Generations," Pew Research Center, April 2, 2018, https://www.pewresearch.org/fact-tank/2018/04/02/most-hispanic-parents-speak-spanish-to-their-children-but-this-is-less-the-case-in-later-immigrant-generations.

211 **While some immigrants have thrived:** Maurice Crul and Jens Schneider, "The Second Generation in Europe: Education and the Transition to the Labor Market," TIES: The Integration of the

European Second Generation University of Amsterdam, June 2009, https://www.migrationpolicy.org/pubs/Crul2010.pdf.

212 **Meanwhile, the Organisation for Economic Co-operation and Development**: Anthony Heath and Wouter Zwysen, "The European Union: Entrenched Disadvantage? Intergenerational Mobility of Young Natives with a Migration Background," in OECD, *Catching Up? Country Studies on Intergenerational Mobility and Children of Immigrants* (Paris: OECD Publishing, 2018), 145, https://doi.org/10.1787/9789264301030-en.

212 **Residents of the European Union**: "Migrant Integration Statistics—at Risk of Poverty and Social Exclusion," European Commission, January 2021, https://ec.europa.eu/eurostat/statistics-explained/index.php?title=Migrant_integration_statistics_-_at_risk_of_poverty_and_social_exclusion.

212 **students with an immigrant background**: "Finding the Way: A Discussion of the Swedish Migrant Integration System," OECD, July 2014, especially pages 5–7, https://www.oecd.org/migration/swedish-migrant-intergation-system.pdf. Some immigrant groups are faring especially poorly. Only about one out of every four Somali immigrants to the country, for example, has a steady job.

213 **When researchers sent fake CVs**: "New CSI Research Reveals High Levels of Job Discrimination Faced by Ethnic Minorities in Britain," Centre for Social Investigation, Nuffield College, Oxford, January 18, 2019, http://csi.nuff.ox.ac.uk/?p=1299.

213 **Around the world, studies have found**: On Japan, see Jonathon Baron, "Mass Attitudes and Discrimination against Hypothetical Job Candidates in Japan: A Resume-based Survey Experiment," Yale University, June 19, 2020, https://papers.ssrn.com/sol3/papers.cfm?abstract_id=3631838. On Switzerland, see Eva Zschirnt and Rosita Fibbi, "Do Swiss Citizens of Immigrant Origin Face Hiring Discrimination in the Labour Market?," February 2019, Working Paper No. 20 in "NCCR—The Migration-Mobility Nexus," https://cadmus.eui.eu/handle/1814/65726. On the Netherlands, see Iris Andriessen, Eline Nievers, and Jaco Dagevos, "Ethnic Discrimination in the Dutch Labor Market: Its Relationship with Job Characteristics and Multiple Group Membership," *Work and Occupations* 39, no. 3 (August 2012): 237–69, https://journals.sagepub.com/doi/10.1177/0730888412444783. On the United States, see Lincoln Quillian, Devah Pager, Ole Hexel, and Arnfinn H. Midtbøen, "Meta-Analysis of Field Experiments Shows No Change in Racial Discrimination in Hiring over Time," *Proceedings of the National Academy of Sciences* 114, no. 41 (September 2017): 10870–875, http://dx.doi.org/10.1073/pnas.1706255114.

213 **account is nevertheless rejected**: See Coulter, *Adios America*; Zemmour, *Le Suicide Francais*; and the books of Ko Bunyu. Though Bunyu himself is from Taiwan, he primarily writes for a Japanese audience. See, for example, Julian Ryall, "China Should Pay Its Respects at Japan's Yasukuni Shrine, Says Taiwan Author Ko Bunyu," *South China Morning Post*, April 24, 2015, https://www.scmp.com/news/asia/article/1774876/taiwanese-author-ko-bunyu-says-china-should-pay-its-respects-japans.

213 **The reason for the persistent gaps in jobs**: See, for example, Sander L. Gilman, "Thilo Sarrazin and the Politics of Race in the Twenty-First Century," *New German Critique* 39, no. 3 (2012): 47–59, https://doi.org/10.2307/j.ctvss3xg0.10.

213 **To them, the socioeconomic disadvantage of minority groups**: For a summary of debates in France, see, for example, Catherine Fieschi, "Muslims and the Secular City: How Right-Wing Populists Shape the French Debate over Islam," Brookings, February 28, 2020, https://www.brookings.edu/research/muslims-and-the-secular-city-how-right-wing-populists-shape-the-french-debate-over-islam/#cancel.

214 **some immigrant groups actually outearn**: Prasun Sonwalkar, "Indians Earn More Than White British Employees in UK, Says Report," *Hindustan Times*, July 9, 2019, https://www.hindustantimes.com/india-news/indians-earn-more-than-whites-in-uk-says-report/story-qd02npVJaFvVjzFvXtQa4I.html.

214　**Chinese, Lebanese, and Nigerian immigrants:** Mark J. Perry, "Chart of the Day," American Enterprise Institute, March 17, 2016, https://www.aei.org/carpe-diem/chart-of-the-day-4.

215　**"provides clear evidence of a narrowing gap":** Doris Oberdabernig and Alyssa Schneebaum, "Catching Up? The Educational Mobility of Migrants' and Natives' Children in Europe," *Applied Economics* 49, no. 37 (2017): 3716, https://doi.org/10.1080/00036846.2016.1267843. Out of eleven countries studied, the two exceptions were Estonia and Latvia. The finding held true in countries including Belgium, Germany, France, and the United Kingdom.

　　Other data sources suggest similar conclusions. While only one out of every eight Sahelian immigrant couples to France hold diplomas that qualify them to study at university, for example, almost half of their children go on to earn an upper secondary degree. See Cris Beauchemin, "Chapter 2: France: Intergenerational Mobility Outcomes of Natives with Immigrant Parents," *Catching Up? Country Studies on Intergenerational Mobility and Children of Immigrants*. OECD. 2017. https://www.oecd-ilibrary.org/sites/9789264301030-4-en/index.html?itemId=/content/component/9789264301030-4-en.

　　Similarly, in the United Kingdom, children from ethnic minorities who have poor parents are now very likely to go to university. In London, two out of every three poor Chinese kids, three out of every five poor Bangladeshi and Indian kids, and one out of every two poor Black-African kids embark on a higher degree. See Tony Sewell CBE, Maggie Aderin-Pocock MBE, and Chughtai, Aftab MBE et al., "Commission on Race and Ethnic Disparities: The Report," UK Government Commission. March 2021. https://assets.publishing.service.gov.uk/government/uploads/system/uploads/attachment_data/file/974507/20210331_-_CRED_Report_-_FINAL_-_Web_Accessible.pdf. See Table 7 "Progression rates to higher education by age 19 – 2018/2019" on page 93.

　　The same is true in North America. In Canada, first- and second-generation immigrants are actually more likely to go to college than Canadians whose ancestors have been in the country for over three generations. See Martin Turcotte, "Education and Labour Market Outcomes of Children with an Immigrant Background by Their Region of Origin," Statistics Canada: Ethnicity, Language and Immigration Thematic Series, November 15, 2019, https://www150.statcan.gc.ca/n1/en/pub/89-657-x/89-657-x2019018-eng.pdf?st=bwLMozx8.

216　**"Children of immigrants from nearly every sending country":** Ran Abramitzky, Leah Platt Boustan, Elisa Jácome, and Santiago Pérez, "Intergenerational Mobility of Immigrants in the US over Two Centuries," National Bureau of Economic Research, Working Paper 26408, October 2019 (quote is on page 30), https://www.nber.org/papers/w26408.

216　**A lot of observers, the economists conclude:** Abramitzky, Platt Boustan, Jácome, and Pérez, "Intergenerational Mobility of Immigrants in the US over Two Centuries," 31.

217　**On average, African Americans earn 75 percent:** Eileen Patten, "Racial, Gender Wage Gaps Persist in U.S. Despite Some Progress," Pew Research Center, July 1, 2016, https://www.pewresearch.org/fact-tank/2016/07/01/racial-gender-wage-gaps-persist-in-u-s-despite-some-progress.

217　**The wealth disparity between white and black:** Kriston McIntosh, Emily Moss, Ryan Nunn, and Jay Shambaugh, "Examining the Black-White Wealth Gap," Brookings, February 27, 2020, https://www.brookings.edu/blog/up-front/2020/02/27/examining-the-black-white-wealth-gap.

217　**For Asian households, who significantly:** Valerie Wilson, "Racial Disparities in Income and Poverty Remain Largely Unchanged amid Strong Income Growth in 2019," Economic Policy Institute, September 16, 2020, https://www.epi.org/blog/racial-disparities-in-income-and-poverty-remain-largely-unchanged-amid-strong-income-growth-in-2019.

217　**much more likely to be incarcerated:** "Criminal Justice Fact Sheet," NAACP, accessed February 22, 2021, https://www.naacp.org/criminal-justice-fact-sheet.

217–18　**Making his electoral pitch to black voters:** Tom LoBianco and Ashley Killough, "Trump Pitches Black Voters: 'What the Hell Do You Have to Lose?,'" CNN, August 19, 2016, https://www.cnn.com/2016/08/19/politics/donald-trump-african-american-voters/index.html.

218 **Raj Chetty's important research demonstrates:** "Racial Disparities in Income Mobility Persist, Especially for Men," Opportunity Insights, accessed September 26, 2021, https://opportunityin sights.org/race.

218 **Of every one hundred black Americans who grew up:** Emily Badger, Claire Cain Miller, Adam Pearce, and Kevin Quealy, "Income Mobility Charts for Girls, Asian-Americans and Other Groups. Or Make Your Own," *New York Times*, March 27, 2018, https://www.nytimes.com/inter active/2018/03/27/upshot/make-your-own-mobility-animation.html. To retrieve these results, input "Follow the lives of [black boys and girls] and [black boys and girls] from [poor] households, using their [individual] incomes as adults and including kids of [only native-born mothers]."

See also Raj Chetty, Nathaniel Hendren, Maggie R. Jones, and Sonya R. Porter, "Race and Economic Opportunity in the United States: An Intergenerational Perspective," NBER Working Paper No. 24441, March 2018, https://www.nber.org/system/files/working_papers/w24441 /w24441.pdf.

218 **And while black boys experience less:** Badger, Miller, Pearce, and Quealy, "Income Mobility Charts for Girls, Asian-Americans and Other Groups. Or Make Your Own." To retrieve these results, input: "Follow the lives of [white girls] and [black girls] from [poor] households, using their [individual] incomes as adults and including kids of [only native-born mothers]."

219 **African American households in the ninety-fifth percentile:** "Historical Income Tables: People," Table United States Censure Bureau: "Historical Income Tables: Income Inequality, Table H-1. Income Limits for Each Fifth and Top 5 Percent [Black]," https://www2.census.gov/programs -surveys/cps/tables/time-series/historical-income-households/h01b.xlsx. Compare also United States Census Buearu: "Historical Income Tables: People, Table P-1Total CPS Population and Per Capita Income [Black]," https://www2.census.gov/programs-surveys/cps/tables/time-series/histori cal-income-people/p01b.xlsx. Note that I cite the data for "Black Alone or In Combination," which includes respondents who checked multiple races, including black. The data for "Black Alone," which excludes African Americans who define as multiracial, shows very similar results.

219 **By 1950, the gap had fallen:** "Black Men in America Are Living Almost as Long as White Men," *Economist*, June 15, 2019, https://www.economist.com/united-states/2019/06/15/black-men -in-america-are-living-almost-as-long-as-white-men.

219 **Over the same period:** "Thomas B. Edsall: "How Strong Is America's Multiracial Democracy?" *New York Times*, September 1, 2021, "https://www.nytimes.com/2021/09/01/opinion/us-multi racial-democracy.html.

219 **Today, in 2021, typical African Americans:** In the descriptions that follow, I paint a picture of the most representative facts about the socioeconomic conditions of African Americans. Some of these apply to over half of the population. Others apply to a plurality. (For example, 46 percent of black Americans are covered by employer-sponsored health care, with the rest consisting of a mix of people who buy health insurance on the open market, are eligible for Medicare or Medicaid, or lack health coverage.)

219 **rather than either the urban core or the countryside:** Alana Semuels, "No, Most Black People Don't Live in Poverty—or Inner Cities," *Atlantic*, October 12, 2016, https://www.theatlantic .com/business/archive/2016/10/trump-african-american-inner-city/503744.

219 **they are below the age of forty:** Jennifer Cheeseman Day, "88% of Blacks Have a High School Diploma, 26% a Bachelor's Degree," US Census Bureau, June 10, 2020, "Gap Narrower among the Young," https://www.census.gov/library/stories/2020/06/black-high-school-attainment-nearly -on-par-with-national-average.html.

220 **They work in white-collar jobs:** See "Report: Labor Force Characteristics by Race and Ethnicity," US Bureau of Labor Statistics, October 2019, especially the "Industry" section, https://www.bls .gov/opub/reports/race-and-ethnicity/2018/home.htm.

220 **They get their health insurance:** Bobbi M. Bittker, "Racial and Ethnic Disparities in Employer-Sponsored Health Coverage," American Bar Association, September 8, 2020. https://www.ameri

canbar.org/groups/crsj/publications/human_rights_magazine_home/health-matters-in-elections/racial-and-ethnic-disparities-in-employer-sponsored-health-coverage.

220 **Consequently, the views of the median black American:** See, for example, Kim Parker, Rich Morin, and Juliana Menasce Horowitz, "America in 2050," Pew Research Center, March 21, 2019, https://www.pewresearch.org/social-trends/2019/03/21/america-in-2050; Russel Berman, "As White Americans Give Up on the American Dream, Blacks and Hispanics Embrace It," *Atlantic*, September 4, 2015, https://www.theatlantic.com/politics/archive/2015/09/the-surprising-optimism-of-african-americans-and-latinos/401054; and Carol Graham, "Why Are Black Poor Americans More Optimistic Than White Ones?" Brookings, January 30, 2018, https://www.brookings.edu/articles/why-are-black-poor-americans-more-optimistic-than-white-ones.

220 **On a cold morning in November 2019:** "Learning Together: What Happens When Students from Universities and Prisons Learn Together?," University of Cambridge, accessed June 1, 2021, https://www.ccgsj.crim.cam.ac.uk/research/learning-together-what-happens-when-students-from-universities-and-prisons-learn-together.

220 **celebrated its fifth anniversary:** "Fishmongers' Hall: Usman Khan Described Education Project as 'Kind of Family,'" BBC, April 23, 2021, https://www.bbc.com/news/uk-england-london-56858078.

220 **elegant rooms of London's Fishmongers' Hall:** "Fishmongers' Hall: Usman Khan Unlawfully Killed Cambridge Graduates," BBC, May 30, 2021, https://www.bbc.com/news/uk-england-london-57260509.

220 **Usman Khan, one of the program's vaunted:** "Fishmongers' Hall: Usman Khan Described Education Project as 'Kind of Family.'"

220 **Over the next ten minutes, he stabbed:** Sebastian Shukla, Nicole Chavez, and Hollie Silverman, "This Is What We Know about London Bridge Stabbing Suspect Usman Khan," CNN, November 30, 2019, https://www.cnn.com/2019/11/29/europe/london-bridge-stabbing-suspect-what-we-know/index.html.

221 **Over the past few decades, homegrown terrorists:** On France, see, for example, "Paris Attacks: Who Were the Attackers?," BBC, April 27, 2016, https://www.bbc.com/news/world-europe-34832512. On Germany, see, for example, Marcel Fürstenau, "Berlin Islamist Terror Attack: A Deadly Story of Failure," DW, December 28, 2020, https://www.dw.com/en/berlin-islamist-terror-attack-a-deadly-story-of-failure/a-55990942. On the United Kingdom, see, for example, "London Attack: Who Were the Attackers?," June 28, 2017, BBC, https://www.bbc.com/news/uk-40173157. On the United States, see, for example, "Profile: Who Is Boston Bomber Dzhokhar Tsarnaev?," BBC, April 8, 2015, https://www.bbc.com/news/world-us-canada-31734557.

221 **there were eighty-one shootings and fifty-eight bomb explosions:** Nancy Isenson, "Bombs, Shootings Are a Part of Life in Swedish City Malmo," DW, November 23, 2019, https://www.dw.com/en/bombs-shootings-are-a-part-of-life-in-swedish-city-malmo/a-51337737.

221 **In the years since then, these bombings:** Richard Orange, "Bombs and Blood Feuds: The Wave of Explosions Rocking Sweden's Cities," *Guardian*, January 25, 2020, https://www.theguardian.com/world/2020/jan/25/bombs-blood-feuds-malmo-explosions-rocking-swedens-cities.

222 **in the summer of 2015, the latest newcomers:** See Yascha Mounk, "Figures of Division," *New Yorker*, January 28, 2019, https://www.newyorker.com/magazine/2019/01/28/how-a-teens-death-has-become-a-political-weapon. See also "Migrant Crisis: Migration to Europe Explained in Seven Charts," BBC, March 4, 2016, https://www.bbc.com/news/world-europe-34131911.

222 **"They are leading a war":** Mounk, "Figures of Division."

222 **From the murder of the journalists at _Charlie Hebdo_:** "Charlie Hebdo Attack: France Seeks Long Jail Terms in Paris Trial," BBC, December 8, 2020, https://www.bbc.com/news/55231200.

222 **the shooting at the Pulse nightclub:** Alyson Hurt and Ariel Zambelich, "3 Hours in Orlando: Piecing Together an Attack and Its Aftermath," NPR, June 26, 2016, https://www.npr.org/2016/06/16/482322488/orlando-shooting-what-happened-update.

222 **"Islam is in itself a political ideology":** "Islam Not Compatible with German Constitution, Says AfD Party," *Reuters*, April 17, 2016, https://www.reuters.com/article/us-germany-afd-islam/islam-not-compatible-with-german-constitution-says-afd-party-idUSKCN0XE0T0.

223 **Desperate for any kind of weapon:** See "Fishmongers' Hall Porter 'Stabbed Usman Khan with Spear,'" *BBC*, April 20, 2021, https://www.bbc.com/news/uk-england-london-56815632, and Daniel Tilles, "Polish Hero Who Confronted London Bridge Terrorist to Be Given Top British Honour," *Notes from Poland*, December 26, 2019, https://notesfrompoland.com/2019/12/26/polish-hero-who-confronted-london-bridge-terrorist-to-be-given-top-british-honour.

225 **"Muslims in France are horrified":** Louise Couvelaire, "After the Conflans Attack, Many Imams Condemn the Assassination of Samuel Paty," *Monde*, October 19, 2020, https://www.lemonde.fr/societe/article/2020/10/19/apres-l-attentat-de-conflans-de-nombreux-imams-condamnent-l-assassinat-de-samuel-paty_6056566_3224.html.

225 **Claims that Islam is somehow incompatible:** In the United Kingdom, for example, 84 percent of Muslims said that it is "always wrong" to "use violent extremism to protest against things they think are very unfair or unjust." The figure for Christians was 88 percent. When specifically asked about violence invoking religious justifications, even more British Muslims rejected the idea, with 92 percent of them saying that it is "always wrong" for people to use "violent extremism in the name of a religion to protest or achieve a goal."

225 **It may, for example, be technically:** John Mueller and Mark G. Stewart, "Terrorism and Bathtubs: Comparing and Assessing the Risks," *Terrorism and Political Violence* 33, no. 1 (2021): 138–63, https://doi.org/10.1080/09546553.2018.1530662.

Chapter Nine: Demography Isn't Destiny

231 **But when the United States Census Bureau:** Sam Roberts, "Minorities in US Set to Become Majority by 2042," *New York Times*, August 14, 2008, https://www.nytimes.com/2008/08/14/world/americas/14iht-census.1.15284537.html.

231 **THE U.S. WHITE MAJORITY WILL SOON:** Dudley Poston, "The U.S. White Majority Will Soon Disappear Forever," *Houston Chronicle*, April 30, 2019, https://www.houstonchronicle.com/local/gray-matters/article/The-US-white-majority-will-soon-disappear-forever-13806738.php.

231 **Other newspapers and magazines explored:** Pavithra Mohan, "How the End of the White Majority Could Change Office Dynamics in 2040," *Fast Company*, January 27, 2020, https://www.fastcompany.com/90450018/how-the-end-of-the-white-majority-could-change-office-dynamics-in-2040.

231 **On the other side, there were members:** Since "white Hispanics" count as so-called people of color for the purpose of these projections, even tens of millions of people with wholly or predominantly European ancestry are included in that category. The only racial group that is almost wholly *excluded* from the category are Arabs, who count as white even though most hail from the continent of Asia. (Since there are some Arabs in Latin America, and a few of them have since migrated to America, a very small number of Arabs would, technically, count as "people of color.")

232 **In its most extreme form, this fear:** See Norimitsu Onishi, "The Man Behind a Toxic Slogan Promoting White Supremacy," *New York Times*, September 20, 2019, https://www.nytimes.com/2019/09/20/world/europe/renaud-camus-great-replacement.html, and Scott Sayare, "French Provocateur Enters Battle over Comments," *New York Times*, February 11, 2011, https://www.nytimes.com/2011/02/12/world/europe/12zemmour.html.

232 **Traitorous politicians, far-right activists claim:** See Lauretta Charlton, "What Is the Great Replacement?," *New York Times*, August 6, 2019, and Nellie Bowles, "'Replacement Theory,' a Racist, Sexist Doctrine, Spreads in Far-Right Circles," *New York Times*, March 18, 2019, https://www.nytimes.com/2019/03/18/technology/replacement-theory.html.

234　**The future size of that group:** This isn't a full list of all the relevant factors. Life expectancy and the age at which people have children, for example, also affect such models.

235　**Three or four decades ago, a majority:** "22% of Americans Have a Relative in a Mixed-Race Marriage," Pew Research Center, March 14, 2006, https://www.pewresearch.org/social-trends /2006/03/14/guess-whos-coming-to-dinner.

236　**In 1980, only three percent of newborns:** Kim Parker, Juliana Menasce Horowitz, Rich Morin, and Mark Hugo Lopez, "Multiracial in America," Pew Research Center, June 11, 2015, https:// www.pewresearch.org/social-trends/2015/06/11/multiracial-in-america.

236　**Only one out of every ten Americans:** Gretchen Livingston and Anna Brown, "Intermarriage in the US: 50 Years after Loving v. Virginia," Pew Research Center, May 17, 2018, https://www.pew research.org/social-trends/2017/05/18/intermarriage-in-the-u-s-50-years-after-loving-v-virginia. Whereas opposition to intermarriage used to be strongest among whites, it is now strongest among African Americans. According to the Pew Research Center, for example, black respondents were twice as likely as white respondents to say that "people of different races marrying each other" is, generally speaking, "a bad thing." Gretchen Livingston and Anna Brown, "Public Views on Inter-marriage," Pew Research Center, May 18, 2017, https://www.pewresearch.org/social-trends/2017 /05/18/2-public-views-on-intermarriage/#americans-are-now-much-more-open-to-the-idea -of-a-close-relative-marrying-someone-of-a-different-race.

236　**By the late 2010s, one out of every seven:** Gretchen Livingston, "The Rise of Multiracial and Multiethnic Babies in the U.S," Pew Research Center, June 6, 2017, https://www.pewresearch.org /fact-tank/2017/06/06/the-rise-of-multiracial-and-multiethnic-babies-in-the-u-s.

236　**Nearly one out of every three Hispanic:** Livingston and Brown, "Intermarriage in the US: 50 Years after Loving v. Virginia."

236　**As Edward Telles and Vilma Ortiz found:** Edward Eric Telles and Vilma Ortiz, *Generations of Ex-clusion: Mexican Americans, Assimilation, and Race* (New York: Russell Sage Foundation, 2008), 281.

237　**As one prominent sociologist summarized:** Richard Alba, "The Likely Persistence of a White Majority," *American Prospect,* January 11, 2016, https://prospect.org/civil-rights/likely-persistence -white-majority. See also the excellent in-depth report by the Pew Charitable Trust: Parker, Me-nasce Horowitz, Morin, and Hugo Lopez, "Multiracial in America."

　　　The one notable exception are mixed-race children who have a black parent. While mixed-race Americans with some Asian ancestry are very likely to "say that they have more in common with whites" (Alba, "The Likely Persistence of a White Majority"), Pew reports that those with African ancestry "have a set of experiences, attitudes and social interactions that are much more closely aligned with the Black community." Parker, Menasce Horowitz, Morin, and Hugo Lopez, "Multiracial in America."

　　　This should not come as a surprise. Historically, enslaved people would count as black—and be denied civil rights—even if they only had one black great-grandparent. This legacy lives on in American conceptions about who counts as black today.

　　　But it is a mistake to assume that the "one-drop rule" has a similarly strong hold over other ethnic groups. The projections of the Census Bureau are, quite simply, wrong to take it for granted that the historical experience of African Americans predicts the future behavior of most mixed-race Americans.

237　**In 2014, there were about 55 million people:** Renne Stepler and Anna Brown, "2014, Hispanics in the United States Statistical Portrait," April 19, 2016, Pew Research Center, https://www.pew research.org/hispanic/2016/04/19/2014-statistical-information-on-hispanics-in-united-states.

237　**the Census Bureau predicted:** Sandra L. Colby and Jennifer M. Ortman, "Projections of the Size and Composition of the U.S. Population: 2014 to 2060," United States Census Bureau, Current Population Reports, P25-1143, March 2015, https://www.census.gov/content/dam/Census/library /publications/2015/demo/p25-1143.pdf.

237 **But while many people of Hispanic origin are black or indigenous:** See Colby and Ortman, "Projections of the Size and Composition of the U.S. Population: 2014 to 2060," page 9, table 2. According to the projection, there will be 285 million whites in the country by 2060, of whom 182 million will be non-Hispanic whites. Note that a combination of factors including a change in the wording of the census form and a greater ability to code handwritten responses has resulted in a significant increase in the share of Hispanics who consider themselves mixed-race or non-white in the 2020 Census. See Sabrina Tavernise, Tariro Mzezewa, and Giulia Heyward, "Behind the Surprising Jump in Multiracial Americans, Several Theories," *New York Times*, August 13, 2021, https://www.nytimes.com/2021/08/13/us/census-multiracial-identity.html. See also Sabrina Tavernise and Robert Gebeloff, "Census Shows Sharply Growing Numbers of Hispanic, Asian and Multiracial Americans," *New York Times*, August 12, 2021, https://www.nytimes.com/2021/08/12/us/us-census-population-growth-diversity.html.

238 **Progressives, López and Gavito concluded:** Ian Hany López and Tory Gavito, "This Is How Biden Should Approach the Latino Vote," *New York Times*, September 18, 2020, https://www.nytimes.com/2020/09/18/opinion/biden-latino-vote-strategy.html.

238 **While Hispanics are adding the greatest numbers:** Colby and Ortman, "Projections of the Size and Composition of the U.S. Population: 2014 to 2060."

238 **Korean Americans have a median household income:** By comparison, whites have a median income of $76,057. See Valerie Wilson, "Racial Disparities in Income and Poverty Remain Largely Unchanged amid Strong Income Growth in 2010," Economic Policy Institute, September 2020, https://www.epi.org/blog/racial-disparities-in-income-and-poverty-remain-largely-unchanged-amid-strong-income-growth-in-2019; Abby Budiman, "Koreans in the U.S. Fact Sheet," Pew Research Center, accessed September 27, 2021, https://www.pewresearch.org/social-trends/fact-sheet/asian-americans-koreans-in-the-u-s; Abby Budiman, "Chinese in the U.S. Fact Sheet," Pew Research Center, accessed September 27, 2021, https://www.pewresearch.org/social-trends/fact-sheet/asian-americans-chinese-in-the-u-s; and Abby Budiman, "Indians in the U.S. Fact Sheet," Pew Research Center, accessed September 27, 2021, https://www.pewresearch.org/social-trends/fact-sheet/asian-americans-indians-in-the-u-s.

239 **The median Asian woman in the United States:** According to the Bureau of Labor Statistics, Asian women over the age of sixteen had median weekly earnings of $1,134. Among white men over the age of sixteen, median weekly earning were $1,118. "Usual Weekly Earnings of Wage and Salary Workers: First Quarter 2021," Bureau of Labor Statistics, table 3, accessed September 27, 2021, https://www.bls.gov/news.release/pdf/wkyeng.pdf.

239 **While Asian Americans currently make up less:** Abby Budiman and Neil G. Ruiz, "Key Facts about Asian Americans, a Diverse and Growing Population," April 29, 2021, Pew Research Center, https://www.pewresearch.org/fact-tank/2021/04/29/key-facts-about-asian-americans.

239 **At Berkeley, for example, nearly half of the domestic:** "Admissions Statistics," Harvard College, accessed September 27, 2021, https://college.harvard.edu/admissions/admissions-statistics, and "UC Berkeley Fall Enrollment Data for New Undergraduates," UC Berkeley, accessed September 27, 2021, https://opa.berkeley.edu/uc-berkeley-fall-enrollment-data-new-undergraduates. (The undergraduate student body is 41.8 percent Asian American. Of those, 11.8 percent are international students, likely including a sizeable Chinese contingent. Another 4.2 percent of students declined to state their ethnicity.)

239 **Because the country will come to be majority minority:** In the fall of 2020, I ran an informal poll on my Twitter feed. Emphasizing that I was including Hispanic whites in the question, I asked what percentage of the American population would, according to the latest projections from the United States Census Bureau, be white by 2060. More than 70 percent of respondents answered that fewer than half of all Americans would, under this definition, be white. Fewer than 5 percent of respondents gave the right response: forty years from now, more than two-thirds of Americans will still be white.

The result of this poll is of course entirely unrepresentative; it by no means captures what average Americans think about this question. But since people who follow political scientists on social media and spend their weekends clicking on polls about the future demographic composition of the country are likely to be highly politically engaged, it does reveal something interesting about how much of America's political class now misperceives its own country.

240 **The social mood was distinctly conservative:** See Richard Wolf, "Timeline: Same-sex Marriage through the Years," *USA Today*, June 24, 2015, https://www.usatoday.com/story/news/politics /2015/06/24/same-sex-marriage-timeline/29173703, and Associated Press, "Voters Pass All 11 Bans on Gay Marriage," NBC, November 1, 2004, https://www.nbcnews.com/id/wbna638 3353.

240 **And though George W. Bush was derided:** Associated Press, "Bush Edges Kerry in 'Regular Guy' Poll," NBC, May 26, 2004, https://www.nbcnews.com/id/wbna5067874.

241 **Soon, this seemingly right-leaning country:** John B. Judis and Ruy A. Teixeira, *The Emerging Democratic Majority* (New York: Scribner, 2002).

241 **Over time, "these groups of voters":** Judis and Teixeira. *The Emerging Democratic Majority*, 35.

242 **Obama won big among the highly educated:** David Paul Kuhn, "Exit Polls: How Obama Won," *Politico*, November 5, 2008, https://www.politico.com/story/2008/11/exit-polls-how-obama-won -015297.

242 **In the minds of many progressive journalists:** To some left-wing activists, the idea of the inevitable demographic majority also contained a second promise. If Democrats needed to hold together a broad coalition to win elections, as campaign strategists had long believed, progressive politicians would face a series of tough trade-offs. Since many of their policies are deeply unpopular among the white working-class voters that have traditionally made up the largest segment of the party's base, they always faced a tension between ideological purity and electoral viability.

The theory of the inevitable demographic majority seemingly liberated Democrats from such constraints. Pressing ahead with a deeply progressive policy program did not just seem to them to be right as a matter of principle; it also looked like the obvious way to build the electoral coalition of the future.

242 **Democrats, Anton warned, are "on the cusp":** Publius Decius Mus (Michael Anton), "The Flight 93 Election," *Claremont Review of Books*, September 5, 2016, https://claremontreviewofbooks.com /digital/the-flight-93-election.

243 **In the lead-up to the election, Trump:** Martin Pengelly, "Trump Predicts Demographics Make 2016 'Last Election Republicans Can Win,'" *Guardian*, September 9, 2016, https://www.the guardian.com/us-news/2016/sep/09/trump-demographics-2016-election-republicans-can-win.

243 **"Demography alone appears to give Clinton":** Sama Khalid, "The 270 Project: Try To Predict Who Will Win the Election," NPR, June 30, 2016, https://www.npr.org/2016/06/30/483687093 /the-270-project-try-to-predict-who-will-win-the-election. *Vox* put it in even starker terms: "There are simply not enough struggling, resentful, xenophobic white people in the US to constitute a national majority sufficient to win a presidential election." David Roberts, "Why I Still Believe Donald Trump Will Never Be President," *Vox*, January 30, 2016, https://www.vox.com/2016/1 /30/10873476/donald-trump-never-president.

243 **When the ballots were counted on the evening:** The demographic forces that had made Obama such an electoral powerhouse, Teixeira predicted in a triumphant post-election report published in March 2009, were only going to accelerate in the following years. Citing the Census Bureau, he pointed out that "the United States will be majority-minority by 2042." And these favorable demographic trends, he argued, would be especially pronounced in states that play a crucial role in the electoral college. Michigan and Pennsylvania, in particular, would soon be characterized by a new "progressive dominance." In the event, it was those very states that delivered Trump his victory. See Ruy Teixeira, "Twenty Years of Demographic, Geographic, and Attitudinal Changes across the Country Herald a New Progressive Majority," Center for American Progress, page 20,

March 11, 2009, https://www.americanprogress.org/issues/democracy/reports/2009/03/11/5783/new-progressive-america.

243 **Enthralled by the growth of the minority vote:** Nate Cohn, "How the Obama Coalition Crumbled, Leaving an Opening for Trump," *New York Times*, December 23, 2016, https://www.nytimes.com/2016/12/23/upshot/how-the-obama-coalition-crumbled-leaving-an-opening-for-trump.html.

243 **As Teixeira recently acknowledged:** Ruy Teixeira, "Democrats Can't Rely on Demographics Alone," Persuasion, June 4, 2021, https://www.persuasion.community/p/demography-is-not-destiny.

244 **When all the ballots were counted, he beat:** Mark Sherman, "Electoral College Makes It Official: Biden Won, Trump Lost," AP News, December 14, 2020, https://apnews.com/article/joe-biden-270-electoral-college-vote-d429ef97af2bf574d16463384dc7cc1e.

244 **But even there, actual vote patterns:** See Nate Cohn, "Why Rising Diversity Might Not Help Democrats as Much as They Hope," *New York Times*, May 4, 2021, https://www.nytimes.com/2021/05/04/us/census-news-republicans-democrats.html, and Teixeira, "Democrats Can't Rely on Demographics Alone."

244 **Over the following four years, he increased:** See, for example, "Understanding The 2020 Electorate: AP VoteCast Survey," NPR, May 21, 2021, https://www.npr.org/2020/11/03/929478378/understanding-the-2020-electorate-ap-votecast-survey; Leila Fadel, "Majority of Muslims Voted for Biden, but Trump Got More Support Than He Did in 2016," NPR, December 4, 2020, https://www.npr.org/2020/12/04/942262760/majority-of-muslims-voted-for-biden-but-trump-got-more-not-less-support; Sean Collins, "Trump Made Gains with Black Voters in Some States. Here's Why," *Vox*, November 4, 2020, https://www.vox.com/2020/11/4/21537966/trump-black-voters-exit-polls; and "An Examination of the 2016 Electorate, Based on Validated Voters," Pew Research Center, accessed September 26, 2021, https://www.pewresearch.org/politics/2018/08/09/an-examination-of-the-2016-electorate-based-on-validated-voters.

244 **This certainly helps to explain why Trump:** Nicole Narea, "How Latinos in Miami-Dade County Helped Trump Win Florida," *Vox*, November 3, 2020, https://www.vox.com/policy-and-politics/2020/11/3/21548510/florida-miami-dade-latinos-cuba.

245 **The overwhelmingly Mexican American counties:** Keith Collins et al., "Hispanic Voters Deliver a Texas Win for Trump," *New York Times*, November 10, 2020, https://www.nytimes.com/interactive/2020/11/05/us/texas-election-results.html.

246 **Forget that countries in which one party:** See, for example, José Maria Marin, "Literature Review: Corruption and One-Party Dominance," *Transparency International*, May 29, 2015, https://knowledgehub.transparency.org/assets/uploads/helpdesk/Corruption_and_one_party_dominance_2015.pdf.

246 **Obama once said that we shouldn't slice:** Barack Obama, "Keynote Address at the 2004 Democratic National Convention," July 27, 2004, https://web.archive.org/web/20080403144623/http://www.barackobama.com/2004/07/27/keynote_address_at_the_2004_de.php.

246 **In the vision that many progressives have:** There is also a second problem with this supposed utopia. Even if the definitions of the United States Census Bureau prove to be right, and the grandchildren of Cameron Diaz, Martin Sheen, and Snooki dutifully identify as "people of color" forty years hence, "white" America will still constitute a little fewer than half of the population. And though this group might then lose every election, it will continue to exercise a lot of power in the country. Even if it proves unable to impose its will on the rest of the population, it will surely be able to make life pretty miserable for the ascendant majority in all kinds of ways.

247 **In *The Great Demographic Illusion*, the eminent sociologist:** Richard D. Alba, *The Great Demographic Illusion: Majority, Minority, and the Expanding American Mainstream* (Princeton, NJ: Princeton University Press, 2020).

251 **In Germany, a recent poll showed:** Bojan Pancevski, "Immigrants and Their Children Shift towards Center-Right in Germany," *Wall Street Journal*, February 9, 2021, https://www.wsj.com/articles/immigrants-and-their-children-shift-toward-center-right-in-germany-11612872336.

251 **And in the United Kingdom, a conservative:** DiversityUK, "Britain's most ethnically diverse Cabinet Ever," July 25, 2019, https://diversityuk.org/britains-most-ethnically-diverse-cabinet-ever.

251–52 **"Rather than ushering in a more tolerant future":** Maureen A. Craig and Jennifer A. Richeson, "On the Precipice of a 'Majority-Minority' America: Perceived Status Threat from the Racial Demographic Shift Affects White Americans' Political Ideology," *Association for Psychological Science* 25, no. 6 (April 2014): 1189–97, http://dx.doi.org/10.1177/0956797614527113.

Chapter Ten: Policies That Can Help

255 **It is easier to cheer on the success:** See, for example, the "deep story" suggested in Arlie Russell Hochschild, *Strangers in Their Own Land: Anger and Mourning on the American Right* (New York: The New Press, 2018).

257 **Sociologists found that the average participant:** Jake Cigainero, "Who Are France's Yellow Vest Protesters, and What Do They Want?," NPR, December 3, 2018, https://www.npr.org/2018/12/03/672862353/who-are-frances-yellow-vest-protesters-and-what-do-they-want.

257 **Though the ideological profile of the yellow vests:** Matt Bradley, Mac William Bishop, and Marguerite Ward, "'Yellow Vests' Find Support among France's Far-Right and Far-Left—but Can They Win Votes?," NBC, February 26, 2019, https://www.nbcnews.com/news/world/yellow-vests-find-support-among-france-s-far-right-far-n976021.

257 **So, increasingly, was an anger bordering:** "Yellow Vest Protests: More Than 100 Arrested as Violence Returns to Paris," BBC, November 16, 2019, https://www.bbc.com/news/world-europe-50447733.

257 **with a growing share of participants identifying:** See Alice Kantor, "Why Are France's Yellow Vest Protests so White?," Al Jazeera, January 28, 2019, https://www.aljazeera.com/features/2019/1/28/why-are-frances-yellow-vest-protests-so-white, and Adam Nossiter, "Anti-Semitic Taunts by Yellow Vests Prompt French Soul-Searching," *New York Times*, February 18, 2019, https://www.nytimes.com/2019/02/18/world/europe/france-antisemitism-yellow-vests-alain-finkielkraut.html.

258 **Building on Rousseau's lament, writers:** For the most subtle explanation of this thesis, see James Scott, *Against the Grain: A Deep History of the Earliest States* (New Haven, CT: Yale University Press, 2017).

258 **When well-heeled westerners return:** This has been beautifully caricatured by Humanitarians of Tinder, a website that features such photographs drawn from the profiles of users of the eponymous dating app. See https://humanitariansoftinder.com.

258 **Looking at twenty different countries:** Manuel Funke, Moritz Schularick, and Christoph Trebesch, "Going to Extremes: Politics after Financial Crisis, 1870–2014," Center for Economic Studies and Ifo Institute, CESifo Working Paper No. 5553, page 2, October 2015, https://www.statewatch.org/media/documents/news/2015/oct/financial-crises-cesifo-wp-5553.pdf.

258 **putting a severe "strain on modern democracies":** Funke, Schularick, and Trebesch, "Going to Extremes: Politics after Financial Crisis, 1870–2014," 35.

258 **According to the World Values Survey:** Brandon Ambrosino, "What the World Values, in One Chart," *Vox*, December 29, 2014, https://www.vox.com/2014/12/29/7461009/culture-values-world-inglehart-welzel. To view and manipulate the data directly, you can access the World Values Survey here: https://www.worldvaluessurvey.org/WVSDocumentationWV7.jsp.

258 **And as Benjamin Friedman, an economist:** Benjamin M. Friedman, *The Moral Consequences of Economic Growth* (New York: Alfred A. Knopf, 2005), 4.

261 **the nations of the Group of Seven (G7) have recently agreed:** Alan Rappeport and Liz Alderman, "Yellen Aims to Win Support for Global Tax Deal," *New York Times*, June 2, 2021, https://www.nytimes.com/2021/06/02/us/politics/yellen-global-tax.html, and Alan Rappeport, "Global Tax Deal Reached among G7 Nations," *New York Times*, June 11, 2021, https://www.nytimes.com/2021/06/05/us/politics/g7-global-minimum-tax.html.

261 **Other ideas whose time may one day:** Noam Scheiber, "The Biden Team Wants to Transform the Economy. Really," *New York Times*, February 11, 2021, https://www.nytimes.com/2021/02/11/magazine/biden-economy.html.

261 **industrial policy or even a basic income:** For an influential philosophical justification of universal basic income, see Philippe van Parijs, *Real Freedom for All: What (If Anything) Can Justify Capitalism?* (Oxford, UK: Oxford University Press, 1997). For a discussion of recent attempts to implement it, see Sigal Samuel, "Guaranteed Income Is Graduating from Charity to Public Policy," *Vox*, June 3, 2021, https://www.vox.com/future-perfect/2021/6/3/22463776/guaranteed-universal-basic-income-charity-policy.

262 **A significant increase in the resources devoted:** Notably, it would boost economic growth for society as a whole, helping diverse democracies generate the growth and tax revenue they need to offer their citizens secure prosperity.

263 **Especially in countries in which the educational:** Rich Motoko, Amanda Cox, and Matthew Bloch, "Money, Race and Success: How Your School District Compares," *New York Times*, April 29, 2016, https://www.nytimes.com/interactive/2016/04/29/upshot/money-race-and-success-how-your-school-district-compares.html.

263 **In the United States, for example, the funding:** The Biden administration has proposed a $20 billion fund to help redress funding inequalities between rich and poor districts. See Kevin Carey, "Rich Schools, Poor Schools and a Biden Plan," *New York Times*, June 9, 2021, https://www.nytimes.com/2021/06/09/upshot/biden-school-funding.html. For an overview of the problem with unequal school funding and a set of proposals for how to redress it, see Carmel Martin, Ulrich Boser, Meg Benner, and Perpetual Baffour, "A Quality Approach to School Funding: Lessons Learned from School Finance Litigation," Center for American Progress, November 13, 2018, https://www.americanprogress.org/issues/education-k-12/reports/2018/11/13/460397/quality-approach-school-funding. Providing a more consistent quality of schooling could also make a contribution to the crucial goals of educational and residential integration because it would reduce the incentives of affluent white residents to move to wealthier neighborhoods once they have school-aged children.

263 **Those who wanted to build a generous welfare:** See, for example, Theda Skocpol, "Universal Appeal," *Brookings Review* 9, no. 3 (1991): 28, https://doi.org/10.2307/20080225, and Theda Skocpol, "Targeting within Universalism: Politically Viable Policies to Combat Poverty in the United States," in Christopher Jencks and Paul E. Peterson, *The Urban Underclass* (Washington, DC: The Brookings Institution, 1991), 411–36.

264 **As questions of race have come to the forefront:** Isabel Sawhill and Richard V. Reeves, "The Case for 'Race-Conscious' Policies," Brookings, February 4, 2016, https://www.brookings.edu/blog/social-mobility-memos/2016/02/04/the-case-for-race-conscious-policies.

264 **from who should get loans at preferential rates:** "Civil Rights, Fair Lending and Consumer Rights Organizations Urge a More Race-Conscious CRA," National Community Reinvestment Coalition, February 16, 2021, https://ncrc.org/civil-rights-fair-lending-and-consumer-rights-organizations-urge-a-more-race-conscious-cra.

264 **who should first get access to life-saving vaccines:** See Isaac Stanley Becker and Lena H. Sun, "Aiming for Fairness in the Coronavirus Fight," *Washington Post*, December 20, 2020, https://www.washingtonpost.com/health/2020/12/18/covid-vaccine-racial-equity/, and Yascha Mounk, "Why I'm Losing Trust in the Institutions," Persuasion, December 23, 2020, https://www.persuasion.community/p/why-im-losing-trust-in-the-institutions.

264 **Joe Biden vowed that his administration's "priority":** The White House (@WhiteHouse), "Our priority will be Black, Latino, Asian, and Native American owned small businesses, women-owned businesses, and finally having equal access to resources needed to re-open and re-build," Twitter, January 10, 2021, 5:55 p.m., https://twitter.com/WhiteHouse/status/1348403213 200990209.

264 **new rules established a racial pecking order:** Associated Press, "Court Rules against Biden Administration's Use of Race, Sex to Allocated COVID-19 Aid," *Oregonian*, May 28, 2021, https:// www.oregonlive.com/business/2021/05/court-rules-against-using-race-sex-to-allocate-federal-aid .html. See also Zaid Jilani, "What's Race Got to Do with It?," Persuasion, May 10, 2021, https:// www.persuasion.community/p/whats-race-got-to-do-with-it.

265 **Thankfully, a federal court held:** See Hailey Konnath, "6th Circ. Blocks SBA's COVID-19 Loan Priority For Minorities," *Law 360*, https://www.law360.com/articles/1389372/6th-circ-blocks -sba-s-covid-19-loan-priority-for-minorities.

265 **In a telling study from the United Kingdom:** Robert Ford and Anouk Kootstra, "Do White Voters Support Welfare Policies Targeted at Ethnic Minorities? Experimental Evidence from Britain," *Journal of Ethnic and Migration Studies* 43, no. 1 (2017): 81, https://doi.org/10.1080/1369183X .2016.1180969.

265 **When Ford and Kootstra asked:** Ford and Kootstra, "Do White Voters Support Welfare Policies Targeted at Ethnic Minorities?," 97.

265 **"reduce inequalities between whites":** Ford and Kootstra, "Do White Voters Support Welfare Policies Targeted at Ethnic Minorities?," 85.

266 **Up to 67 percent now opposed them:** Ford and Kootstra, "Do White Voters Support Welfare Policies Targeted at Ethnic Minorities?," 87.

266 **As a result, policies that disproportionately:** See, for example, Marc Novicoff, "Stop Marketing Race-Blind Policies as Racial Equity Initiatives," *Slow Boring*, February 20, 2020, http://slowbor ing.com/p/race-blind-policies-racial-equity, and Brink Lindsey, "Moderation in Pursuit of Social Justice Is an Indispensable Virtue," Niskanen Center, April 20, 2021, https://www.niskanencenter .org/moderation-in-pursuit-of-social-justice-is-an-indispensable-virtue.

266 **A recent paper by two political scientists:** Micah English and Joshua Kalla, "Racial Equality Frames and Public Policy Support: Survey Experimental Evidence," OSF Preprints, April 23, 2021, https://doi.org/10.31219/osf.io/tdkf3.

266 **"explicitly use racial justice framing":** English and Kalla, "Racial Equality Frames and Public Policy Support," 1.

266 **Strikingly, these race-based justifications:** See English and Kalla, "Racial Equality Frames and Public Policy Support," table A4 and table A5. Multiple other polls and studies come to the same result. When a left-leaning polling firm presented voters with a proposal to make it easier to build multifamily housing that was cast in universal terms, for example, it elicited strong support. A plurality of voters favored the policy when its stated purpose was to "drive economic growth as more people will be able to move to high-opportunity regions with good jobs." Voters who were presented with an explicitly race-conscious justification for the same policy, by contrast, were significantly less likely to support the measure. When told that the policy "is a matter of racial justice" because current regulations "lock in America's system of racial segregation, blocking Black Americans from pursuing economic opportunity," opposition to the measure grew stronger among both Democrats and Republicans. See Jerusalem Demsas, "How to Convince a NIMBY to Build More Housing," *Vox*, February 24, 2021, https://www.vox.com/22297328/affordable-housing-nimby -housing-prices-rising-poll-data-for-progress.

267 **They often fail to attract the majority:** For an example of a race-conscious policy that likely backfired by harming the very group whose interests it was supposed to prioritize, see Mounk, "Why I'm Losing Trust in the Institutions."

268 **Ever since a giant corruption scandal:** For one of the best accounts of Silvio Berlusconi's rise to power, see Alexander Stille, *The Sack of Rome: Media + Money + Celebrity = Power = Silvio Berlusconi* (New York: Penguin, 2007).

268 **he offered a giant seat bonus:** Ian Fisher, "Berlusconi Changes Rules to His Benefit," *New York Times*, December 15, 2005, https://www.nytimes.com/2005/12/15/world/europe/berlusconi -changes-rules-to-his-benefit.html.

269 **The opposition strenuously opposed the reforms:** "Italy Moves to Change Electoral System," *New York Times*, October 13, 2005, https://www.nytimes.com/2005/10/13/world/europe/italy -moves-to-change-electoral-system.html.

269 **But when Italians finally went:** Elisabetta Povoledo, "An Overseas Surprise for Berlusconi," *New York Times*, April 13, 2006, https://www.nytimes.com/2006/04/13/world/europe/an-overseas -surprise-for-berlusconi.html.

269 **the newly created Unione beat Berlusconi's:** Corinne Deloy, "The Left Wins Both Houses in Italian Parliamentary Elections in a Ballot Marked by Much Confusion and Division in the Country," Robert Schuman Fondation, April 12, 2006, https://www.robert-schuman.eu/en/eem /0513-the-left-wins-both-houses-in-italian-parliamentary-elections-in-a-ballot-marked-by-much -confusion-and-division-in-the-country.

269 **Under the new electoral rules, those 24,700:** "Top Court Confirms Prodi's Win in Italian Election," *New York Times*, April 19, 2006, https://www.nytimes.com/2006/04/19/world/europe /top-court-confirms-prodis-win-in-italian-election.html.

269 **Some believe that popular anger:** Lee Drutman, *Breaking the Two-Party Doom Loop: The Case for Multiparty Democracy in America* (New York: Oxford University Press, 2020). For a legislative proposal, see "The Fair Representation Act," Fair Vote, accessed September 26, 2021, https://www .fairvote.org/fair_rep_in_congress#why_rcv_for_congress.

269 **Others argue that Democrats would finally:** See, for example, Quinta Jurecic and Susan Hennessey, "The Reckless Race to Confirm Amy Coney Barrett Justifies Court Packing," *Atlantic*, October 4, 2020, https://www.theatlantic.com/ideas/archive/2020/10/skeptic-case-court-packing /616607, and Adam Serwer, "The Supreme Court Is Helping Republicans Rig Elections," *Atlantic*, October 22, 2020, https://www.theatlantic.com/ideas/archive/2020/10/dont-let-supreme-court -choose-its-own-electorate/616808. In April 2021, senior Democrats including Jerrold Nadler, the chairman of the House Judiciary Committee, introduced a naked court-packing bill into Congress. Carl Hulse, "Democrats' Supreme Court Expansion Plan Draws Resistance," *New York Times*, April 15, 2021, https://www.nytimes.com/2021/04/15/us/politics/democrats-supreme -court-expansion.html.

269 **Like Silvio Berlusconi—and many other politicians:** Examples of such failures are legion. In 1950, for example, the American Political Science Association convened the most eminent scholars of the day to discuss the problems plaguing the institutions of the United States. Their report concluded that the country suffered from having two political parties that didn't have a clear ideological profile. It would be much better, they suggested, if Democrats and Republicans disagreed more sharply on the key issues of the day.

Over the next decades, their wish came true. By making it easier for Americans to vote for politicians that represented their core values, these changes undoubtedly had some positive effects. But as the last years painfully demonstrated, they also created huge problems of their own. American politics is now deeply polarized. With every election, the stakes seem to grow more existential. Preoccupied with the problems of their own time, the eminent members of the panel vastly underestimated the new problems that their desired changes would bring about.

The democratic transition of postcommunist regimes offers another instructive example of the difficulty of predicting the impact of institutions. As a rich literature in political science shows, the political systems of many Central and Eastern European countries were deeply influenced by their leaders' perception of what rules would benefit them. And yet most of these leaders rapidly lost power. In a rapidly shifting political landscape, institutional features that were designed to serve them frequently came to harm them instead.

271 **In keeping with the informal "Hastert Rule":** See, for example, Tara Golshan, "The 'Hastert Rule,' the Reason a DACA Deal Could Fail in the House, Explained," *Vox*, January 24, 2018, https://www.vox.com/policy-and-politics/2018/1/24/16916898/hastert-rule-daca-could-fail-house-ryan, and Yascha Mounk, "The Rise of McPolitics," *New Yorker*, June 25, 2018, https://www.newyorker.com/magazine/2018/07/02/the-rise-of-mcpolitics.

272 **Maine, for example, allows voters:** Patrick Whittle, "Maine's Ranked Choice Voting Rules and Procedures, Explained," AP News, November 2, 2020, https://apnews.com/article/election-2020-senate-elections-voting-maine-united-states-355f2859cf5dabf25bb0bb953f9c66bd.

272 **In California, meanwhile, the two candidates:** "How California's 'Jungle Primary' System Works," NPR, June 5, 2018, https://www.npr.org/2018/06/05/617250124/how-californias-jungle-primary-system-works.

272 **Both reforms can give politicians:** Another proposed reform to change the duopoly of American political parties consists in introducing "multi-member districts," which would supposedly make it easier for third parties to gain representation in Congress. This would introduce an attenuated form of proportional representation to the United States without the need to a change the constitution. For an argument against proportional representation in the U.S. Congress, see "Two Cheers for Two Parties," Intelligence^2 Debates, February 13, 2020, https://www.intelligencesquaredus.org/debates/two-cheers-two-parties.

274 **And while five out of every ten respondents:** Philip Connor and Jens Manuel Krogstad, "Many Worldwide Oppose More Migration—Both into and out of Their Countries," Pew Research Center, December 10, 2018, https://www.pewresearch.org/fact-tank/2018/12/10/many-worldwide-oppose-more-migration-both-into-and-out-of-their-countries.

274 **In part because of widespread revulsion:** William A. Galston, "As Trump's Zero-Tolerance Immigration Policy Backfires, Republicans Are in Jeopardy," Brookings, June 18, 2018, https://www.brookings.edu/blog/fixgov/2018/06/18/trumps-zero-tolerance-immigration-policy-puts-republicans-in-jeopardy.

274 **after his first hundred days in office:** Joel Rose, "Despite Concerns about Border, Poll Finds Support for More Pathways to Citizenship," NPR, May 20, 2021, https://www.npr.org/2021/05/20/998248764/despite-concerns-about-border-poll-finds-support-for-more-pathways-to-citizenshi.

274 **Many also believe that high levels of immigration:** Ana Gonzalez-Barrera and Phillip Connor, "Around the World, More Say Immigrants Are a Strength Than a Burden," Pew Research Center, March 14, 2019, https://www.pewresearch.org/global/2019/03/14/around-the-world-more-say-immigrants-are-a-strength-than-a-burden.

276 **Lutherans are now very likely:** Michael Lipka, "U.S. Religious Groups and Their Political Leanings," Pew Research Center, February 23, 2016, https://www.pewresearch.org/fact-tank/2016/02/23/u-s-religious-groups-and-their-political-leanings.

276 **If two Americans are divided by one socially:** See Lilliana Mason, *Uncivil Agreement: How Politics Became Our Identity* (Chicago: University of Chicago Press, 2018).

277 **seek to establish a kind of domestic Peace Corps:** Theodore Johnson, *When the Stars Begin to Fall: Overcoming Racism and Renewing the Promise of America* (New York: Atlantic Monthly Press, 2021).

277 **Others have called for schools to recommit:** See, for example, Jill Lepore, *This America: The Case for the Nation* (New York: Liverlight, 2019), and Rebecca Winthrop, "The Need for Civic Education in 21st-Century Schools," Brookings, June 4, 2020, https://www.brookings.edu/policy2020/bigideas/the-need-for-civic-education-in-21st-century-schools.

277 **Others still emphasize the importance for elite institutions:** Michael Lind, *The New Class War: Saving Democracy from the Managerial Elite* (New York: Portfolio, 2020).

Conclusion

282 **The Great Recession took an especially heavy toll:** See, for example, Christopher Famighetti and Darrick Hamilton, "The Great Recession, Education, Race, and Homeownership," Economic Policy Institute, May 15, 2019, https://www.epi.org/blog/the-great-recession-education-race-and-homeownership, and Amanda Logan and Christian E. Weller, "The State of Minorities: The Recession Issue," Center for American Progress, January 16, 2009, https://www.americanprogress.org/issues/race/news/2009/01/16/5482/the-state-of-minorities-the-recession-issue.

282 **Opposition to the country's first black president:** Anthony Zurcher, "The Birth of the Obama 'Birther' Conspiracy," BBC, September 16, 2016, https://www.bbc.com/news/election-us-2016-37391652.

282 **The spread of cell phones:** Nicol Turner-Lee, "Where Would Racial Progress in Policing Be without Camera Phones?," Brookings, June 5, 2020, https://www.brookings.edu/blog/fixgov/2020/06/05/where-would-racial-progress-in-policing-be-without-camera-phones.

286 **Even comparatively homogeneous democracies:** Bruce Stokes and Kat Devlin, "Perceptions of Immigrants, Immigration and Emigration," Pew Research Center, November 12, 2018, https://www.pewresearch.org/global/2018/11/12/perceptions-of-immigrants-immigration-and-emigration.

289 **Manu Chao was born in France:** See Marcos Hassan, "At 20, Manu Chao's 'Clandestino' Remains a Radical and Compassionate Work of Art," *Remezcla*, October 5, 2018, https://remezcla.com/features/music/manu-chao-clandestino-album-20th-anniversary, and Jasmine Garsd and Manu Chao, "This Week on Alt.Latino: Special Guest Manu Chao," September 8, 2011, on *Alt. Latino*, NPR, interview, relevant time stamp 1:33–2:31, https://www.npr.org/sections/altlatino/2011/09/08/140257279/this-week-on-alt-latino-special-guest-manu-chao.

289 **He grew up in the highly diverse suburbs:** See Garsd and Chao, "This Week on Alt.Latino: Special Guest Manu Chao," relevant time stamp 2:35–4:11, and Hassan, "At 20, Manu Chao's 'Clandestino' Remains a Radical and Compassionate Work of Art."

289 **His is the sound of encounter:** Richard Harrington, "Seeing the World through Manu Chao's Eyes," *Washington Post*, June 22, 2007, https://www.washingtonpost.com/wp-dyn/content/article/2007/06/21/AR2007062100690.html. As Manu Chao told *The Guardian*, he cut his teeth playing music in the Parisian subway: "The people using the subway in Paris were very eclectic—there was people from a lot of different countries, different cultures—so we have to be able to play all kinds of music to please all the people on the subway. It was the perfect school to learn a lot of different styles of music." Garsd and Chao, "This Week on Alt.Latino: Special Guest Manu Chao."

290 **Much of *Clandestino*, his first album:** Peter Culshaw, "Clandestino: The Story of Manu Chao's Classic Album," *Guardian*, May 9, 2013, https://www.theguardian.com/music/2013/may/09/manu-chao-clandestino-culshaw. Though *Clandestino* is the first album Chao had published under this name, he had previously published records under the name of *Mano Negra*.

290 ***They call me the one who's disappearing:*** Manu Chao, "El Desaparecido," Genius, accessed June 6, 2021, https://genius.com/Manu-chao-el-desaparecido-lyrics, translation mine.

INDEX